PERCY BYSSHE SHELLEY

Political Writings

Crofts Classics

PERCY BYSSHE SHELLEY

Political Writings

including

"A Defence of Poetry"

EDITED BY

Roland A. Duerksen

MIAMI UNIVERSITY, OHIO

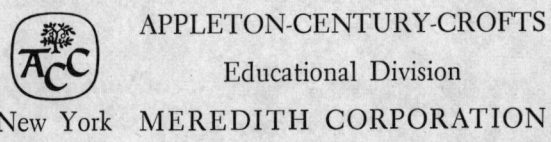

APPLETON-CENTURY-CROFTS

Educational Division

New York MEREDITH CORPORATION

6119–1

Library of Congress Card Number: 75–102035

PRINTED IN THE UNITED STATES OF AMERICA

390–23890–2

contents

introduction vii

principal dates in the life of Percy Bysshe Shelley xxiii

An Address to the Irish People (1812) 1

Proposals for an Association
of Philanthropists (1812) 36

Declaration of Rights (1812) 53

A Letter to Lord Ellenborough (1812) 59

On the Punishment of Death (1813–1814?) 72

An Address to the People on the Death of
the Princess Charlotte (1817) 78

From Essay on Christianity (1812–1819?) 89

The Moral Teaching of Jesus Christ
(1812–1819?) 95

A Proposal for Putting Reform to the Vote
Throughout the Kingdom (1817) 97

A Philosophical View of Reform
(1819) 104

Fragments on Reform (1819–1820?) 158

A System of Government by Juries
(1819–1820?) 160

A Defence of Poetry (1821) 164

Fragments (1820) 198

appendix a: selected prefaces to poems 199

appendix b: selections from Shelley's letters 213

bibliography 223

introduction

Readers who know Percy Bysshe Shelley as the author of "To a Skylark," "Indian Serenade," and other frequently anthologized poems may be startled to learn that in his sensitivity to, and his articulate enthusiasm for, social reform he anticipated and challenged later radicals. Some groups of political activists today appear motivated by the same inner urgency that impelled Shelley. In all English literature, Shelley was one of the first prophetic voices of a movement which in the twentieth century has attained vast proportions in the struggle for human rights and individual dignity—a movement for nonviolent reform that some observers believe could yet become a worldwide alternative to nuclear destruction. A. Stanley Walker has declared that in the modern world Shelley shines forth "as one of the few balanced writers on Reform, as an unbiased thinker of no mean calibre, and finally as a prophet born out of his time." [1]

An example is seen in Queen Mab (1813), Shelley's youthful poem on reform. Widely read by members of the Chartist Movement, it came to be known as the "Chartists' bible." That this movement remained essentially nonviolent was a major factor in England's avoiding a revolutionary civil war in the turbulent first half of the nineteenth century. Although the Chartists' goals were not attained immediately, almost all were achieved peacefully in England before 1870.

Shelley was brought up in a family with a strong Whig commitment at a time when the events, methods, and excesses of the French Revolution were fresh in public memory. His grandfather had been a vigorous agitator for Whig-sponsored reform and his father was a Whig Member of Parliament. Shelley was expected to assume his father's role, but certainly not to become a radical. His

[1] "Peterloo, Shelley and Reform," PMLA, XL (March 1925), 164.

training included thorough inculcation of the views of Whig reform leaders. Although not a Cobbett, a Cartwright, a Bentham, or a Burdett in the sense of rational economic planning, Shelley was scarcely to be outdone as an activist in the romantic current of the reform movement. He became an early and lifelong enthusiast of William Godwin's basic principles as set forth in An Enquiry Concerning Political Justice (1793). Shelley's imaginative powers incorporated into sublime artistic form the concepts that Godwin presented in the context of unrelenting rationality. And whatever disillusionment Shelley later had to face as Godwin's son-in-law, he never lost faith in Godwin's concept that truth has meaning only as the mind of an individual perceives it. Upon this premise Shelley, as a philosophical poet and essayist, founded his belief in the possibility of man's social and political progress, and wrote energetically for the cause of reform in England.

Like most liberals of his day, Shelley was sympathetic to the aims of the French Revolution. He came, however, to realize that the advancement of freedom was hindered rather than helped by the violence of the liberators. The emancipation of downtrodden people became his primary concern, accompanied by a certainty that vengeful retaliation must not be the motive or method of reforms. Shelley declared emphatically that love is the only means of achieving a satisfactory new social order or of creating anything good. The conception of love as the supreme spirit of human advancement pervades and unifies his poems, essays, and letters.

In Queen Mab Shelley foretells the doom of selfishness when man's awakened reason will have brought him back to his natural self. The distinctions of poverty and wealth, the desire for fame, the fear of disease, infamy, and woe, and the horrors of war will disappear when man cooperates with "changeless nature" to take up the work of regeneration. Love will induce mankind not to "fear the cure" but to abandon lust, revenge, murder, discord, war, and misery, the "playthings of its childhood." When, years later, Shelley wrote to the editor of the Examiner protesting the publication of a pirated edition of Queen Mab, he did not deplore the work's message, but rather its general immaturity of expression, which he feared was likely rather "to *injure than to serve the sacred cause of freedom.*" He never ceased to urge man to look at himself rationally and strive for a reasoned, nonviolent way out of his social dilemma. While the artistry and poetic expression of his later poems improve immeasurably, the theme of man's struggle against oppression remains constant. In studying Shelley's political essays, we should bear in mind that their spirit of sweeping reform is paralleled in "Hymn to Intellectual Beauty," The Revolt of Islam, "Ode to the West Wind," Prometheus Unbound, "Song to the Men of England," "England in 1819," The Masque of Anarchy, Swellfoot the Tyrant, and Hellas. Of these we may, in passing, single out two: The Masque of Anarchy, in which an indignant outburst against a specific act of despotism is followed by an emphatic injunction to nonviolent resistance, and Prometheus Unbound, in which the concept of reform is presented on a universal scale and given cosmic proportions.

As Queen Mab set forth Shelley's poetic expression of reform attitudes, so his first political essay, An Address, to the Irish People, had a year earlier presented the basic concepts that were to pervade the reform essays. Shortly after their marriage, Shelley and his wife Harriet went to Ireland to engage in the struggle there for separation from England and for political and religious freedom. Writing to Elizabeth Hitchener on January 26, 1812, before his departure for Ireland, Shelley said of the Address to the Irish People, "It is intended to familiarize to uneducated apprehensions ideas of liberty, benevolence, peace, and toleration. It is secretely intended also as a preliminary to other pamphlets to shake Catholicism at its basis, and induce Quakerish and Socinian principles of politics, without objecting to the Christian religion." Although Shelley did not succeed in making the Irish situation the nucleus of a worldwide reform movement, his Address became essentially what he envisioned for it. It is the first of a series of political essays culminating in the comprehensive Philosophical View of Reform and followed by the Defence of Poetry, which clearly expresses the unity Shelley found in poetry and social concern.

Writing in a simple style, designed especially to appeal to workers barely able to read, Shelley maintains in the

Address that the primary issues in the cause of Irish freedom are Catholic Emancipation, Universal Suffrage, and the Repeal of the Union. The Address is certainly an oversimplification, but Shelley's note to Miss Hitchener, his specific purpose of getting the Irish workingmen to act, and two short essays composed before he left Ireland, Proposals for an Association of Philanthropists and Declaration of Rights, all show that Shelley recognized it as such. The Proposals, addressed to a literate audience, reasserts and extends the basic principles of the Address, and urges the founding of societies to achieve the goals set forth. Declaration of Rights, which Shelley published as a broadside, restates the ideas developed in the other two essays but, unlike the necessarily simpler Address, indicates his awareness of their implications. Yet it is the Address that contains the essence of Shelley's political philosophy at this early stage, the philosophy from which developed his later more substantial theories.

In the Address, which he distributed personally in the streets of Dublin, Shelley calls upon Irishmen to awaken and restore their rights as citizens. He emphasizes his belief that freedom is produced by thought and coolness—resistence of the mind, not of the body, is the essence of successful revolution. This belief remained a primary aspect of his political view. Although repeatedly cautioning Irishmen against the use of violence, Shelley is not unmindful of human emotions and conditioning. He recognizes that certain cases may seem to demand violent action, but he in no way condones it:

> Many circumstances, I will own, may excuse what is called rebellion, but no circumstances can ever make it good for your cause, and however honourable to your feelings, it will reflect no credit on your judgments. It will bind you more closely to the block of the oppressor, and your children's children, whilst they talk of your exploits, will feel that you have done them injury instead of benefit.

Shelley explains the excuse for rebellion later, in A Philosophical View of Reform: "Right government being an institution for the purpose of securing such a moderate degree of happiness to men as has been experimentally practicable, the sure character of misgovernment is misery, and first discontent and, if that be despised, then insurrection, as the legitimate expression of that misery." For evidence to support this analysis, we need only hear the cry of minority groups in the latter half of the twentieth century. Shelley realized that in cases of desperation, to condemn or to condone is not relevant—last resorts are clear indications that society has failed to do what is good.

The proposals of the Address created hardly a stir in Ireland, and it appeared that Shelley had made an unpardonable blunder. The suppressed Irish, having long and timidly turned the other cheek, had lost faith in their meek, passive waiting for the demise of English political and religious discrimination. Shelley concluded, however, that instead of being dangerous or unworkable, his scheme was ill-timed—the Irish were not ready to comprehend the assertive or activistic emphasis in his program. He withdrew his pamphlets from circulation and returned to England. Although his spirit may have been dampened, he had not lost faith in his cause. He remained convinced of the truth of his declaration to the Irish, and in one of his notes on Queen Mab reaffirmed his conviction that "the falsehood of a proposition is felt by those who use coercion, not reasoning, to procure its admission."

Back in England, Shelley soon found an issue that would extend his political involvement. Daniel Isaac Eaton, an elderly London bookseller and publisher, was brought to trial on March 6, 1812 for having published Part Three of Paine's Age of Reason. On May 15, Lord Ellenborough sentenced him to imprisonment for eighteen months and to stand once a month for two hours in the pillory. Shelley's letter of June 11 to William Godwin contains the following reaction:

What do you think of Eaton's trial and sentence? I mean not to insinuate that this poor bookseller has any characteristics in common with Socrates or Jesus Christ; still the spirit that pillories and imprisons him is the same that brought them to an untimely end. Still, even in this enlightened age, the moralist and reformer may expect coercion analogous to that used with the humble, zealous imitator of their en-

> deavors. I have thought of addressing the public on
> the subject and indeed have begun an outline of the
> address. May I be favored with your remarks on it
> before I send it to the world?

There must have been little delay in the composition of
the Letter to Lord Ellenborough, for on July 29 Shelley
announced to the London bookseller Thomas Hookham
that it had been printed.

Drawing on his earlier essay The Necessity of Atheism,
on Paine's Age of Reason, and on Hume's Essays, Shelley
argues in the Letter that neither an individual nor a nation can fully develop without absolute freedom of speech
and of the press. After first charging that, through the admission of purely emotional religious arguments, the jury
had been prejudiced against Eaton, Shelley contends that
Eaton was really convicted because of his deism. And he
enters wholeheartedly into the accusation of Ellenborough:
"Ha then! the mask is fallen off; you persecute him because his faith differs from yours." Asserting that belief is
involuntary, Shelley declares that a man "can only be accountable for those actions which are influenced by his
will." Morality being determined by society, that morality
is shown to be weak, Shelley argues, that requires force or
coercion for its establishment. Especially incongruent is
the reliance upon coercion exhibited in this case by Christians, the proclaimed followers of "the meek reformer
Jesus."

Kenneth Neill Cameron says of A Letter to Lord Ellenborough that it is "Shelley's first important work of literature, a work to be ranked among the classics of the struggle for freedom of speech. It succeeds in transcending—
as the Irish pamphlets do only partially—the issues of the
day into a universal application." [2] In a letter to Leigh
Hunt on November 3, 1819, on the occasion of Richard
Carlile's being tried on a similar charge, Shelley restated
much of the Letter's argument.

On the issue of capital punishment Shelley is no less
incisive and clear than on the need for freedom of speech.
His fragmentary essay On the Punishment of Death
(1814?) advocates emphasizing preventive measures rather

[2] The Young Shelley (New York, 1950), p. 186.

than punishment of crime. Capital punishment, Shelley believes, has a brutalizing effect on society as well as on the criminal and should, therefore, be abolished along with all torture. Death is so elusive a subject that no man can take upon himself to assert whether the mind or soul survives it and that we cannot know whether it is good or evil, punishment or reward. In this respect his argument against capital punishment is very much like his argument against censorship of speech and of the press. It is based on a strong belief in freedom from restriction in all matters that cannot be supported or challenged by demonstrable evidence.

Related also to the Letter to Lord Ellenborough is Shelley's Address to the People on the Death of Princess Charlotte, written in November 1817, immediately after the death of the princess in whom liberals had seen some hope for support of needed governmental reforms. The real purpose of the essay, however, was to make Englishmen, especially the poor, see to what extent the freedom to voice their grievances had been eroded. The Address effectively compares the general mourning for the beautiful princess with the deep grief that should be expressed by a nation whose government, on trumped-up charges, hangs and quarters three poor laborers for speaking out on the need for change. Subtly, Shelley moves from the death of the princess to the death of Freedom, until near the end of the essay, the Princess Charlotte is no longer the subject of the essay at all:

> A beautiful Princess is dead: she who should have been the Queen of her beloved nation and whose posterity should have ruled it for ever. She loved the domestic affections and cherished arts which adorn and valour which defends. She was amiable and would have become wise, but she was young, and in the flower of youth the despoiler came. LIBERTY is dead. . . . Man has murdered Liberty.

The essay ends with the thought that Liberty might yet be resurrected. There is a parallel between this closing note of hope and the concluding lines of Shelley's sonnet "England in 1819," in which the evils of the times are "graves, from which a glorious Phantom may/Burst, to illumine our tempestuous day." The Address, with its vigorous, forth-right style, its dignified thought, and its eloquence of pow-erfully simple phrasing, marks another advance in Shelley's expression of a political philosophy.

Shelley nowhere expresses more pointedly his views on political power than in his fragmentary and undated Essay on Christianity. Religion being historically linked to polit-ical power, and the two together having largely determined the trends of social organization, it is not surprising to find political and social considerations paramount in Shelley's essay on Christianity. (More accurately, it is an essay on various pronouncements attributed to Jesus Christ—not an analysis or explanation of historical Christianity.) Several excerpts are so concerned with society and government that they cannot be omitted from a collection of Shelley's polit-ical essays. The doctrines that Shelley finds distinctive of Christ's teaching are: the superiority of universal love over group loyalties, the need for at least approximate equality of possessions, the irrelevance of revenge and punishment to the problems of crime, and the implicit necessity that moral revolution precede political advancement. "It is not too much to assert," he declares, "that they have been the doctrines of every just and compassionate mind that ever speculated on the social nature of man."

Another fragment, closely related in thought to An Essay on Christianity, though not composed in the same notebook, is The Moral Teaching of Jesus Christ. In addi-tion to generally supporting the Essay, it asserts that Jesus Christ exposed the essential wickedness and ultimate fu-tility of power politics. Shelley declares Christ's reform pro-posals so radical as to make Plato's Republic and Godwin's Political Justice appear "probable and practical systems in comparison."

Shelley himself repeatedly gives evidence that he wished not only to propose radical or ideal reforms, but also to sug-gest immediately attainable reforms in government. A Proposal for Putting Reform to the Vote Throughout the Kingdom, written in early 1817, is a link in the chain of such suggestions, from the early Address to the Irish Peo-ple to the much later and more comprehensive Philosophi-cal View of Reform. In its appeal to moderation in imme-diate demands, the Proposal is a direct descendant of the

Address to the Irish People. *The emphasis on gradualism is clearly summarized in its conclusion:*

> A pure Republic may be shewn, by inferences the most obvious and irresistible, to be that system of social order the fittest to produce the happiness and promote the genuine eminence of man. Yet nothing can less consist with reason or afford smaller hopes of any beneficial issue than the plan which should abolish the regal and the aristocratical branches of our constitution before the public mind, through many gradations of improvement, shall have arrived at the maturity which can disregard these symbols of its childhood.

Shelley's nonapocalyptic approach to the attainment of a new social order must not be overlooked. Although he stresses the importance of preparing "the public mind" for the great change, he explains that this preparation comes about "through many gradations of improvement." The implication is that the enlightened reformer will urge political improvement in all particular cases that come to his attention but will view each of these cases as one phase in the radical education of the human mind, which is the primary means of achieving genuine, lasting renewal.

The Philosophical View of Reform is most clearly anticipated when the Proposal singles out a particularly necessary measure—the reform of the House of Commons. Shelley raises direct or leading questions about it, and gives suggestions:

> The question now at issue is whether the majority of the adult individuals of the United Kingdom of Great Britain and Ireland desire or no a complete representation in the Legislative Assembly. . . . The House of Commons does not represent the will of the people of the British Nation; . . . that House should originate such measures of Reform as would render its Members the actual Representatives of the Nation.

In the Philosophical View of Reform the pronouncement is direct and is supported by argumentation: "The House of Commons ought questionless to be immediately nominated by the great mass of the people. The aristocracy and those who unite in their own persons the vast privileges conferred by the possession of inordinate wealth are sufficiently represented by the House of Peers and by the King." This declaration compares well with an excerpt from Shelley's November 1819 letter to Leigh Hunt:

> The great thing to do is to hold the balance between popular impatience and tyrannical obstinacy, to inculcate with fervour both the right of resistance and the duty of forbearance. You know my principles incite me to take all the good I can get in politics, for ever aspiring to something more. I am one of those whom nothing will fully satisfy, but who [are] ready to be partially satisfied [by] all that is practicable.

Shelley's most ambitious project for aid to governmental and social renovation was the Philosophical View of Reform. How clearly the essay, although encompassing the author's theory of history, reflects a responsiveness to immediate situations is shown by its relationship to The Masque of Anarchy,[3] written at about the same time. This poem was generated by what Shelley called a "torrent of indignation . . . boiling in my veins" when, in Italy, he received news of the notorious Manchester Massacre. A protest meeting of English workingmen peaceably assembled in St. Peter's Field, Manchester, on August 16, 1819, had in advance been declared illegal. The authorities had ruthlessly planned a cavalry charge against the persistent crowd, and a number of persons were killed and many wounded. The poet's indignation blazes, especially in the first nine stanzas, but throughout the poem he never counsels violent retaliation. Instead, he advises men who seek freedom to stand together as a great unarmed company

[3] Walker, p. 161. Notes for Prometheus Unbound and "Ode to the West Wind," jotted on the manuscript of A Philosophical View of Reform, indicate (as does the content of the poems) that the essay is also closely related to these poems. See T. W. Rolleston's edition of A Philosophical View of Reform (London: Oxford University Press, 1920), pp. 93–94.

against the tyrant. They are to stand "like a forest close and mute" and fearlessly face the advancing hordes.

> And if then the tyrants dare
> Let them ride among you there,
> Slash, and stab, and maim, and hew,—
> What they like, that let them do.
>
> With folded arms and steady eyes,
> And little fear, and less surprise,
> Look upon them as they slay
> Till their rage has died away.

The tyrant's troops will return with shame, and the unified demonstration of nonviolent resistance will sound "Oppression's thundered doom." The Masque of Anarchy, written on the spur of the moment and prompted by deep feeling, is in emphasis identical to the deliberate and rational, though fragmentary, Philosophical View of Reform, first edited and published by T. W. Rolleston in 1920, about one hundred years after its composition. Had this essay been published earlier, it might have done a great deal to remove from Shelley's image the imputation of ineffectual idealism, which has been generally attributed to him.

In the essay Shelley seeks to set forth clearly how freedom from oppression may be achieved. History, he says, has been a struggle vacillating between dictatorship and liberty. Yet the general tendency has been toward liberty. The forces of art and culture have raised man always slightly higher during democratic periods than the forces of despotic restriction could depress them in the totalitarian periods. The true patriot, Shelley declares, will constantly promulgate humane political truth and will educate others to meet the onslaughts of tyrants nonviolently—to "wait with folded arms the event of the fire of the artillery and receive with unshrinking bosoms the bayonets of the charging battalions." To avoid this ultimate confrontation, however, he will work ardently for reform, beginning with minor improvements and building up to greater advances. When reform has been obtained, he will refrain from seeking revenge against his former oppressors.

Shelley expresses great enthusiasm for the Constitution of the United States of America, especially for its adaptability. In the American and French revolutions (even though they were violent) he sees such great advancements of freedom that progress to a better society must continue despite all opposition. Although the higher social order may be many generations coming, it will be achieved. As shown above, his first concern for immediate change in England is the reform of Parliament. The progression then will be to a republican state and from that to an egalitarian society. After gradual reforms of franchise and tax systems, as well as the elimination of a standing army, courageously active minds, led by philosophers, prophets, and poets, will continue to resist oppression and to assert human freedoms in new areas and evolving conditions.

The role of these progressive leaders is presented comprehensively in A Defence of Poetry (1821), Shelley's great expression on his art. A response to Peacock's half-serious Four Ages of Poetry, which argues that poetry has become obsolescent, the Defence, though complete and finely wrought, is only the first of three projected parts—the latter two, regrettably, were never written. Shelley defines poetry and traces its historical development, regressions, and reassertions. Poetry, he declares, is imaginative thought, whether this be expressed in verse, prose, or other art forms. It combines reason and imagination to create in the reader an apprehension that is attuned to progress and not to a static condition of prescribed order. Its ultimate accomplishment is to urge men away from selfishness and toward an acceptance of humanity. As an outgrowth of man's most essential being, poetry becomes the highest form of reason, and the poet therefore is the creator of that which the mechanist uses.

Historically, poets have initiated the new ages, and poetry has remained, to the end of every civilization, the expression of the noblest and highest potentiality still left in that system. By a direct warning against an unimaginative society, Shelley strongly asserts the continuing usefulness of poetry.

Whilst the mechanist abridges and the political economist combines labour, let them beware that their speculations, for want of correspondence with those first principles which belong to the imagination, do

not tend, as they have in modern England, to exasperate at once the extremes of luxury and want. . . .
The rich have become richer, and the poor have become poorer; and the vessel of the state is driven
between the Scylla and Charybdis of anarchy and
despotism. Such are the effects which must ever flow
from the unmitigated exercise of the calculating
faculty.

Sensing that an aggressively selfish and primarily industrial
society is gradually adapting men to function as parts of a
vast production-consumption machine, and anticipating
the gargantuan growth of the problem, Shelley urges the
increase of love and identification among individuals and
groups as a necessary corrective to this disruptive trend.

The great secret of morals is love, or a going out of
our own nature, and an identification of ourselves with
the beautiful which exists in thought, action, or person not our own. A man, to be greatly good, must
imagine intensely and comprehensively; he must put
himself in the place of another and of many others;
the pains and pleasures of his species must become
his own. The great instrument of moral good is the
imagination; and poetry administers to the effect by
acting upon the cause.

In defining poetry as socially responsive and useful, and in
devoting two-thirds of the essay to an examination of
poetry's effects upon society, Shelley makes of the Defence
a well-ordered summing-up of important views expressed
in his political essays. In the political essays he has shown
men how easily they can know what is right; in the Defence he explains that only the poet (the imaginative
thinker) can accomplish the most difficult task of making
men voluntary doers of right.

We have more moral, political, and historical wisdom
than we know how to reduce into practice; we have
more scientific and economical knowledge than can
be accommodated to the just distribution of the produce which it multiplies. The poetry in these systems

of thought is concealed by the accumulation of facts and calculating processes. There is no want of knowledge respecting what is wisest and best in morals, government, and political economy, or at least what is wiser and better than what men now practice and endure. . . . To what but a cultivation of the mechanical arts in a degree disproportioned to the presence of the creative faculty, which is the basis of all knowledge, is to be attributed the cause of all invention for abridging and combining labour to the exasperation of the inequality of mankind? From what other cause has it arisen that these inventions which should have lightened, have added a weight to the curse imposed on Adam? Thus Poetry and the principle of Self, of which Money is the visible incarnation, are the God and Mammon of the world.

In the twentieth-century world of mass automation, threatened by worldwide destruction, these words have a prophetic ring. Shelley's point is that it is in their service to the god of imaginative identification with all that is not the self that poets gain the right to the grand, though generally unacknowledged title, "legislators of the world." They alone point the way out of the morass of a self-seeking, power-mad society.

There is no certainty that the aims of Shelley's "legislators" can be achieved, but neither is their ineffectuality certain. Reformers since Shelley's time have been affected by his invincible belief that universal equality and the freedom of each individual are essential tenets in the law of progress toward an enlightened, beautified world. Henry David Thoreau, the great exponent of civil disobedience, read Shelley appreciatively. Karl Marx is said to have judged that Shelley "was essentially a revolutionist and . . . would always have been one of the advanced guard of socialism." [4] The seed of failure which Shelley would have detected in Marx's socialism—as he detected it in all materialistic systems of power—is, as expressed in his own words, "the most fatal error that ever happened in the

---

[4] Shelley Society, Publications, Ser. 1, no. 1, vol. 1, pt. 2 (London: Reeves and Turner, 1888).

world—the separation of political and ethical science." [5] Tolstoy, recognizing the need of a spiritual weapon against the root evil embodied in the pursuit of power, used this statement by Shelley as an epigraph to his late work, An Appeal to Social Reformers (first published in 1900).[6] Shelley transmitted to later thinkers and political innovators the radical thought that the leading force in history is generated not by materialism (whether collectivist or capitalist) nor by "rational" politics or "scientific" economics, but by the power of the imaginative identification. This power was illustrated when Mohandas Gandhi, an oriental in upbringing and belief, selected Shelley's very English reform poem The Masque of Anarchy for reading to a vast audience during the campaign for India's freedom.[7] And today's largely unstructured challenge to traditional power structures, manifested especially on campuses the world over, is infused with essentially the same imaginative power that Shelley so consistently acclaimed.

The text of the essays in this edition is based primarily on that in The Complete Works of Percy Bysshe Shelley, edited by Roger Ingpen and Walter E. Peck (Julian Editions), ten volumes (New York: Charles Scribner's Sons, 1926–30) and has been checked against that in Shelley's Prose: or The Trumpet of a Prophecy (corrected edition), edited by David Lee Clark (Albuquerque: The University of New Mexico Press, 1966). The earlier editions that have been useful as authoritative sources are: Essays, Letters from Abroad, Translations, and Fragments, edited by Mary Shelley (London: Edward Moxon, 1840); Prose

[5] In context, the statement appears thus in Shelley's January 7, 1812, letter to Elizabeth Hitchener: "Southey says Expediency ought to [be] made the ground of politics, but not of morals. I urged that the most fatal error that ever happened in the world was the separation of political and ethical science; that the former ought to be entirely regulated by the latter, as whatever was a right criterion of action for an individual must be so for society, which was but an assemblage of individuals; 'that politics were morals more comprehensively enforced.'" [6] See Essays from Tula (London, 1948), p. 137. [7] See Louis Fischer Gandhi: His Life and Message for the World (New York, 1954), p. 49.

Works of Percy Bysshe Shelley, *edited by H. Buxton Forman* (London: Reeves, 1880); Shelley's Prose in the Bodleian Manuscripts, *edited by A. H. Koszul* (London: Henry Frowde, 1910); and A Philosophical View of Reform, *edited by T. W. Rolleston* (London: Oxford University Press, 1920).

principal dates in the life
of Percy Bysshe Shelley

1792   Born August 4 at Field Place, Warnham, in Sussex. Eldest son of Timothy Shelley, a country squire who becomes a baronet in 1815.

1798–1802   Attends day school at Warnham.

1802–04   Attends Sion House Academy near Brentford. Proves himself a sensitive, open-hearted, but temperamental student, excelling in intellectual rather than social aspects of his schooling.

1804–10   Studies at Eton, where he gains a reputation as a rebel against establishment regulations and against orthodox religion. Writes juvenile novels and poems.

1810–11   Enters Oxford in October; is expelled in March after he and his friend T. J. Hogg publish a pamphlet, *The Necessity of Atheism*. Resides in London. In August, elopes with Harriet Westbrook, aged sixteen, and marries her in Edinburgh. Alienation from his father because of expulsion from Oxford and marriage to Harriet. In November settles at Keswick, Cumberland.

1812   In January, writes introductory letter to William Godwin, expressing his enthusiasm over *Political Justice*. Spends February to April in Ireland for the cause of reform. Writes *An Address to the Irish People* and *Proposals for an Association of Philanthropists*. From April to October moves from place to place in England, finally becoming involved in Tremadoc land reclamation project. Publishes *Declaration of Rights* and *A Letter to Lord Ellenborough*. Under government surveillance as reform activist. Begins *Queen Mab*. Meets Godwin and T. L. Peacock.

1813   After short trip to Ireland, returns to London in April. Privately prints *Queen Mab*, his first influential poem. Daughter Ianthe born in June. In financial distress because of estrangement from his father. Becomes vegetarian. Moves in July to Bracknell, Berkshire.

1814   Gradual estrangement of interests between Shelley and Harriet. Publishes *A Refutation of Deism*. Frequently meets Mary Godwin, seventeen-year-old daughter of William Godwin and Mary Wollstonecraft. Elopes with her in July, touring France and Switzerland for six weeks, then returns to London. Second child, Charles, born to Harriet in November. Moves about to avoid creditors.

1815   After death of his grandfather Sir Bysshe Shelley in January, receives an annual allowance of £1000, of which he allots £200 annually to Harriet. In summer takes up residence at Bishopsgate, near Windsor. Is closely associated with Peacock. Composes *Alastor* (autumn).

1816   His son William born to Mary. Publishes *Alastor* (March). Spends May to September with Byron in Switzerland, near Geneva. Composes *Hymn to Intellectual Beauty* and *Mont Blanc*. Settles at Bath. In December learns of Harriet's suicide by drowning. Immediately marries Mary Godwin. Begins literary association with Leigh Hunt, Keats, Hazlitt, and Horace Smith.

1817   Moves to Marlow. By court order (issued in March by Lord Chancellor Eldon), is deprived of custody of his children by Harriet. Daughter Clara born (September). Writes *A Proposal for Putting Reform to the Vote*; begins *The Revolt of Islam*. Develops close friendship with Leigh Hunt

and Horace Smith. Rapidly composes *An Address
to the People on the Death of the Princess Charlotte* (November).

1818   Publishes *The Revolt of Islam* (January). In March,
leaves England for Italy; there moves from place
to place. Renews association with Byron (then
residing in Venice). Daughter Clara dies (September). Writes *Julian and Maddalo* and *Lines
Written Among the Euganean Hills;* begins
Prometheus Unbound. Visits Rome and moves
to Naples (December).

1819   Publishes *Rosalind and Helen.* Lives in Rome
(March to June). Completes Acts II and III of
Prometheus Unbound. Son William dies (June).
Resides near Leghorn (June to October). Writes
his stage play *The Cenci.* Moves to Florence in
October. Son Percy Florence born (November).
Writes *A Philosophical View of Reform; The
Masque of Anarchy;* letter to *The Examiner* on
Carlile; *Peter Bell the Third; Ode to the West
Wind; Prometheus Unbound,* Act IV.

1820   Settles at Pisa, remaining in that area (except for
short absences) until his death. Publishes *The
Cenci.* Writes *Ode to Liberty, To a Skylark, The
Sensitive Plant, Oedipus Tyrannus,* and *The
Witch of Atlas.* Forms friendship with Greek
Prince Mavrocordato. Publishes *Prometheus Un-
bound.*

1821   Writes *Epipsychidion.* In February and March
writes *A Defence of Poetry.* Hearing of death of
Keats, begins *Adonais* in April; prints it at Pisa
in July. Writes *Hellas* (autumn). Renews fel-
lowship with Byron upon latter's move to Pisa
in November.

1822   Works on composition of *Charles I.* Publishes
Hellas. In May moves for the summer to Casa
Magni, near Lerici on Gulf of Spezzia, sharing
the residence with Mary, Edward Williams, and
Williams's wife Jane. Writes *The Triumph of*

Life (left unfinished). Meets Hunt at Leghorn in June. With Williams, drowns on July 8 in storm while returning from Leghorn in Shelley's boat.

An Address to the Irish People

Fellow men, I am not an Irishman, yet I can feel for you. I hope there are none among you who will read this address with prejudice or levity, because it is made by an Englishman; indeed, I believe there are not. The Irish are a brave nation. They have a heart of liberty in their breasts, but they are much mistaken if they fancy that a stranger cannot have as warm a one. Those are my brothers and my countrymen, who are unfortunate. I should like to know what there is in a man being an Englishman, a Spaniard, or a Frenchman, that makes him worse or better than he really is. He was born in one town, you in another, but that is no reason why he should not feel for you, desire your benefit, or be willing to give you some advice which may make you more capable of knowing your own interest, or acting so as to secure it. There are many Englishmen who cry down the Irish and think it answers their ends to revile all that belongs to Ireland; but it is not because these men are Englishmen

Title page advertisement The lowest possible price is set on this publication, because it is the intention of the Author to awaken in the minds of the Irish poor, a knowledge of their real state, summarily pointing out the evils of that state, and suggesting rational means of remedy. Catholic Emancipation, and a Repeal of the Union Act (the latter, the most successful engine that England ever wielded over the misery of fallen Ireland) being treated of in the following address, as grievances which unanimity and resolution may remove, and associations conducted with peaceable firmness, being earnestly recommended, as means for embodying that unanimity and firmness which must finally be successful.

1

that they maintain such opinions, but because they wish to get money, and titles, and power. They would act in this manner to whatever country they might belong, until mankind is much altered for the better, which reform, I hope, will one day be effected. I address you, then, as my brothers and my fellow men, for I should wish to see the Irishman who, if England was persecuted as Ireland is, who, if France was persecuted as Ireland is, who, if any set of men that helped to do a public service were prevented from enjoying its benefits as Irishmen are—I should like to see the man, I say, who would see these misfortunes and not attempt to succour the sufferers when he could, just that I might tell him that he was no Irishman, but some bastard mongrel bred up in a court, or some coward fool who was a democrat to all above him and an aristocrat to all below him. I think there are few true Irishmen who would not be ashamed of such a character, still fewer who possess it. I know that there are some, not among you my friends, but among your enemies, who seeing the title of this piece, will take it up with a sort of hope that it may recommend violent measures and thereby disgrace the cause of freedom, that the warmth of an heart desirous that liberty should be possessed equally by all will vent itself in abuse on the enemies of liberty, bad men who deserve the contempt of the good, and ought not to excite their indignation to the harm of their cause. But these men will be disappointed—I know the warm feeling of an Irishman sometimes carries him beyond the point of prudence. I do not desire to root out, but to moderate this honourable warmth. This will disappoint the pioneers of oppression, and they will be sorry that through this address nothing will occur which can be twisted into any other meaning but what is calculated to fill you with that moderation which they have not, and make you give them that toleration which they refuse to grant you. You profess the Roman Catholic religion which your fathers professed before you. Whether it is the best religion or not, I will not here inquire; all religions are good which make men good; and the way that a person ought to prove that his method of worshipping God is best is for himself to be better than all other men. But we will consider what your religion was in old times and what it is now; you may say it is not a fair way for me to proceed as a Protestant, but I am not a Protestant nor am I a Catholic, and therefore not being a follower of either of these religions, I am better able to judge between them. A Protestant is my brother, and a Catholic is my brother. I am happy when I can do either of them a service, and no pleasure is so great to me than that which I should feel if my advice could make men of any professions of faith, wiser, better, and happier.

The Roman Catholics once persecuted the Protestants, the Protestants now persecute the Roman Catholics— should we think that one is as bad as the other? No, you are not answerable for the faults of your fathers any more than the Protestants are good for the goodness of their fathers. I must judge of people as I see them; the Irish Catholics are badly used. I will not endeavour to hide from them their wretchedness; they would think that I mocked at them if I should make the attempt. The Irish Catholics now demand for themselves and profess for others unlimited toleration, and the sensible part among them, which I am willing to think constitutes a very large portion of their body, know that the gates of Heaven are open to people of every religion, provided they are good. But the Protestants, although they may think so in their hearts, which certainly, if they think at all, they must seem to act as if they thought that God was better pleased with them than with you; they trust the reins of earthly government only to the hands of their own sect. In spite of this, I never found one of them impudent enough to say that a Roman Catholic, or a Quaker, or a Jew, or a Mahometan, if he was a virtuous man and did all the good in his power, would go to Heaven a bit the slower for not subscribing to the thirty-nine articles[1]—and if he should say so, how ridiculous in a foppish courtier not six feet high to direct the spirit of universal harmony[2] in what manner to conduct the affairs of the universe!

The Protestants say that there was a time when the Roman Catholics burnt and murdered people of different

1 **thirty-nine articles** articles of faith adopted by the Church of England in 1562 2 **spirit of universal harmony** Shelley's consistently-held concept of God

sentiments, and that their religious tenets are now as they were then. This is all very true. You certainly worship God in the same way that you did when these barbarities took place, but is that any reason that you should now be barbarous? There is as much reason to suppose it as to suppose that because a man's great-grandfather, who was a Jew, had been hung for sheep-stealing, that I, by believing the same religion as he did, must certainly commit the same crime. Let us then see what the Roman Catholic religion has been. No one knows much of the early times of the Christian religion, until about three hundred years after its beginning, two great churches, called the Roman and the Greek Churches, divided the opinions of men. They fought for a very long time; a great many words were wasted and a great deal of blood shed.

This as you may suppose, did no good. Each party, however, thought they were doing God a service, and that he would reward them. If they had looked an inch before their noses, they might have found that fighting and killing men, and cursing them and hating them, was the very worst way for getting into favour with a Being who is allowed by all to be best pleased with deeds of love and charity. At last, however, these two Religions entirely separated, and the Popes reigned like Kings and Bishops at Rome, in Italy. The inquisition was set up, and in the course of one year 30,000 people were burnt in Italy and Spain for entertaining different opinions from those of the Pope and the Priests. There was an instance of shocking barbarity which the Roman Catholic Clergy committed in France by order of the Pope. The bigoted Monks of that country, in cold blood, in one night massacred 80,000 Protestants;[3] this was done under the authority of the Pope, and there was only one Roman Catholic Bishop who had virtue enough to refuse to help. The vices of Monks and Nuns in their convents were in those times shameful. People thought that they might commit any sin, however monstrous, if they had money .

3 **massacred 80,000 Protestants**   the Massacre of Saint Bartholomew (August 24 to September 17, 1572) in which thousands of French Huguenots died at the hands of Catholics, an event solemnly celebrated by the Pope

enough to prevail upon the Priests to absolve them. In truth, at that time the Priests shamefully imposed upon the people, they got all the power into their own hands, they persuaded them that a man could not be entrusted with the care of his own soul, and by cunningly obtaining possession of their secrets, they became more powerful than Kings, Princes, Dukes, Lords, or Ministers. This power made them bad men; for although rational people are very good in their natural state, there are now, and ever have been, very few whose good dispositions despotic power does not destroy. I have now given a fair description of what your religion was; and, Irishmen, my brothers! will you make your friend appear a liar when he takes upon himself to say for you that you are not now what the professors of the same faith were in times of yore? Do I speak false when I say that the inquisition is the object of your hatred? Am I a liar if I assert that an Irishman prizes liberty dearly, that he will preserve that right, and if it be wrong, does not dream that money can give to a Priest, or the talking of another man erring like himself, can in the least influence the judgment of the eternal God? I am not a liar if I affirm in your name that you believe a Protestant equally with yourself to be worthy of the Kingdom of Heaven, if he be equally virtuous; that you will treat men as brethren wherever you may find them, and that difference of opinion in religious matters shall not, does not in the least on your part, obstruct the most perfect harmony on every other subject. Ah! no, Irishmen, I am not a liar. I seek your confidence, not that I may betray it, but that I may teach you to be happy, and wise, and good. If you will not repose any trust in me I shall lament, but I will do everything in my power that is honourable, fair, and open, to gain it. Some teach you that others are heretics, that you alone are right; some teach that rectitude consists in religious opinions, without which no morality is good; some will tell you that you ought to divulge your secrets to one particular set of men; beware, my friends, how you trust those who speak in this way. They will, I doubt not, attempt to rescue you from your present miserable state, but they will prepare a worse. It will be out of the frying-pan into the fire. Your present oppressors, it is true, will then oppress you no longer, but you will feel the lash of a master a thousand times more blood-thirsty and cruel. Evil designing men will spring up who will prevent your thinking as you please, will burn you if you do not think as they do. There are always bad men who take advantage of hard times. The monks and priests of old were very bad men; take care no such abuse your confidence again. You are not blind to your present situation, you are villainously treated, you are badly used. That this slavery shall cease, I will venture to prophesy. Your enemies dare not to persecute you longer; the spirit of Ireland is bent, but it is not broken, and that they very well know. But I wish your views to embrace a wider scene; I wish you to think for your children and your children's children, to take great care (for it all rests with you) that whilst one tyranny is destroyed another more fierce and terrible does not spring up. Take care then of smooth-faced impostors, who talk indeed of freedom, but who will cheat you into slavery. Can there be worse slavery than the depending for the safety of your soul on the will of another man? Is one man more favored than another by God? No, certainly, they are all favored according to the good they do, and not according to the rank and profession they hold. God values a poor man as much as a Priest, and has given him a soul as much to himself; the worship that a kind Being must love, is that of a simple affectionate heart, that shews its piety in good works, and not in ceremonies, or confessions, or burials, or processions, or wonders. Take care then, that you are not led away. Doubt every thing that leads you not to charity, and think of the word "heretic" as a word which some selfish knave invented for the ruin and misery of the world, to answer his own paltry and narrow ambition. Do not inquire if a man be a heretic, if he be a Quaker, or a Jew, or a Heathen; but if he be a virtuous man, if he loves [love] liberty and truth, if he wish the happiness and peace of human kind. If a man be ever so much a believer and love not these things, he is a heartless hypocrite, a rascal, and a knave. Despise and hate him, as ye despise a tyrant and a villain. Oh! Ireland, thou emerald of the ocean, whose sons are generous and brave, whose daughters are honourable, and frank, and fair; thou art the isle on whose green shores I have desired to see the standard of liberty erected, a flag of fire, a beacon at which the world shall light the torch of Freedom!

We will now examine the Protestant Religion. Its origin is called the Reformation. It was undertaken by some bigoted men who shewed how little they understood the spirit of Reform, by burning each other. You will observe that these men burnt each other; indeed they universally betrayed a taste for destroying and vied with the chiefs of the Roman Catholic Religion in not only hating their enemies, but those men who least of all were their enemies, or anybody's enemies. Now, do the Protestants, or do they not, hold the same tenets as they did when Calvin burnt Servetus? They swear that they do. We can have no better proof. Then with what face can the Protestants object to Catholic Emancipation on the plea that Catholics once were barbarous, when their own establishment is liable to the very same objections, on the very same grounds? I think this is a specimen of bare-faced intoleration, which I had hoped would not have disgraced this age; this age, which is called the age of reason, of thought diffused, of virtue acknowledged, and its principles fixed. Oh! that it may be so. I have mentioned the Catholic and Protestant Religions more to shew that any objection to the toleration of the one forcibly applies to the non-permission of the other, or rather to shew that there is no reason why both might not be tolerated, why every Religion, every form of thinking might not be tolerated. But why do I speak of *toleration?* This word seems to mean that there is some merit in the person who tolerates; he has this merit if it be one, of refraining to do an evil act, but he will share the merit with every other peaceable person who pursues his own business and does not hinder another of his rights. It is not a merit to tolerate, but it is a crime to be intolerant; it is not a merit in me that I sat [sit] quietly at home without murdering any one, but it is a crime if I do so. Besides, no act of a National representation can make any thing wrong which was not wrong before; it cannot change virtue and truth, and for a very plain reason: because they are unchangeable. An Act passed in the British Parliament to take away the rights of Catholics to act in that assembly, does not really take them away. It prevents them from doing it by force. This is in such cases the last and only efficacious way. But force is not the test of truth; they will never have recourse to violence who acknowledge no other rule of behaviour but virtue and justice.[4]

The folly of persecuting men for their religion will appear if we examine it. Why do we persecute them? to make them believe as we do. Can anything be more barbarous or foolish? For although we may make them say they believe as we do, they will not in their hearts do any such thing, indeed they cannot; this devilish method can only make them false hypocrites. For what is belief? We cannot believe just what we like, but only what we think to be true; for you cannot alter a man's opinion by beating or burning, but by persuading him that what you think is right, and this can only be done by fair words and reason. It is ridiculous to call a man a heretic because he thinks differently from you; he might as well call you one. In the same sense, the word orthodox is used; it signifies "to think rightly" and what can be more vain and presumptuous in any man or any set of men, to put themselves so out of the ordinary course of things as to say, "What we think is right; no other people throughout the world have opinions any thing like equal to ours." Anything short of unlimited toleration and complete charity with all men, on which you will recollect that Jesus Christ principally insisted, is wrong, and for this reason—what makes a man to be a good man? not his religion, or else there could be no good men in any religion but one, when yet we find that all ages, countries, and opinions have produced them. Virtue and wisdom always so far as they went produced liberty or happiness long before any of the religions now in the world were ever heard of. The only use of a religion that ever I could see is to make men wiser or better; so far as it does this, it is a good one. Now, if people are good and yet have sentiments differing from you, then all the purposes are answered which any reasonable man could want, and whether he thinks like you or not is of too little consequence to employ means which must be disgusting and hateful to candid minds; nay they cannot approve of

4 **I have mentioned . . . . justice** theme of Godwin's *Political Justice*, Bk. II, ch. ii–iii

such means. For as I have before said, you cannot believe or disbelieve what you like—perhaps some of you may doubt this, but just try. I will take a common and familiar instance. Suppose you have a friend of whom you wish to think well; he commits a crime, which proves to you that he is a bad man. It is very painful to you to think ill of him, and you would still think well of him if you could. But, mark the word, you *cannot* think well of him, not even to secure your own peace of mind can you do so. You try, but your attempts are vain. This shews how little power a man has over his belief, or rather, that he cannot believe what he does not think true. And what shall we think now? What fools and tyrants must not those men be who set up a particular religion, say that this religion alone is right, and that everyone who disbelieves it ought to be deprived of certain rights which are really his, and which would be allowed him if he believed. Certainly, if you cannot help disbelief, it is not any fault in you. To take away a man's rights and privileges, to call him a heretic or to think worse of him, when at the same time you cannot help owning that he has committed no fault, is the grossest tyranny and intoleration. From what has been said I think we may be justified in concluding that people of all religions ought to have an equal share in the state, that the words heretic and orthodox were invented by a vain villain and have done a great deal of harm in the world, and that no person is answerable for his belief whose actions are virtuous and moral, that the religion is best whose members are the best men, and that no person can help either his belief or disbelief. Be in charity with all men. It does not therefore, signify what your Religion *was*, or what the Protestant Religion *was;* we must consider them as we find them. What are they *now?* Yours is not intolerant; indeed, my friends, I have ventured to pledge myself for you that it is not. You merely desire to go to Heaven in your own way, nor will you interrupt fellow travellers, although the road which you take may not be that which they take. Believe me that goodness of heart and purity of life are things of more value in the eye of the Spirit of Goodness than idle earthly ceremonies and things which have any thing but charity for their object. And is it for the first or the last of these things that you or the Protestants contend? It is for the last. Prejudiced people indeed are they who grudge to the happiness and comfort of your souls things which can do harm to no one. They are not compelled to share in these rites. Irishmen, knowledge is more extended than in the early period of your religion; people have learned to think, and the more thought there is in the world, the more happiness and liberty will there be. Men begin now to think less of idle ceremonies and more of realities. From a long night have they risen, and they can perceive its darkness. I know no men of thought and learning who do not consider the Catholic idea of purgatory much nearer the truth than the Protestant one of eternal damnation. Can you think that the Mahometans and the Indians who have done good deeds in this life will not be rewarded in the next? The Protestants believe that they will be eternally damned—at least they swear that they do. I think they appear in a better light as perjurers than believers in a falsehood so hurtful and uncharitable as this. I propose unlimited toleration, or rather the destruction both of toleration and intoleration. The act permits certain people to worship God after such a manner, which, in fact, if not done, would as far as in it lay prevent God from hearing their address. Can we conceive anything more presumptuous, and at the same time more ridiculous, than a set of men granting a licence to God to receive the prayers of certain of his creatures? Oh Irishmen! I am interested in your cause, and it is not because you are Irishmen or Roman Catholics that I feel with you and feel for you, but because you are men and sufferers. Were Ireland at this moment peopled with Brahmins, this very same address would have been suggested by the same state of mind. You have suffered not merely for your religion, but some other causes which I am equally desirous of remedying. The Union of England with Ireland has withdrawn the Protestant aristocracy and gentry from their native country, and with these their friends and connections. Their resources are taken from this country, although they are dissipated in another; the very poor people are most infamously oppressed by the weight of burden which the superior ranks lay upon their shoulders. I am no less desirous of the reform of these evils (with many others) than for the Catholic Emancipation.

Perhaps you all agree with me on both these subjects; we now come to the method of doing these things. I agree with the Quakers so far as they disclaim violence and trust their cause wholly and solely to its own truth. If you are convinced of the truth of your cause, trust wholly to its truth; if you are not convinced, give it up. In no case employ violence; the way to liberty and happiness is never to transgress the rules of virtue and justice. Liberty and happiness are founded upon virtue and justice; if you destroy the one, you destroy the other. However ill others may act, this will be no excuse for you if you follow their example; it ought rather to warn you from pursuing so bad a method. Depend upon it, Irishmen, your cause shall not be neglected. I will fondly hope that the schemes for your happiness and liberty, as well as those for the happiness and liberty of the world, will not be wholly fruitless. One secure method of defeating them is violence on the side of the injured party. If you can descend to use the same weapons as your enemy, you put yourself on a level with him on this score; you must be convinced that he is on these grounds your superior. But appeal to the sacred principles of virtue and justice; then how is he awed into nothing! How does truth shew him in his real colours and place the cause of toleration and reform in the clearest light! I extend my view not only to you as Irishmen, but to all of every persuasion, of every country. Be calm, mild, deliberate, patient; recollect that you can in no measure more effectually forward the cause of reform than by employing your leisure time in reasoning or the cultivation of your minds. Think and talk, and discuss. The only subjects you ought to propose are those of happiness and liberty. Be free and be happy, but first be wise and good. For you are not all wise or good. You are a great and a brave nation, but you cannot yet be all wise or good. You may be at some time, and then Ireland will be an earthly Paradise. You know what is meant by a mob; it is an assembly of people who, without foresight or thought, collect themselves to disapprove of by force any measure which they dislike. An assembly like this can never do anything but harm; tumultuous proceedings must retard the period when thought and coolness will produce freedom and happiness, and that to the very people who make the mob. But if a number of human beings, after thinking of their own interests, meet together for any conversation on them and employ resistance of the mind, not resistance of the body, these people are going the right way to work. But let no fiery passions carry them beyond this point; let them consider that in some sense the whole welfare of their countrymen depends on their prudence and that it becomes them to guard the welfare of others as their own. Associations for purposes of violence are entitled to the strongest disapprobation of the real reformist. Always suspect that some knavish rascal is at the bottom of things of this kind, waiting to profit by the confusion. All secret associations are also bad. Are you men of deep designs, whose deeds love darkness better than light; dare you not say what you think before any man, can you not meet in the open face of day in conscious innocence? Oh, Irishmen, ye can! Hidden arms, secret meetings, and designs violently to separate England from Ireland are all very bad. I do not mean to say the very end of them is bad; the object you have in view may be just enough, whilst the way you go about it is wrong, may be calculated to produce an opposite effect. Never do evil that good may come; always think of others as well as yourself, and cautiously look how your conduct may do good or evil when you yourself shall be mouldering in the grave. Be fair, open, and you will be terrible to your enemies. A friend cannot defend you, much as he may feel for your sufferings, if you have recourse to methods of which virtue and justice disapprove. No cause is in itself so dear to liberty as yours. Much depends on you; far may your efforts spread either hope or despair; do not then cover in darkness wrongs at which the face of day and the tyrants who bask in its warmth ought to blush. Wherever has violence succeeded? The French Revolution, although undertaken with the best intentions, ended ill for the people; because violence was employed, the cause which they vindicated was that of truth, but they gave it the appearance of a lie by using methods which will suit the purposes of liars as well as their own. Speak boldly and daringly what you think. An Irishman was never accused of cowardice; do not let it be thought possible that he is a coward.

Let him say what he thinks, a lie is the basest and meanest employment of men; leave lies and secrets to courtiers and lordlings; be open, sincere, and single-hearted. Let it be seen that the Irish votaries of Freedom dare to speak what they think; let them resist oppression, not by force of arms, but by power of mind, and reliance on truth and justice. Will any be arraigned for libel—will imprisonment or death be the consequences of this mode of proceeding? Probably not. But if it were so? Is danger frightful to an Irishman who speaks for his own liberty and the liberty of his wife and children? No, he will steadily persevere, and sooner shall pensioners cease to vote with their benefactors than an Irishman swerve from the path of duty. But steadily persevere in the system above laid down; its benefits will speedily be manifested. Persecution may destroy some, but cannot destroy all, or nearly all; let it do its will, ye have appealed to truth and justice—show the goodness of your religion by persisting in a reliance on these things, which must be the rules even of the Almighty's conduct. But before this can be done with any effect, habits of SOBRIETY, REGULARITY, and THOUGHT must be entered into and firmly resolved upon.

My warm-hearted friends, who meet together to talk of the distresses of your countrymen until social chat induces you to drink rather freely, as ye have felt passionately, so reason coolly. Nothing hasty can be lasting; lay up the money with which you usually purchase drunkenness and ill-health, to relieve the pains of your fellow-sufferers. Let your children lisp of Freedom in the cradle—let your death-bed be the school for fresh exertions—let every street of the city and field of the country be connected with thoughts which liberty has made holy. Be warm in your cause, yet rational, and charitable, and tolerant—never let the oppressor grind you into justifying his conduct by imitating his meanness.

Many circumstances, I will own, may excuse what is called rebellion, but no circumstances can ever make it good for your cause, and however honourable to your feelings, it will reflect no credit on your judgments. It will bind you more closely to the block of the oppressor, and your children's children, whilst they talk of your exploits, will feel that you have done them injury instead of benefit.

A crisis is now arriving which shall decide your fate. The King of Great Britain has arrived at the evening of his days. He has objected to your emancipation; he has been inimical to you; but he will in a certain time be no more.[5] The present Prince of Wales will then be king. It is said that he has promised to restore you to freedom; your real and natural right will, in that case, be no longer kept from you. I hope he has pledged himself to this act of justice, because there will then exist some obligation to bind him to do right. Kings are but too apt to think, little as they should do.[6] They think everything in the world is made for them; when the truth is that it is only the vices of men that make such people necessary, and they have no other right of being kings but in virtue of the good they do.

The benefit of the governed is the origin and meaning of government. The Prince of Wales has had every opportunity of knowing how he ought to act about Ireland and liberty. That great and good man Charles Fox, who was your friend and the friend of freedom, was the friend of the Prince of Wales. He never flattered or disguised his sentiments but spoke them *openly* on every occasion, and the Prince was the better for his instructive conversation. He saw the truth, and he believed it. Now I know not what to say; his staff is gone, and he leans upon a broken reed; his present advisers are not like Charles Fox; they do not plan for liberty and safety, not for the happiness but for the glory of their country; and what, Irishmen, is the glory of a country divided from their happiness? It is a false light hung out by the enemies of freedom to lure the unthinking into their net. Men like these surround the Prince, and whether or no he has really promised to emancipate you, whether or no he will consider the promise of a Prince of Wales binding to a King of England, is yet a matter of doubt. We cannot at least be quite certain of it: on this you cannot certainly rely. But there are men who, wherever they find a tendency to freedom, go there to increase, support, and regulate that tendency. These men who join

5 **The King . . . . no more** King George III died January 29, 1820, nearly eight years later 6 **Kings are . . . should do** thinking and acting very quickly is excessive, even dangerous, in kings

to a rational disdain of danger a practice of speaking the truth and defending the cause of the oppressed against the oppressor, these men see what is right and will pursue it. On such as these you may safely rely; they love you as they love their brothers; they feel for the unfortunate and never ask whether a man is an Englishman or an Irishman, a Catholic, a heretic, a Christian, or a heathen, before their hearts and their purses are opened to feel with their misfortunes and relieve their necessities; such are the men who will stand by you for ever. Depend then not upon the promises of Princes, but upon those of virtuous and disinterested men; depend not upon force of arms or violence, but upon the force of the truth of the rights which you have to share equally with others, the benefits and the evils of Government.

The crisis to which I allude as the period of your emancipation, is not the death of the present king, or any circumstance that has to do with kings, but something that is much more likely to do you good: it is the increase of virtue and wisdom which will lead people to find out that force and oppression is wrong and false; and this opinion, when it once gains ground, will prevent government from severity. It will restore those rights which government has taken away. Have nothing to do with force or violence, and things will safely and surely make their way to the right point. The Ministers have now in Parliament a very great majority, and the Ministers are against you. They maintain the falsehood that, were you in power you would persecute and burn, on the plea that you once did so. They maintain many other things of the same nature. They command the majority of the House of Commons, or rather the part of that assembly who receive pensions from Government, or whose relatives receive them. These men of course are against you, because their employers are. But the sense of the country is not against you, the people of England are not against you—they feel warmly for you— in some respects they feel with you. The sense of the English and of their governors is opposite—there must be an end of this; the goodness of a Government consists in the happiness of the Governed. If the Governed are wretched and dissatisfied, the Government has failed in its end. It wants altering and mending. It will be mended, and a reform of English government will produce good to the Irish—good to all human kind, excepting those whose happiness consists in others' sorrows, and it will be a fit punishment for these to be deprived of their devilish joy. This I consider as an event which is approaching, and which will make the beginning of our hopes for that period which may spread wisdom and virtue so wide as to leave no hole in which folly or villainy may hide themselves. I wish you, O Irishmen, to be as careful and thoughtful of your interests as are your real friends. Do not drink, do not play, do not spend any idle time, do not take everything that other people say for granted—there are numbers who will tell you lies to make their own fortunes. You cannot more certainly do good to your own cause than by defeating the intentions of these men. Think, read, and talk; let your own condition and that of your wives and children fill your minds; disclaim all manner of alliance with violence; meet together if you will, but do not meet in a mob. If you think and read and talk with a real wish of benefiting the cause of truth and liberty, it will soon be seen how true a service you are rendering, and how sincere you are in your professions; but mobs and violence must be discarded. The certain degree of civil and religious liberty which the usage of the English Constitution allows is such as the worst of men are entitled to, although you have it not; but that liberty which we may one day hope for, wisdom and virtue can alone give you a right to enjoy. This wisdom and this virtue I recommend on every account that you should *instantly begin* to practise. Lose not a day, not an hour, not a moment. Temperance, sobriety, charity, and independence will give you virtue; and reading, talking, thinking and searching, will give you wisdom; when you have those things you may defy the tyrant. It is not going often to chapel, crossing yourselves, or confessing, that will make you virtuous; many a rascal has attended regularly at Mass, and many a good man has never gone at all. It is not paying Priests or believing in what they say that makes a good man, but it is doing good actions or benefiting other people; this is the true way to be good, and the prayers, and confessions, and masses of him who does not these things, are good for nothing at all. Do your work regularly and quickly; when you have done, think, read, and talk; do not spend your money in idleness and drinking, which so far from doing good to your cause, will do it harm. If you have anything to spare from your wife and children, let it do some good to other people, and put them in a way of getting wisdom and virtue, as the pleasure that will come from these good acts will be much better than the head-ache that comes from a drinking bout. And never quarrel between each other; be all of one mind as nearly as you can; do those things, and I will promise you liberty and happiness. But if, on the contrary of these things, you neglect to improve yourselves, continue to use the word heretic, and demand from others the toleration which you are unwilling to give, your friends and the friends of liberty will have reason to lament the death-blow of their hopes. I expect better things from you; it is for yourselves that I fear and hope. Many Englishmen are prejudiced against you, they sit by their own fire-sides, and certain rumours, artfully spread are ever on the wing against you. But these people who think ill of you and of your nation are often the very men who, if they had better information, would feel for you most keenly. Wherefore are these reports spread? How do they begin? They originate from the warmth of the Irish character, which the friends of the Irish nation have hitherto encouraged rather than repressed; this leads them, in those moments when their wrongs appear so clearly, to commit acts which justly excite displeasure. They begin therefore from yourselves, although falsehood and tyranny artfully magnify and multiply the cause of offence. Give no offence.

I will for the present dismiss the subject of the Catholic Emancipation; a little reflection will convince you that my remarks are just. Be true to yourselves, and your enemies shall not triumph. I fear nothing, if charity and sobriety mark your proceedings. Everything is to be dreaded, you yourselves will be unworthy of even a restoration to your rights, if you disgrace the cause, which I hope is that of truth and liberty, by violence, if you refuse to others the toleration which you claim for yourselves. But this you will not do. I rely upon it, Irishmen, that the warmth of your characters will be shewn as much in union with Englishmen and what are called heretics, who feel for you and love you, as in avenging your wrongs or forwarding their annihilation. It is the heart that glows and not the cheek. The firmness, sobriety, and consistence of your outward behaviour will not at all shew any hardness of heart, but will prove that you are determined in your cause, and are going the right way to work. I will repeat that virtue and wisdom are necessary to true happiness and liberty. The Catholic Emancipation, I consider, is certain.[7] I do not see that anything but violence and intolerance among yourselves can leave an excuse to your enemies for continuing your slavery. The other wrongs under which you labor will probably also soon be done away. You will be rendered equal to the people of England in their rights and privileges and will be in all respects, so far as concerns the state, as happy. And now, Irishmen, another and a more wide prospect opens to my view. I cannot avoid, little as it may appear to have any thing to do with your present situation, to talk to you on the subject. It intimately concerns the well-being of your children and your children's children and will, perhaps more than anything, prove to you the advantage and necessity of being thoughtful, sober, and regular; of avoiding foolish and idle talk, and thinking of yourselves as of men who are able to be much wiser and happier than you now are; for habits like these will not only conduce to the successful putting aside your present and immediate grievances, but will contain a seed which in future times will spring up into the tree of liberty and bear the fruit of happiness.

There is no doubt but the world is going wrong, or rather that it is very capable of being much improved. What I mean by this improvement is the inducement of a more equal and general diffusion of happiness and liberty. Many people are very rich and many are very poor. Which do you think are happiest? I can tell you that neither are happy, so far as their station is concerned. Nature never intended that there should be such a thing as a poor man or a rich one. Being put in an unnatural situation, they can neither of them be happy, so far as their situation is concerned. The poor man is born to obey

---

7 **The Catholic Emancipation . . . certain** Catholic Emancipation bill was passed by English Parliament in 1829, seven years after Shelley's death

the rich man, though they both come into the world equally helpless and equally naked. But the poor man does the rich no service by obeying him—the rich man does the poor no good by commanding him. It would be much better if they could be prevailed upon to live equally like brothers—they would ultimately both be happier. But this can be done neither to-day nor to-morrow; much as such a change is to be desired, it is quite impossible. Violence and folly in this, as in the other case, would only put off the period of its event. Mildness, sobriety, and reason, are the effectual methods of forwarding the ends of liberty and happiness.

Although we may see many things put in train during our lifetime, we cannot hope to see the work of virtue and reason finished now; we can only lay the foundation for our posterity. Government is an evil; it is only the thoughtlessness and vices of men that make it a necessary evil. When all men are good and wise, Government will of itself decay; so long as men continue foolish and vicious, so long will Government, even such a Government as that of England, continue necessary in order to prevent the crimes of bad men. Society is produced by the wants, Government by the wickedness, and a state of just and happy equality by the improvement and reason of man. It is in vain to hope for any liberty and happiness without reason and virtue—for where there is no virtue there will be crime, and where there is crime there must be Government. Before the restraints of Government are lessened, it is fit that we should lessen the necessity for them. Before Government is done away with, we must reform ourselves. It is this work which I would earnestly recommend to you, O Irishmen; REFORM YOURSELVES— and I do not recommend it to you particularly because I think that you most need it, but because I think that your hearts are warm and your feelings high, and you will perceive the necessity of doing it more than those of a colder and more distant nature.

I look with an eye of hope and pleasure on the present state of things, gloomy and incapable of improvement as they may appear to others. It delights me to see that men begin to think and to act for the good of others. Extensively as folly and selfishness has predominated in this age, it gives me hope and pleasure, at least, to see that many know what is right. Ignorance and vice commonly go together; he that would do good must be wise—a man cannot be truly wise who is not truly virtuous. Prudence and wisdom are very different things. The prudent man is he who carefully consults for his own good; the wise man is he who carefully consults for the good of others.

I look upon Catholic Emancipation and the restoration of the liberties and happiness of Ireland, so far as they are compatible with the English Constitution, as great and important events. I hope to see them soon. But if all ended here, it would give me little pleasure—I should still see thousands miserable and wicked; things would still be wrong. I regard, then, the accomplishment of these things as the road to a greater reform—that reform after which virtue and wisdom shall have conquered pain and vice, when no government will be wanted but that of your neighbour's opinion. I look to these things with hope and pleasure because I consider that they will certainly happen and because men will not then be wicked and miserable. But I do not consider that they will or can immediately happen; their arrival will be gradual, and it all depends upon yourselves how soon or how late these great changes will happen. If all of you to-morrow were virtuous and wise, government which to-day is a safeguard, would then become a tyranny. But I cannot expect a rapid change. Many are obstinate and determined in their vice, whose selfishness makes them think only of their own good, when in fact, the best way even to bring that about is to make others happy. I do not wish to see things changed now, because it cannot be done without violence, and we may assure ourselves that none of us are fit for any change however good, if we condescend to employ force in a cause which we think right. Force makes the side that employs it directly wrong, and as much as we may pity, we cannot approve the headstrong and intolerant zeal of adherents.

Can you conceive, O Irishmen! a happy state of society —conceive men of every way of thinking living together like brothers? The descendant of the greatest Prince would there be entitled to no more respect than the son of a peasant. There would be no pomp and no parade, but that which the rich now keep to themselves would then be distributed among the people. None would be in magnificence, but the superfluities then taken from the rich would be sufficient, when spread abroad, to make everyone comfortable. No lover would then be false to his mistress, no mistress would desert her lover. No friend would play false, no rents, no debts, no taxes, no frauds of any kind would disturb the general happiness. Good as they would be, wise as they would be, they would be daily getting better and wiser. No beggars would exist, nor any of those wretched women who are now reduced to a state of the most horrible misery and vice by men whose wealth makes them villainous and hardened. No thieves or murderers, because poverty would never drive men to take away comforts from another, when he had enough for himself. Vice and misery, pomp and poverty, power and obedience, would then be banished altogether. It is for such a state as this, Irishmen, that I exhort you to prepare. "A camel shall as soon pass through the eye of a needle, as a rich man enter the Kingdom of Heaven." [8] This is not to be understood literally; Jesus Christ appears to me only to have meant that riches have generally the effect of hardening and vitiating the heart; so has poverty. I think those people then are very silly, and cannot see one inch beyond their noses, who say that human nature is depraved; when at the same time wealth and poverty, those two great sources of crime, fall to the lot of a great majority of people; and when they see that people in moderate circumstances are always most wise and good. People say that poverty is no evil—they have never felt it, or they would not think so. That wealth is necessary to encourage the arts—but are not the arts very inferior things to virtue and happiness—the man would be very dead to all generous feelings who would rather see pretty pictures and statues than a million free and happy men.

It will be said that my design is to make you dissatisfied with your present condition, and that I wish to raise a Rebellion. But how stupid and sottish must those men be who think that violence and uneasiness of mind have anything to do with forwarding the views of peace, harmony, and happiness. They should know that nothing was so

8 **"A camel . . . Heaven"** Matt. 19:23–24 (misquoted)

well-fitted to produce slavery, tyranny, and vice as the violence which is attributed to the friends of liberty and which the real friends of liberty are the only persons who disdain. As to your being dissatisfied with your present condition, anything that I may say is certainly not likely to increase that dissatisfaction. I have advanced nothing concerning your situation, but its real case, but what may be proved to be true. I defy any one to point out a false-hood that I have uttered in the course of this address. It is impossible but the blindest among you must see that every thing is not right. This sight has often pressed some of the poorest among you to take something from the rich man's store by violence to relieve his own necessities. I cannot justify, but I can pity him. I cannot pity the fruits of the rich man's intemperance. I suppose some are to be found who will justify him. This sight has often brought home to a day-labourer the truth which I wish to impress upon you, that all is not right. But I do not merely wish to convince you that our present state is bad, but that its alteration for the better depends on your own exertions and resolutions.

But he has never found out the method of mending it, who does not first mend his own conduct and then pre-vail upon others to refrain from any vicious habits which they may have contracted—much less does the poor man suppose that wisdom as well as virtue is necessary and that the employing his little time in reading and thinking is really doing all that he has in his power to do towards the state, when pain and vice shall perish altogether.

I wish to impress upon your minds that without virtue or wisdom there can be no liberty or happiness and that temperance, sobriety, charity, and independence of soul will give you virtue—as thinking, enquiring, reading, and talking will give you wisdom. Without the first, the last is of little use, and without the last, the first is a dreadful curse to yourselves and others.

I have told you what I think upon this subject, because I wish to produce in your minds an awe and caution nec-essary before the happy state of which I have spoken can be introduced. This cautious awe is very different from the prudential fear which leads you to consider yourself as the first object, as on the contrary it is full of that warm and ardent love for others that burns in your hearts, O Irishmen! and from which I have fondly hoped to light a flame that may illumine and invigorate the world.

I have said that the rich command, and the poor obey, and that money is only a kind of sign, which shews that according to government the rich man has a right to command the poor man, or rather that the poor man being urged by having no money to get bread, is forced to work for the rich man, which amounts to the same thing. I have said that I think all this very wrong, and that I wish the whole business was altered. I have also said that we can expect little amendment in our own time, and that we must be contented to lay the foundation of liberty and happiness by virtue and wisdom. This then, shall be my work; let this be yours, Irishmen. Never shall that glory fail which I am anxious that you shall deserve. The glory of teaching to a world the first lessons of virtue and wisdom.

Let poor men still continue to work. I do not wish to hide from them a knowledge of their relative condition in society; I esteem it next [to] impossible to do so. Let the work of the labourer, of the artificer—let the work of every one, however employed, still be exerted in its accustomed way. The public communication of this truth ought in no manner to impede the established usages of society; however, it is fitted in the end to do them away. For this reason it ought not to impede them, because if it did, a violent and unaccustomed and sudden sensation would take place in all ranks of men, which would bring on violence and destroy the possibility of the event of that which in its own nature must be gradual, however rapid, and rational, however warm. It is founded on the reform of private men, and without individual amendment it is vain and foolish to expect the amendment of a state or government. I would advise them therefore whose feelings this address may have succeeded in affecting (and surely those feelings which charitable and temperate remarks excite can never be violent and intolerant), if they be, as I hope, those whom poverty has compelled to class themselves in the lower orders of society, that they will as usual attend to their business and the discharge of those public or private duties which custom has ordained. Nothing can be more rash and thoughtless than to shew in ourselves singular instances of any particular doctrine before the general mass of the people are so convinced by the reasons of the doctrine that it will be no longer singular. That reasons as well as feeling may help the establishment of happiness and liberty on the basis of wisdom and virtue is our aim and intention. Let us not be led into any means which are unworthy of this end, nor, as so much depends upon yourselves, let us cease carefully to watch over our conduct, that when we talk of reform it be not objected to us that reform ought to begin at home. In the interval that public or private duties and necessary labours allow, husband your time so that you may do to others and yourselves the most real good. To improve your own minds is to join these two views; conversation and reading are the principal and chief methods of awakening the mind to knowledge and goodness. Reading or thought will principally bestow the former of these—the benevolent exercise of the powers of the mind in communicating useful knowledge will bestow an habit of the latter; both united will contribute so far as lies in your individual power to that great reform which will be perfect and finished the moment everyone is virtuous and wise. Every folly refuted, every bad habit conquered, every good one confirmed, as [is] so much gained in this great and excellent cause.

To begin to reform the Government is immediately necessary, however good or bad individuals may be; it is the more necessary if they are eminently the latter in some degree to palliate or do away the cause as political institution has even [ever] the greatest influence on the human character and is that alone which differences the Turk from the Irishman.

I write now not only with a view for Catholic Emancipation, but for universal emancipation; and this emancipation complete and unconditional, that shall comprehend every individual of whatever nation or principles, that shall fold in its embrace all that think and all that feel. The Catholic cause is subordinate, and its success preparatory to this great cause, which adheres to no sect but society, to no cause but that of universal happiness, to no party but the people. I desire Catholic Emancipation, but I desire not to stop here, and I hope there are few who, having

perused the preceding arguments, will not concur with me
in desiring a complete, a lasting, and a happy amendment.
That all steps, however good and salutary, which may be
taken, all reforms consistent with the English constitution
that may be effectuated can only be subordinate and preparatory to the great and lasting one which shall bring
about the peace, the harmony, and the happiness of Ireland, England, Europe, the World. I offer merely an out-
line of that picture which your own hopes may gift with
the colors of reality.

Government will not allow a peaceable and reasonable
discussion of its principles by any association of men who
assemble for that express purpose. But have not human
beings a right to assemble to talk upon what subject they
please? Can anything be more evident than that, as government is only of use as it conduces to the happiness of
the governed, those who are governed have a right to talk
on the efficacy of the safeguard employed for their benefit? Can any topic be more interesting or useful than on
discussing how far the means of government is or could
be made in a higher degree effectual to producing the end?
Although I deprecate violence and the cause which depends for its influence on force, yet I can by no means
think that assembling together merely to talk of how
things go on, I can by no means think that societies
formed for talking on any subject however government
may dislike them, come in any way under the head of
force or violence. I think that associations conducted in the
spirit of sobriety, regularity, and thought, are one of the
best and most efficient of those means which I would
recommend for the production of happiness, liberty, and
virtue.

Are you slaves, or are you men? If slaves, then crouch
to the rod, and lick the feet of your oppressors, glory [in]
your shame; it will become you, if brutes, to act according
to your nature. But you are men; a real man is free, so far
as circumstances will permit him. Then firmly, yet quietly,
resist. When one cheek is struck, turn the other to the
insulting coward. You will be truly brave; you will resist
and conquer. The discussion of any subject is a right that
you have brought into the world with your heart and
tongue. Resign your heart's blood before you part with this

inestimable privilege of man. For it is fit that the governed should enquire into the proceedings of Government, which is of no use the moment it is conducted on any other principle but that of safety. You have much to think of. Is war necessary to your happiness and safety? The interests of the poor gain nothing from the wealth or extension of a nation's boundaries; they gain nothing from glory, a word that has often served as a cloak to the ambition or avarice of Statesmen. The barren victories of Spain, gained in behalf of a bigoted and tyrannical Government, are nothing to them. The conquests in India, by which England has gained glory indeed, but a glory which is not more honourable than that of Buonaparte, are nothing to them. The poor purchase this glory and this wealth at the expense of their blood and labor, and happiness, and virtue. They die in battle for this infernal cause. Their labor supplies money and food for carrying it into effect; their happiness is destroyed by the oppression they undergo; their virtue is rooted out by the depravity and vice that prevail throughout the army, and which under the present system is perfectly unavoidable. Who does not know that the quartering of a regiment on any town will soon destroy the innocence and happiness of its inhabitants? The advocates for the happiness and liberty of the great mass of the people, who pay for war with their lives and labor, ought never to cease writing and speaking until nations see, as they must feel, the folly of fighting and killing each other in uniform for nothing at all. Ye have much to think of. The state of your representation in the house, which is called the collective representation of the country, demands your attention.

It is horrible that the lower classes must waste their lives and liberty to furnish means for their oppressors to oppress them yet more terribly. It is horrible that the poor must give in taxes what would save them and their families from hunger and cold; it is still more horrible that they should do this to furnish further means of their own abjectedness and misery; but what words can express the enormity of the abuse that prevents them from choosing representatives with authority to enquire into the manner in which their lives and labor, their happiness and innocence, is expended, and what advantages result from their expenditure which may counterbalance so horrible and monstrous an evil? There is an outcry raised against amendment; it is called innovation and condemned by many unthinking people who have a good fire and plenty to eat and drink; hard-hearted or thoughtless beings, how many are famishing whilst you deliberate, how many perish to contribute to your pleasures? I hope that there are none such as these native Irishmen, indeed I scarcely believe that there are.

Let the object of your associations (for I conceal not my approval of assemblies conducted with regularity, *peaceableness* and thought for any purpose) be the amendment of these abuses; it will have for its object universal Emancipation, liberty, happiness, and virtue. There is yet another subject, "the Liberty of the Press." The liberty of the press consists in a right to publish any opinion on any subject which the writer may entertain. The Attorney General in 1793 on the trial of Mr. Perry, said, "I never will dispute the right of any man fully to discuss topics respecting government and honestly to point out what he may consider a proper remedy of grievances." The liberty of the Press is placed as a sentinel to alarm us when any attempt is made on our liberties. It is this Sentinel, O Irishmen, whom I now awaken! I create to myself a freedom which exists not. There is no liberty of the press for the subjects of British government.

It is really ridiculous to hear people yet boasting of this inestimable blessing when they daily see it successfully muzzled and outraged by the lawyers of the crown, and by virtue of what are called ex officio informations. Blackstone says that "if a person publishes what is improper, mischievous, or illegal, he must take the consequences of his own temerity"; and Lord Chief Baron Comyns defines libel as "a contumely, or reproach, published to the defamation of the Government, of a magistrate, or of a private person." Now, I beseech you to consider the words, mischievous, improper, illegal, contumely, reproach, or defamation. May they not make that mischievous or improper which they please? Is not law with them, as clay in the potter's hand? Do not the words, contumely, reproach, or defamation, express all degrees and forces of disapprobation? It is impossible to express yourself displeased at certain proceedings of Government, or the individuals who conduct it, without uttering a reproach. We cannot honestly point out a proper remedy of grievances with safety, because the very mention of these grievances will be reproachful to the personages who countenance them and therefore will come under a definition of libel. For the persons who thus directly or indirectly undergo reproach will say for their own sakes that the exposure of their corruption is mischievous and improper; therefore, the utterer of the reproach is a fit subject for three years' imprisonment. Is there anything like the Liberty of the Press in restrictions so positive yet pliant as these? The little freedom which we enjoy in this most important point comes from the clemency of our rulers, or their fear lest public opinion, alarmed at the discovery of its enslaved state, should violently assert a right to extension and diffusion. Yet public opinion may not always be so formidable, rulers may not always be so merciful or so timid. At any rate, evils, and great evils, do result from the present system of intellectual slavery, and you have enough to think of if this grievance alone remained in the constitution of society. I will give but one instance of the present state of our Press.

A countryman of yours is now confined in an English gaol.[9] His health, his fortune, his spirits suffer from close confinement. The air which comes through the bars of a prison-gate does not invigorate the frame nor cheer the spirits. But Mr. Finnerty, much as he has lost, yet retains the fair name of truth and honour. He was imprisoned for persisting in the truth. His judge told him on his trial that truth and falsehood were indifferent to the law, and that if he owned the publication any consideration, whether the facts that it related were well or ill-founded, was totally irrelevant. Such is the libel law. Such the liberty of the Press—there is enough to think of. The right of withholding your individual assent to war, the right of choosing

9 **A countryman . . . gaol** Peter Finnerty, Irish journalist convicted without privilege of defending himself in court, and sentenced to eighteen months' imprisonment for publishing a "libelous" letter in London *Morning Chronicle*. Shelley contributed to a relief fund for Finnerty

delegates to represent you in the assembly of the nation, and that of freely opposing intellectual power to any measures of Government of which you may disapprove are, in addition to the indifference with which the legislative and the executive power ought to rule their conduct towards professors of every religion, enough to think of.

I earnestly desire peace and harmony: peace, that whatever wrongs you may have suffered, benevolence and a spirit of forgiveness should mark your conduct towards those who have persecuted you; harmony, that among yourselves may be no divisions, that Protestants and Catholics unite in a common interest, and that whatever be the belief and principles of your countryman and fellow-sufferer, you desire to benefit his cause at the same time that you vindicate your own. Be strong and unbiassed by selfishness or prejudice—for, Catholics, your religion has not been spotless; crimes in past ages have sullied it with a stain, which let it be your glory to remove. Nor, Protestants, hath your religion always been characterized by the mildness of benevolence, which Jesus Christ recommended. Had it anything to do with the present subject, I could account for the spirit of intolerance which marked both religions; I will, however, only adduce the fact and earnestly exhort you to root out from your own minds everything which may lead to uncharitableness, and to reflect that yourselves as well as your brethren may be deceived. Nothing on earth is infallible. The Priests that pretend to it are wicked and mischievous impostors; but it is an imposture which everyone, more or less, assumes, who encourages prejudice in his breast against those who differ from him in opinion, or who sets up his own religion as the only right and true one, when no one is so blind as [not] to see that every religion is right and true which makes men beneficent and sincere. I therefore earnestly exhort both Protestants and Catholics to act in brotherhood and harmony, never forgetting, because the Catholics alone are heinously deprived of religious rights, that the Protestants and a certain rank of people of every persuasion share with them all else that is terrible, galling, and intolerable in the mass of political grievance.

In no case employ violence or falsehood. I cannot too often or too vividly endeavour to impress upon your minds that these methods will produce nothing but wretchedness and slavery—that they will at the same time rivet the fetters with which ignorance and oppression bind you to abjectness, and deliver you over to a tyranny which shall render you incapable of renewed efforts. Violence will immediately render your cause a bad one. If you believe in a Providential God, you must also believe that he is a good one; and it is not likely a merciful God would befriend a bad cause. Insincerity is no less hurtful than violence; those who are in the habit of either would do well to reform themselves. A lying bravo will never promote the good of his country—he cannot be a good man. The courageous and sincere may, at the same time, successfully oppose corruption by uniting their voice with that of others, or individually raise up intellectual opposition to counteract the abuses of Government and society. In order to benefit yourselves and your country to any extent, habits of sobriety, regularity, and thought are previously so necessary that without these preliminaries all that you have done falls to the ground. You have built on sand. Secure a good foundation, and you may erect a fabric to stand for ever—the glory and the envy of the world!

I have purposely avoided any lengthened discussion on those grievances to which your hearts are from custom and the immediate interest of the circumstances probably most alive at present. I have not however wholly neglected them. Most of all have I insisted on their instant palliation and ultimate removal; nor have I omitted a consideration of the means which I deem most effectual for the accomplishment of this great end. How far you will consider the former worthy of your adoption, so far shall I deem the latter probable and interesting to the lovers of human kind. And I have opened to your view a new scene—does not your heart bound at the bare possibility of your posterity possessing that liberty and happiness of which during our lives powerful exertions and habitual abstinence may give us a foretaste? Oh! if your hearts do not vibrate at such as this, then ye are dead and cold—ye are not men.

I now come to the application of my principles, the conclusion of my address; and, O Irishmen, whatever conduct ye may feel yourselves bound to pursue, the path which duty points to lies before me clear and unobscured. Dangers may lurk around it, but they are not the dangers which lie beneath the footsteps of the hypocrite or temporizer.

For I have not presented to you the picture of happiness on which my fancy doats as an uncertain meteor to mislead honorable enthusiasm, or blindfold the judgment which makes virtue useful. I have not proposed crude schemes which I should be incompetent to mature, or desired to excite in you any virulence against the abuses of political institution; where I have had occasion to point them out, I have recommended moderation whilst yet I have earnestly insisted upon energy and perseverance; I have spoken of peace, yet declared that resistance is laudable; but the intellectual resistance which I recommend I deem essential to the introduction of the millennium of virtue, whose period every one can, so far as he is concerned, forward by his own proper power. I have not attempted to shew that the Catholic claims or the claims of the people to a full representation in Parliament, or any of those claims to real rights which I have insisted upon as introductory to the ultimate claim of *all*, to universal happiness, freedom, and equality; I have not attempted, I say, to shew that these can be granted consistently with the spirit of the English Constitution.[10] This is a point which I do not feel myself inclined to discuss, and which I consider foreign to my subject. But I have shewn that these claims have for their basis truth and justice, which are immutable, and which in the ruin of Governments shall rise like a Phœnix from their ashes.

Is any one inclined to dispute the possibility of a happy change in society? Do they say that the nature of man is corrupt, and that he was made for misery and wickedness? Be it so. Certain as are opposite conclusions, I will concede the truth of this for a moment. What are the means which I take for melioration? Violence, corruption, rapine, crime? Do I do evil that good may come? I have recom-

10 The excellence of the Constitution of Great Britain appears to me to be its indefiniteness and versatility, whereby it may be unresistingly accommodated to the progression of wisdom and virtue. Such accommodation I desire; but I wish for the cause before the effect. [Shelley's note]

mended peace, philanthropy, wisdom. So far as my arguments influence, they will influence to these—and if there is any one *now* inclined to say that "private vices are public benefits," [11] and that peace, philanthropy, and wisdom will, if once they gain ground, ruin the human race, he may revel in his happy dreams; though were *I* this man I should envy Satan's Hell. The wisdom and charity of which I speak are the *only* means which I will countenance for the redress of your grievances and the grievances of the world. So far as they operate, I am willing to stand responsible for their *evil* effects. I expect to be accused of a desire for renewing in Ireland the scenes of revolutionary horror which marked the struggles of France twenty years ago. But it is the renewal of that unfortunate æra which I strongly deprecate, and which the tendency of this address is calculated to obviate. For can burthens be borne forever, and the slave crouch and cringe the while? Is misery and vice so consonant to man's nature that he will hug it to his heart? But when the wretched one in bondage beholds the emancipation near, will he not endure his misery awhile with hope and patience, then spring to his preserver's arms, and start into a man?

It is my intention to observe the effect on your minds, O Irishmen! which this address, dictated by the fervency of my love and hope, will produce. I have come to this country to spare no pains where expenditure may purchase you real benefit. The present is a crisis, which of all others is the most valuable for fixing the fluctuation of public feeling; as far as my poor efforts may have succeeded in fixing it to virtue, Irishmen, so far shall I esteem myself happy. I intend this address as introductory to another. The organization of a society whose institution shall serve as a bond to its members for the purposes of virtue, happiness, liberty, and wisdom, by the means of intellectual opposition to grievances, would probably be useful. For the formation of such society I avow myself anxious.

Adieu, my friends! May every Sun that shines on your green Island see the annihilation of an abuse, and the birth of an Embryon of melioration! Your own hearts—may

11 **"private vices are public benefits"**   the subtitle of Mandeville's *Fable of the Bees* (1714) is *Private Vices, Public Benefits*

they become the shrines of purity and freedom, and never may smoke to the Mammon of unrighteousness ascend from the unpolluted altar of their devotion.

No. 7, Sackville Street, Feb. 22.

Postscript

I have now been a week in Dublin, during which time I have endeavoured to make myself more accurately acquainted with the state of the public mind on those great topics of grievances which induced me to select Ireland as a theatre, the widest and fairest, for the operations of the determined friend of religious and political freedom.

The result of my observations has determined me to propose an association for the purposes of restoring Ireland to the prosperity which she possessed before the Union Act, and the religious freedom which the involuntariness of faith ought to have taught all monopolists of Heaven long, long ago that every one had a right to possess.

For the purpose of obtaining the emancipation of the Catholics from the penal laws that aggrieve them, and a Repeal of the Legislative Union Act, and grounding upon the remission of the church-craft and oppression which caused these grievances: *a plan of amendment and regeneration in the moral and political state of society, on a comprehensive and systematic philanthropy, which shall be sure though slow in its projects; and as it is without the rapidity and danger of revolution, so will it be devoid of the time-servingness of temporizing reform*—which in its deliberate capacity, having investigated the state of the government of England, shall oppose those parts of it by intellectual force which will not bear the touch-stone of reason.

For information respecting the principles which I possess, and the nature and spirit of the association which I propose, I refer the reader to a small pamphlet which I shall publish on the subject in the course of a few days.

I have published the above address (written in England) in the cheapest possible form and have taken pains that the remarks which it contains should be intelligible to the most uneducated minds. Men are not slaves and brutes because they are poor; it has been the policy of the thoughtless or wicked of the higher ranks (as a proof of the decay of which policy I am happy to see the rapid success of a comparatively enlightened system of education) to conceal from the poor the truths which I have endeavoured to teach them. In doing so, I have but translated my thoughts into another language; and as language is only useful as it communicates ideas, I shall think my style so far good as it is successful as a means to bring about the end which I desire on any occasion to accomplish.

A Limerick Paper, which I suppose professes to support certain *loyal* and *John Bullish* principles of freedom, has in an essay for advocating the Liberty of the Press, the following clause: "For lawless license of discussion never did we advocate, nor do we now." What is lawless license of discussion? Is it not as indefinite as the words, *contumely, reproach, defamation,* that allow at present such latitude to the outrages that are committed on the free expression of individual sentiment? Can they not see that what is rational will stand by its reason, and what is true stand by its truth, as all that is foolish will fall by its folly, and all that is false be controverted by its own falsehood? Liberty gains nothing by the reform of politicians of this stamp, any more than it gains from a change of Ministers in London. What at present is contumely and defamation would at the period of this Limerick amendment be "lawless license of discussion," and such would be the mighty advantage which this doughty champion of liberty proposes to effect.

I conclude with the words of Lafayette, a name endeared by its peerless bearer to every lover of the human race, "For a nation to love Liberty it is sufficient that she knows it, to be free it is sufficient that she wills it."

Proposals for an Association of Philanthropists

I propose an association which shall have for its immediate objects Catholic Emancipation and the Repeal of the Act of Union between Great Britain and Ireland; and grounding on the removal of these grievances, an annihilation or palliation of whatever moral or political evil it may be within the compass of human power to assuage or eradicate.

Man cannot make occasions, but he may seize those that offer. None are more interesting to Philanthropy than those which excite the benevolent passions that generalize and expand private into public feelings and make the hearts of individuals vibrate not merely for themselves, their families, and their friends, but for posterity, *for a people*; till their country becomes the world and their family the sensitive creation.[1]

A recollection of the absent and a taking into consideration the interests of those unconnected with ourselves is a principal source of that feeling which generates occa-

Complete title Proposals for an Association of Philanthropists who convinced of the inadequacy of the Moral and Political State of Ireland to Produce Benefits which are nevertheless Attainable are Willing to Unite to Accomplish its Regeneration
1 **None are more . . . creation** Shelley's genuine internationalism, opposed to nationalism as the cause of war and other dissension (see *Essay on Christianity*, pp. 92–93)

sions wherein a love for human kind may become eminently useful and active. Public topics of fear and hope, such as sympathize with general grievance or hold out hopes of general amendment, are those on which the Philanthropist would dilate with the warmest feeling. Because these are accustomed to place individuals at a distance from self; for in proportion as he is absorbed in public feeling, so will a consideration of his proper benefit be generalized. In proportion as he feels with or for a nation or a world, so will man consider himself less as that centre to which we are but too prone to believe that every line of human concern does or ought to converge.

I should not here make the trite remark that selfish motive biasses, brutalizes, and degrades the human mind, did it not thence follow that to seize those occasions wherein the opposite spirit predominates, is a duty which Philanthropy imperiously exacts of her votaries, that occasions like these are the proper ones for leading mankind to their own interest by awakening in their minds a love for the interest of their fellows—a plant that grows in every soil, though too often it is choked by tares before its lovely blossoms are expanded. Virtue produces pleasure; it is as the cause to the effect; I feel pleasure in doing good to my friend, because I love him. I do not love him for the sake of that pleasure.

I regard the present state of the public mind in Ireland to be one of those occasions which the ardent votary of the religion of Philanthropy dare not leave unseized. I perceive that the public interest is excited; I perceive that individual interest has, in a certain degree, quitted individual concern to generalize itself with universal feeling. Be the Catholic Emancipation a thing of great or of small misfortune,[2] be it a means of adding happiness to four millions of people, or a reform which will only give honor to a few of the higher ranks, yet a benevolent and disinterested feeling has gone abroad, and I am willing that it should never subside. I desire that means should be taken with energy and expedition, in this important yet fleeting crisis, to feed the unpolluted flame at which nations and ages may light the torch of Liberty and Virtue!

2 **Be . . . misfortune** even if it were not successfully carried out

It is my opinion that the claims of the Catholic inhabitants of Ireland, if gained to-morrow, would in a very small degree aggrandize their liberty and happiness. The disqualifications principally affect the higher orders of the Catholic persuasion; these would principally be benefited by their removal. Power and wealth do not benefit, but injure the cause of virtue and freedom. I am happy, however, at the near approach of this emancipation, because I am inimical to all disqualifications for opinion. It gives me pleasure to see the approach of this enfranchisement, not for the good which it will bring with it, but because it is a sign of benefits approaching, a prophet of good about to come; and therefore do I sympathize with the inhabitants of Ireland in this great cause; a cause which though in its own accomplishment will add not one comfort to the cottager, will snatch not one from the dark dungeon, will root not out one vice, alleviate not one pang, yet it is the fore-ground of a picture, in the dimness of whose distance I behold the lion lay [lie] down with the lamb and the infant play with the basilisk. For it supposes the extermination of the eyeless monster bigotry, whose throne has tottered for two hundred years. I hear the teeth of the palsied beldame Superstition chatter, and I see her descending to the grave! Reason points to the open gates of the Temple of Religious Freedom; Philanthropy kneels at the altar of the common God! There wealth and poverty, rank and abjectness, are names known but as memorials of past time: meteors which play over the loathsome pool of vice and misery, to warn the wanderer where dangers lie. Does a God rule this illimitable universe; are you thankful for his beneficence—do you adore his wisdom— do you hang upon his altar the garland of your devotion? Curse not your brother, though he hath enwreathed with his flowers of a different hue; the purest religion is that of Charity; its loveliness begins to proselyte the hearts of men. The tree is to be judged of by its fruit. I regard the admission of the Catholic claims and the Repeal of the Union Act as blossoms of that fruit which the Summer Sun of improved intellect and progressive virtue is destined to mature.

I will not pass unreflected on the Legislative Union of Great Britain and Ireland, nor will I speak of it as a grievance so tolerable or unimportant in its own nature as that of Catholic disqualification. The latter affects few, the former affects thousands. The one disqualifies the rich from power; the other impoverishes the peasant, adds beggary to the city, famine to the country, multiplies abjectedness, whilst misery and crime play into each other's hands under its withering auspices. I esteem, then, the annihilation of this second grievance to be something more than a mere sign of coming good. I esteem it to be in itself a substantial benefit. The aristocracy of Ireland—for much as I may disapprove other distinctions than those of virtue and talent, I consider it useless, hasty, and violent, not for the present to acquiesce in their continuance—the aristocracy of Ireland suck the veins of its inhabitants and consume the blood in England. I mean not to deny the unhappy truth that there is much misery and vice in the world. I mean to say that Ireland shares largely of both. England has made her poor; and the poverty of a rich nation will make its people very desperate and wicked.

I look forward, then, to the redress of both these grievances, or rather, I perceive the state of the public mind that precedes them as the crisis of beneficial innovation. The latter I consider to be the cause of the former, as I hope it will be the cause of more comprehensively beneficial amendments. It forms that occasion which should energetically and quickly be occupied. The voice of the whole human race, their crimes, their miseries, and their ignorance, invoke us to the task. For the miseries of the Irish poor, exacerbated by the union of their country with England, are not peculiar to themselves. England, the whole civilized world, with few exceptions, is either sunk in disproportioned abjectness or raised to unnatural elevation. The Repeal of the Union Act will place Ireland on a level, so far as concerns the well-being of its poor, with her sister nation. Benevolent feeling has gone out in this country in favor of the happiness of its inhabitants—may this feeling be corroborated, methodized, and continued! May it never fail! But it will not be kept alive by each citizen sitting quietly by his own fire-side, and saying that things are going on well because the rain does not beat on *him*, because *he* has books and leisure to read them, because *he* has money and is at liberty to accumulate luxuries to *himself*. Generous feeling dictates no such sayings. When the heart recurs to the thousands who have no liberty and no leisure, it must be rendered callous by long contemplation of wretchedness, if after such recurrence it can beat with contented evenness. Why do I talk thus? Is there anyone who doubts that the present state of politics and morals is wrong? They say, Shew us a safe method of improvement. There is no safer than the corroboration and propagation of generous and Philanthropic feeling, than the keeping continually alive a love for the human race, than the putting in train causes which shall have for their consequences virtue and freedom; and because I think that individuals acting singly, with whatever energy, can never effect so much as a society, I propose that all those whose views coincide with those that I have avowed, who perceive the state of the public mind in Ireland, who think the present a fit opportunity for attempting to fix its fluctuations at Philanthropy, who love all mankind, and are willing actively to engage in its cause, or passively to endure the persecutions of those who are inimical to its success; I propose to these to form an association for the purposes, first, of debating on the propriety of whatever measures may be agitated, and secondly, for carrying, by united or individual exertion, such measures into effect when determined on. That it should be an association for discussing[3] knowledge and virtue throughout the poorer classes of society in Ireland, for co-operating with any enlightened system of education, for discussing topics calculated to throw light on any methods of alleviation of moral and political evil, and as far as lays [lies] in its power, actively interesting itself in whatever occasions may arise for benefiting mankind.

When I mention Ireland, I do not mean to confine the influence of the association to this or to any other country, but for the time being. Moreover, I would recommend that this association should attempt to form others and to actuate them with a similar spirit; and I am thus indeterminate in my description of the association which I propose, because I conceive that an assembly of men meeting to do all the good that opportunity will permit

3 **discussing** intended word perhaps "diffusing"

them to do, must be in its nature as indefinite and vary-
ing as the instances of human vice and misery that precede,
occasion, and call for its institution.

As political institution and its attendant evils constitute
the majority of those grievances which Philanthropists desire to remedy, it is probable that existing Governments
will frequently become the topic of their discussion, the
results of which may little coincide with the opinions
which those who profit by the supineness of human belief desire to impress upon the world. It is probable that
this freedom may excite the odium of certain well-meaning
people who pin their faith upon their grandmother's apron-
string. The minority in number are the majority in intellect and power. The former govern the latter, though it
is by the sufferance of the latter that this originally delegated power is exercised. This power is become hereditary
and hath ceased to be necessarily united with intellect.

It is certain, therefore, that any questioning of established principles would excite the abhorrence and opposition of those who derived power and honour (such as it is)
from their continuance.

As the association which I recommend would question
those principles (however they may be hedged in with
antiquity and precedent) which appeared ill adapted for
the benefit of human kind, it would probably excite the
odium of those in power. It would be obnoxious to the
government, though nothing would be farther from the
views of associated philanthropists than attempting to
subvert establishments forcibly, or even hastily. Aristocracy
would oppose it, whether oppositionists or ministerialists
(for philanthropy is of no party) because its ultimate views
look to a subversion of all factitious distinctions, although
from its immediate intentions I fear that aristocracy can
have nothing to dread. The priesthood would oppose it
because a union of church and state—contrary to the
principles and practice of Jesus, contrary to that equality
which he fruitlessly endeavoured to teach mankind—is
of all institutions that from the rust of antiquity are called
venerable, the least qualified to stand free and cool reasoning, because it least conduces to the happiness of human
kind; yet did either the minister, the peer, or the bishop,
know their true interest, instead of that virulent opposition

which some among them have made to freedom and philanthropy, they would rejoice and co-operate with the diffusion and corroboration of those principles that would
remove a load of paltry equivocation, paltrier grandeur,
and of wigs that crush into emptiness the brains below
them from their shoulders; and by permitting them to
reassume the degraded and vilified title of man would
preclude the necessity of mystery and deception, would
bestow on them a title more ennobling and a dignity
which, though it would be without the gravity of an
ape, would possess the ease and consistency of a man.

For the reasons above alleged, falsely, prejudicedly, and
narrowly will those very persons whose ultimate benefit
is included in the general good, whose promotion is the
essence of a philanthropic association, will they persecute
those who have the best intentions towards them, malevolence towards none.

I do not, therefore, conceal that those who make the
favour of government the sunshine of their moral day
confide in the political creed makers of the hour, are
willing to think things that are rusty and decayed venerable, and are uninquiringly satisfied with evils as these are,
because they find them established and unquestioned as
they do sunlight and air when they come into existence;
that they had better not even think of philanthropy. I
conceal not from them that the discountenance which
government will show to such an association as I am
desirous to establish will come under their comprehensive
definition of danger: that virtue and any assembly instituted under its auspices demands a voluntariness on the
part of its devoted individuals to sacrifice personal to
public benefit; and that it is possible that a party of beings
associated for the purposes of disseminating virtuous principles may, considering the ascendency which long custom
has conferred on opposite motives to action, meet with
inconveniences that may amount to personal danger. These
considerations are, however, to the mind of the philanthropist as is a drop to an ocean; they serve by their
possible existence as tests whereby to discover the really
virtuous man from him who calls himself a patriot for
dishonourable and selfish purposes. I propose then to such

as think with me, a Philanthropic Association, in spite of the danger that may attend the attempt. I do not this beneath the shroud of mystery and darkness. I propose not an Association of Secrecy. Let it [be] open as the beam of day. Let it rival the sunbeam in its stainless purity, as in the extensiveness of its effulgence.

I disclaim all connexion with insincerity and concealment. The latter implies the former as much as the former stands in need of the latter. It is a very latitudinarian system of morality that permits its professor to employ bad means for any end whatever. Weapons which vice *can* use are unfit for the hands of virtue. Concealment implies falsehood; it is bad and can therefore never be serviceable to the cause of philanthropy.

I propose, therefore, that the association shall be established and conducted in the open face of day, with the utmost possible publicity. It is only vice that hides itself in holes and corners, whose effrontery shrinks from scrutiny, whose cowardice lets *I dare not* wait upon *I would*, like the poor cat in the adage.[4] But the eye of virtue, eagle-like, darts through the undazzling beam of eternal truth, and from the undiminished fountain of its purity gathers wherewith to vivify and illuminate a universe.

I have hitherto abstained from inquiring whether the association which I recommend be or be not consistent with the English constitution. And here it is fit briefly to consider what a constitution is.

Government can have no rights; it is a delegation for the purpose of securing them to others. Man becomes a subject of government, not that he may be in a worse but that he may be in a better state than that of unorganized society. The strength of government is the happiness of the governed. All government existing for the happiness of others is just only so far as it exists by their consent, and useful only so far as it operates to their well-being. Constitution is to government what government is to law. Constitution may, in this view of the subject, be defined to be not merely something constituted for the benefit of

---

4 **I dare not . . . adage** *Macbeth*, I, 7, 44–45 (the same expression appears in *A Letter to Lord Ellenborough*, p. 61, and *A Defence of Poetry*, see p. 190)

any nation or class of people, but something constituted by themselves for their own benefit.[5] The nations of England and Ireland have no constitution, because at no one time did the individuals that compose them constitute a system for the general benefit. If a system determined on by a very few, at a great length of time; if magna charta, the bill of rights, and other usages for whose influence the improved state of human knowledge is rather to be looked to than any system which courtiers pretend to exist and perhaps believe to exist; a system whose spring of agency they represent as something secret, undiscoverable and awful as the law of nature; if these make a constitution, then England has one. But if (as I have endeavoured to show they do not) a constitution is something else, then the speeches of kings or commissioners, the writings of courtiers, and the journals of parliament, which teem with its glory, are full of political cant, exhibit the skeleton of national freedom, and are fruitless attempts to hide evils in whose favour they cannot prove an alibi. As therefore, in the true sense of the expression, the spot of earth on which we live is destitute of constituted Government, it is impossible to offend against its principles, or to be with justice accused of wishing to subvert what has no real existence. If a man was accused of setting fire to a house, which house never existed, and from the nature of things could not have existed, it is impossible that a jury in their senses would find him guilty of arson. The English constitution, then, could not be offended by the principles of virtue and freedom. In fact, the manner in which the Government of England has varied since its earliest establishment proves that its present form is the result of a progressive accommodation to existing principles. It has been a continual struggle for liberty on the part of the people and an uninterrupted attempt at tightening the reins of oppression and encouraging ignorance and imposture by the oligarchy to whom the first William parcelled out the property of the aborigines at the conquest of England by the Normans. I hear much of its being a

5 **Government can . . . own benefit** typical of ideas in this essay closely resembling Godwin's *Political Justice*, Bks. I–II; also closely related to Paine's writings

tree so long growing which to cut down is as bad as cutting down an oak where there are no more. But the best way on topics similar to these is to tell the plain truth, without the confusion and ornament of metaphor. I call expressions similar to these political cant, which, like the songs of Rule Britannia and God save the king, are but abstracts of the caterpillar creed of courtiers, cut down to the taste and comprehension of a mob; the one to disguise to an alehouse politician the evils of that devilish practice of war, and the other to inspire among clubs of all descriptions a certain feeling which some call loyalty and others servility. A philanthropic association has nothing to fear from the English constitution, but it may expect danger from its government. So far however from thinking this an argument against its institution, establishment, and augmentation, I am inclined to rest much of the weight of the cause which my duties call upon me to support on the very fact that government forcibly interferes when the opposition that is made to its proceedings is professedly and undeniably nothing but intellectual. A good cause may be shown to be good; violence instantly renders bad what might before have been good. "Weapons that falsehood can use are unfit for the hands of truth." Truth can reason, and falsehood cannot.

A political or religious system may burn and imprison those who investigate its principles, but it is an invariable proof of their falsehood and hollowness. Here then is another reason for the necessity of a Philanthropic Association, and I call upon any fair and rational opponent to controvert the argument which it contains; for there is no one who even calls himself a philanthropist that thinks personal danger or dishonour terrible in any other light than as it affects his usefulness.

Man has a heart to feel, a brain to think, and a tongue to utter. The laws of his moral as of his physical nature are immutable, as is everything of nature; nor can the ephemeral institutions of human society take away those rights, annihilate or strengthen the duties that have for their basis the imperishable relations of his constitution.

Though the parliament of England were to pass a thousand bills to inflict upon those who determined to utter their thoughts, a thousand penalties, it could not render that criminal which was in its nature innocent before the passing of such bill.

Man has a right to feel, to think, and to speak, nor can any acts of legislature destroy that right. He will feel, he must think, and he *ought* to give utterance to those thoughts and feelings with the readiest sincerity and the strictest candour. A man must have a right to do a thing before he can have a duty; this right must permit before his duty can enjoin him to any act. Any law is bad which attempts to make it criminal to do what the plain dictates within the breast of every man tells [tell] him that he ought to do.

The English Government permits a fanatic to assemble any number of persons to teach them the most extravagant and immoral systems of faith; but a few men meeting to consider its own principles are marked with its hatred and pursued by its jealousy.

The religionist who agonizes the death-bed of the cottager, and by picturing the hell, which hearts black and narrow as his own alone could have invented, and which exists but in their cores, spreads the uncharitable doctrines which devote *heretics* to eternal torments, and represents heaven to be what earth is, a monopoly in the hands of certain favoured ones whose merit consists in slavishness, whose success is the reward of sycophancy. Thus much is permitted, but a public inquiry that involves any doubt of their rectitude into the principles of government is not permitted. When Jupiter and a countryman were one day walking out, conversing familiarly on the affairs of earth, the countryman listened to Jupiter's assertions on the subject for some time in acquiescence, at length happening to hint a doubt. Jupiter threatened him with his thunder; ah, ah, says the countryman, now Jupiter I know that you are wrong; you are always wrong when you appeal to your thunder. The essence of virtue is disinterestedness. Disinterestedness is the quality which preserves the character of virtue distinct from that of either innocence or vice. This, it will be said, is mere assertion. It is so: but it is an assertion, whose truth, I believe, the hearts of philanthropists are disinclined to deny. Those who have been convinced by their grandam of the doctrine of an original hereditary sin, or by the apostles of a degrading philosophy of the necessary and universal selfishness of man cannot be philanthropists. Now as an action, or a motive to action, is only virtuous so far as it is disinterested or partakes (I adopt this mode of expression to suit the taste of some) of the nature of generalized self-love, then reward or punishment, attached even by omnipotence to any action, can in no wise make it either good or bad.

It is no crime to act in contradiction to an English judge or an English legislator, but it is a crime to transgress the dictates of a monitor which feels the spring of every motive, whose throne is the human sensorium, whose empire the human conduct. Conscience is a Government before which all others sink into nothingness; it surpasses, and where it can act, supersedes all other, as nature surpasses art, as God surpasses man.

In the preceding pages, during the course of an investigation of the possible objections which might be urged by Philanthropy, to an association such as I recommend, as I have rather sought to bring forward than conceal my principles, it will appear that they have their origin from the discoveries in the sciences of politics and morals which preceded and occasioned the revolutions of America and France. It is with openness that I confess, nay with pride I assert, that they are so. The names of Paine and Lafayette will outlive the poetic aristocracy of an expatriated Jesuit,[6] as the executive of a bigoted policy will die before the disgust at the sycophancy of their eulogists can subside.

It will be said, perhaps, that much as principles such as these may appear marked on the outside with peace, liberty, and virtue, that their ultimate tendency is to a Revolution, which, like that of France, will end in bloodshed, vice, and slavery. I must offer, therefore, my thoughts on that event, which so suddenly and so lamentably extinguished the overstrained hopes of liberty which it excited. I do not deny that the Revolution of France was occasioned by the literary labors of the Encyclopædists. When we see two events together, in certain cases, we speak of one as the cause, the other the effect. We have no

6 See *Memoires de Jacobinisme,* par l'Abbe Baruel. [Shelley's note]

other idea of cause and effect but that which arises from necessary connection; it is therefore still doubtful whether D'Alembert, Boulanger, Condorcet, and other celebrated characters were the causes of the overthrow of the ancient monarchy of France. Thus much is certain, that they contributed greatly to the extension and diffusion of knowledge, and that knowledge is incompatible with slavery. The French nation was bowed to the dust by ages of uninterrupted despotism. They were plundered and insulted by a succession of oligarchies, each more bloodthirsty and unrelenting than the foregoing. In a state like this, her soldiers learned to fight for Freedom on the plains of America, whilst at this very conjuncture, a ray of science burst through the clouds of bigotry that obscured the moral day of Europe. The French were in the lowest state of human degradation, and when the truth, unaccustomed to their ears, that they were men and equals was promulgated, they were the first to vent their indignation on the monopolizers of earth, because they were most glaringly defrauded of the immunities of nature.

Since the French were furthest removed by the sophistications of political institution from the genuine condition of human beings, they must have been most unfit for that happy state of equal law which proceeds from consummated civilization and which demands habits of the strictest virtue before its introduction.

The murders during the period of the French Revolution, and the despotism which has since been established, prove that the doctrines of Philanthropy and Freedom were but shallowly understood. Nor was it until after that period that their principles became clearly to be explained and unanswerably to be established.

Voltaire was the flatterer of Kings, though in his heart he despised them; so far has he been instrumental in the present slavery of his country. Rousseau gave licence by his writings to passions that only incapacitate and contract the human heart; so far hath he prepared the necks of his fellow-beings for that yoke of galling and dishonourable servitude, which at this moment it bears. Helvetius and Condorcet established principles, but if they drew conclusions, their conclusions were unsystematical and devoid of the luminousness and energy of method; they were little understood in the Revolution. But this age of ours is not stationary. Philosophers have not developed the great principles of the human mind that conclusions from them should be unprofitable and impracticable. We are in a state of continually progressive improvement. One truth that had [has] been discovered can never die, but will prevent the revivification of its apportioned opposite false-hood. By promoting truth and discouraging its opposite, the means of Philanthropy are principally to be forwarded. Godwin wrote during the Revolution of France, and cer-tainly his writings were totally devoid of influence, with regard to its purposes. Oh! that they had not! In the Revolution of France were engaged men whose names are inerasible from the records of Liberty. Their genius pene-trated with a glance the gloom and glare which Church-craft and State-craft had spread before the imposture and villainy of their establishments. They saw the world—were they men? Yes! They felt for it! They risked their lives and happiness for its benefit! Had there been more of those men, France would not now be a beacon to warn us of the hazard and horror of Revolutions, but a pattern of society, rapidly advancing to a state of perfection and holding out an example for the gradual and peaceful regeneration of the world. I consider it to be one of the effects of a Philanthropic Association to assist in the production of such men as these, in an extensive developement of those germs of excellence whose favourite soil is the cultured garden of the human mind.

Many well-meaning persons may think that the attain-ment of the good which I propose as the ultimatum of Philanthropic exertion is visionary and inconsistent with human nature; they would tell me not to make people happy, for fear of overstocking the world, and to permit those who found dishes placed before them on the table of partial nature to enjoy their superfluities in quietness, though millions of wretches crowded around but to pick a morsel,[7] which morsel was still refused to the prayers of agonizing famine.

I cannot help thinking this an evil, nor help endeavour-ing by the safest means that I can devise to palliate at

7 See Malthus on *Population*. [Shelley's note]

present and in fine to eradicate this evil; war, vice, and misery are undeniably bad; they embrace all that we can conceive of temporal and eternal evil. Are we to be told that these are remedyless because the earth would, in case of their remedy, be overstocked? That the rich are still to glut, that the ambitious are still to plan, that the fools whom these knaves mould are still to murder their brethren and call it glory, and that the poor are to pay with their blood, their labor, their happiness, and their innocence for the crimes and mistakes which the hereditary monopolists of earth commit? Rare sophism! How will the heartless rich hug thee to their bosoms and lull their conscience into slumber with the opiate of thy reconciling dogmas! But when the Philosopher and Philanthropist contemplates the universe, when he perceives existing evils that admit of amendment, and hears tell of other evils which in the course of sixty centuries may again derange the system of happiness which the amendment is calculated to produce, does he submit to prolong a positive evil because, if that were eradicated, after a millennium of 6000 years (for such space of time would it take to people the earth) another evil would take place?

To how contemptible a degradation of grossest credulity will not prejudice lower the human mind! We see in Winter that the foliage of the trees is gone, that they present to the view nothing but leafless branches, we see that the loveliness of the flower decays, though the root continues in the earth. What opinion should we form of that man who, when he walked in the freshness of the spring, beheld the fields enamelled with flowers and the foliage bursting from the buds, should find fault with this beautiful order and murmur his contemptible discontents because winter must come, and the landscape be robbed of its beauty for a while again? Yet this man is Mr. Malthus. Do we not see that the laws of nature perpetually act by disorganization and reproduction, each alternately becoming cause and effect? The analyses that we can draw from physical to moral topics are of all others the most striking.

Does anyone yet question the possibility of inducing radical reform of moral and political evil? Does he object, from that impossibility, to the association which I propose, which I frankly confess to be one of the means whose instrumentality I would employ to attain this reform? Let them look to the methods which I use. Let me put my object out of their view and propose their own, how would they accomplish it? By diffusing virtue and knowledge, by promoting human happiness. Palsied be the hand, forever dumb be the tongue that would by one expression convey sentiments differing from these; I will use no bad means for any end whatever. Know then, ye philanthropists, to whatever profession of faith, or whatever determination of principles, chance, reason, or education, may have conducted you, that the endeavours of the truly virtuous necessarily converge to one point, though it be hidden from them what point that is; they all labour for one end, and that controversies concerning the nature of that end serve only to weaken the strength which for the interest of virtue should be consolidated.

The diffusion of true and virtuous principles (for in the first principles of morality *none* disagree) will produce the best of possible terminations.

I invite to an Association of Philanthropy those, of whatever ultimate expectations, who will employ the same means that I employ; let their designs differ as much as they may from mine, I shall rejoice at their co-operation; because if the ultimatum of my hopes be founded on the unity of truth, I shall then have auxiliaries in its cause, and if it be false I shall rejoice that means are not neglected for forwarding that which is true.

The accumulation of evil which Ireland has for the last twenty years sustained, and considering the unremittingness of its pressure I may say patiently sustained; the melancholy prospect which the unforeseen conduct of the Regent of England holds out of its continuance demands of every Irishman whose pulses have not ceased to throb with the life-blood of his heart, that he should individually consult and unitedly determine on some measures for the liberty of his countrymen. That those measures should be pacific though resolute, that their movers should be calmly brave and temperately unbending, though the whole heart and soul should go with the attempt, is the opinion which my principles command me to give.

And I am induced to call an Association such as this

occasion demands, an Association of Philanthropy, because good men ought never to circumscribe their usefulness by any name which denotes their exclusive devotion to the accomplishment of its signification.

When I began the preceding remarks, I conceived that on the removal of the restrictions from the Regent a ministry less inimical than the present to the interests of liberty would have been appointed. I am deceived and the disappointment of the hopes of freedom on this subject afford an additional argument towards the necessity of an Association.

I conclude these remarks which I have indited principally with a view of unveiling my principles with a proposal for an Association for the purposes of Catholic Emancipation, a repeal of the Union Act, and grounding upon the attainment of these objects a reform of whatever moral or political evil may be within its compass of human power to remedy.

Such as are favourably inclined towards the institution would highly gratify the proposer if they would personally communicate with him on this important subject, by which means the plan might be matured, errors in the proposer's original system be detected, and a meeting for the purpose convened with that resolute expedition which the nature of the present crisis demands.

No. 7, Lower Sackville Street.

Declaration of Rights

I

Government has no rights; it is a delegation from several individuals for the purpose of securing their own. It is therefore just only so far as it exists by their consent, useful only so far as it operates to their well-being.

II

If these individuals think that the form of government which they or their forefathers constituted is ill adapted to produce their happiness, they have a right to change it.

III

Government is devised for the security of rights. The rights of man are liberty and an equal participation of the commonage of nature.

IV

As the benefit of the governed is, or ought to be, the origin of government, no men can have any authority that does not expressly emanate from their will.

V

Though all governments are not so bad as that of Turkey, yet none are so good as they might be; the majority of every country have a right to perfect their government; the minority should not disturb them; they ought to secede and form their own system in their own way.

VI

All have a right to an equal share in the benefits and burdens of Government. Any disabilities for opinion imply by their existence barefaced tyranny on the side of government, ignorant slavishness on the side of the governed.

VII

The rights of man, in the present state of society, are only to be secured by some degree of coercion to be exercised on their violator. The sufferer has a right that the degree of coercion employed be as slight as possible.

VIII

It may be considered as a plain proof of the hollowness of any proposition if power be used to enforce instead of reason to persuade its admission. Government is never supported by fraud until it cannot be supported by reason.

IX

No man has a right to disturb the public peace by personally resisting the execution of a law however bad. He ought to acquiesce, using at the same time the utmost powers of his reason to promote its repeal.

X

A man must have a right to act in a certain manner before it can be his duty. He may, before he ought.[1]

XI

A man has a right to think as his reason directs; it is a duty he owes to himself to think with freedom, that he may act from conviction.

1 **A man . . . . ought** an outstanding example of the close accord between Shelley's ideas and those of Godwin and Paine

XII

A man has a right to unrestricted liberty of discussion; falsehood is a scorpion that will sting itself to death.

XIII

A man has not only a right to express his thoughts, but it is his duty to do so.

XIV

No law has a right to discourage the practice of truth. A man ought to speak the truth on every occasion; a duty can never be criminal; what is not criminal cannot be injurious.

XV

Law cannot make what is in its nature virtuous or innocent to be criminal, any more than it can make what is criminal to be innocent. Government cannot make a law; it can only pronounce that which was the law before its organization, viz. the moral result of the imperishable relations of things.

XVI

The present generation cannot bind their posterity. The few cannot promise for the many.

XVII

No man has a right to do an evil thing that good may come.

XVIII

Expediency is inadmissible in morals. Politics are only sound when conducted on principles of morality. They are, in fact, the morals of nations.

XIX

Man has no right to kill his brother; it is no excuse that he does so in uniform. He only adds the infamy of servitude to the crime of murder.

XX

Man, whatever be his country, has the same rights in one place as another, the rights of universal citizenship.

XXI

The government of a country ought to be perfectly indifferent to every opinion. Religious differences, the bloodiest and most rancorous of all, spring from partiality.

XXII

A delegation of individuals for the purpose of securing their rights can have no undelegated power of restraining the expression of their opinion.

XXIII

Belief is involuntary; nothing involuntary is meritorious or reprehensible. A man ought not to be considered worse or better for his belief.

XXIV

A Christian, a Deist, a Turk, and a Jew have equal rights: they are men and brethren.

XXV

If a person's religious ideas correspond not with your own, love him nevertheless. How different would yours have been had the chance of birth placed you in Tartary or India!

XXVI

Those who believe that Heaven is what earth has been, a monopoly in the hands of a favoured few, would do well to reconsider their opinion; if they find that it came from their priest or their grandmother, they could not do better than reject it.

XXVII

No man has a right to be respected for any other possessions but those of virtue and talents. Titles are tinsel, power a corruptor, glory a bubble, and excessive wealth a libel on its possessor.

XXVIII

No man has a right to monopolise more than he can enjoy; what the rich give to the poor, whilst millions are starving, is not a perfect favour, but an imperfect right.

XXIX

Every man has a right to a certain degree of leisure and liberty, because it is his duty to attain a certain degree of knowledge. He may before he ought.

XXX

Sobriety of body and mind is necessary to those who would be free; because, without sobriety, a high sense of philanthropy cannot actuate the heart, nor cool and determined courage execute its dictates.

XXXI

The only use of government is to repress the vices of man. If man were today sinless, to-morrow he would have a right to demand that government and all its evils should cease.[2]

2 **If man were . . . should cease** note conditional phrasing, too frequently overlooked by critics of Shelley's philosophy

Man! thou whose rights are here declared, be no longer forgetful of the loftiness of thy destination. Think of thy rights; of those possessions which will give thee virtue and wisdom, by which thou mayest arrive at happiness and freedom. They are declared to thee by one who knows thy dignity,[3] for every hour does his heart swell with honourable pride in the contemplation of what thou mayest attain, by one who is not forgetful of thy degeneracy, for every moment brings home to him the bitter conviction of what thou art.

Awake!—arise!—or be for ever fallen.[4]

3 **Think . . . . dignity** a declaration fully supported by Shelley's best poetry and essays 4 **Awake . . . fallen** Milton, *Paradise Lost*, l. 330

A Letter to Lord Ellenborough

My Lord,

As the station to which you have been called by your country is important, so much the more awful is your responsibility, so much the more does it become you to watch lest you inadvertently punish the virtuous and reward the vicious.

You preside over a court which is instituted for the suppression of crime and to whose authority the people submit on no other conditions than that its decrees should be conformable to justice.

If it should be demonstrated that a judge had condemned an innocent man, the bare existence of laws in conformity to which the accused is punished, would but little extenuate his offence. The inquisitor when he burns an obstinate heretic may set up a similar plea, yet few are

Continuation of title page Occasioned by the sentence which he passed on Mr. D. I. Eaton, as publisher of the third part of Paine's *Age of Reason. Deorum offensa, Diis curae.* "It is contrary to the mild spirit of the Christian religion, for no sanction can be found under that dispensation which will warrant a government to impose disabilities and penalties upon any man on account of his religious opinions." [*Hear, Hear.*] Marquis Wellesley's Speech, Globe, July 2.

Advertisement: *I have waited impatiently for these last four months, in the hopes that some pen, fitter for the important task, would have spared me the perilous pleasure of becoming the champion of an innocent man. This may serve as an excuse for the delay to those who think that I have let pass the aptest opportunity, but it is not to be supposed that in four short months the public indignation raised by Mr. Eaton's unmerited suffering can have subsided.*

sufficiently blinded by intolerance to acknowledge its validity. It will less avail such a judge to assert the policy of punishing one who has committed no crime. Policy and morality ought to be deemed synonymous in a court of justice, and he whose conduct has been regulated by the latter principle is not justly amenable to any penal law for a supposed violation of the former. It is true, my Lord, laws exist which suffice to screen you from the animadversion of any constituted power, in consequence of the unmerited sentence which you have passed upon Mr. Eaton; but there are no laws which screen you from the reproof of a nation's disgust, none which ward off the just judgment of posterity, if that posterity will deign to recollect you.

By what right do you punish Mr. Eaton? What but antiquated precedents, gathered from times of priestly and tyrannical domination, can be adduced in palliation of an outrage so insulting to humanity and justice? Whom has he injured? What crime has he committed? Wherefore may he not walk abroad like other men and follow his accustomed pursuits? What end is proposed in confining this man, charged with the commission of no dishonourable action? Wherefore did his aggressor avail himself of popular prejudice and return no answer but one of commonplace contempt to a defence of plain and simple sincerity? Lastly, when the prejudices of the jury, as Christians, were strongly and unfairly inflamed [1] against this injured man as a Deist, wherefore did not you, my Lord, check such unconstitutional pleading and desire the jury to pronounce the accused innocent or criminal [2] without reference to the particular faith which he professed?

In the name of justice, what answer is there to these questions? The answer which Heathen Athens made to Socrates is the same with which Christian England must attempt to silence the advocates of this injured man—"He has questioned established opinions." Alas! the crime of inquiry is one which religion never has forgiven. Implicit faith and fearless inquiry have in all ages been irreconcile-

1 See the Attorney-General's speech. [Shelley's note]   2 By Mr. Fox's bill (1791) juries are, in cases of libel, judges both of the law and the fact. [Shelley's note]

able enemies. Unrestrained philosophy has in every age opposed itself to the reveries of credulity and fanaticism. The truths of astronomy demonstrated by Newton have superseded astrology; since the modern discoveries in chemistry, the philosopher's stone has no longer been deemed attainable. Miracles of every kind have become rare in proportion to the hidden principles which those who study nature have developed. That which is false will ultimately be controverted by its own falsehood. That which is true needs but publicity to be acknowledged. It is ever a proof that the falsehood of a proposition is felt by those who use power and coercion, not reasoning and persuasion, to procure its admission. Falsehood skulks in holes and corners, "it lets I dare not wait upon I would, like the poor cat in the adage," [3] except when it has power, and then, as it was a coward, it is a tyrant; but the eagle-eye of truth darts thro' the undazzling sunbeam of the immutable and just, gathering thence wherewith to vivify and illuminate a universe!

Wherefore, I repeat, is Mr. Eaton punished? Because he is a Deist? And what are you, my Lord? A Christian. Ha then! the mask has fallen off; you persecute him because his faith differs from yours. You copy the persecutors of Christianity in your actions and are an additional proof that your religion is as bloody, barbarous, and intolerant as theirs. If some deistical Bigot in power (supposing such a character for the sake of illustration) should in dark and barbarous ages have enacted a statute making the profession of Christianity criminal, if you, my Lord, were a Christian bookseller and Mr. Eaton a judge, those arguments which you consider adequate to justify yourself for the sentence you have passed must likewise suffice in the suppositionary case to justify Mr. Eaton in sentencing you to Newgate and the pillory for being a Christian. Whence is any right derived but that which power confers for persecution? Do you think to convert Mr. Eaton to your religion by embittering his existence? You might force him by torture to profess your tenets, but he could not believe them except you should make them credible, which perhaps exceeds your power. Do you think to please the

3 "it lets . . . adage" *Macbeth*, I, 7, 44–45

God you worship by this exhibition of your zeal? If so, the Demon to whom some nations offer human hecatombs is less barbarous than the Deity of civilised society.

You consider man as an accountable being—but he can only be accountable for those actions which are influenced by his will.[4]

Belief and disbelief are utterly distinct from and unconnected with volition. They are the apprehension of the agreement or disagreement of the ideas which compose any proposition. Belief is an involuntary operation of the mind, and, like other passions, its intensity is purely proportionate to the degrees of excitement. Volition is essential to merit or demerit. How then can merit or demerit be attached to what is distinct from that faculty of the mind whose presence is essential to their being? I am aware that religion is founded on the voluntariness of belief, as it makes it a subject of reward and punishment; but before we extinguish the steady ray of reason and common sense, it is fit that we should discover, which we cannot do without their assistance, whether or no there be any other which may suffice to guide us through the labyrinth of life.

If the law *de heretico comburendo*[5] had not been formally repealed, I conceive that from the promise held out by your Lordship's zeal, we need not despair of beholding the flames of persecution rekindled in Smithfield. Even now the lash that drove Descartes and Voltaire from their native country, the chains which bound Galileo, the flames which burned Vanini[6] again resound. And where? In a nation that presumptuously calls itself the sanctuary of freedom. Under a government which, whilst it infringes the very right of thought and speech, boasts of permitting the liberty of the press, a man is pilloried and imprisoned because he is a Deist, and no one raises his voice in the indignation of outraged humanity. Does the Christian God, whom his followers eulogize as the Deity of humility and peace—he, the regenerator of the world, the meek

---

4 **he can . . . will** one of the important concepts which Shelley found very attractive in Godwin's *Political Justice* (see especially Bk. II, ch. v)　5 "on the burning of heretics"　6 **Lucilio Vanini** (1585–1619)　Italian sceptic burned at the stake for atheism

reformer—authorize one man to rise against another and, because lictors are at his beck, to chain and torture him as an Infidel?

When the Apostles went abroad to convert the nations, were they enjoined to stab and poison all who disbelieved the divinity of Christ's mission? Assuredly they would have been no more justifiable in this case than he is at present who puts into execution the law which inflicts pillory and imprisonment on the Deist.

Has not Mr. Eaton an equal right to call your Lordship an Infidel as you have to imprison him for promulgating a different doctrine from that which you profess? What do I say! Has he not even a stronger plea? The word *Infidel* can only mean anything when applied to a person who professes that which he disbelieves. The test of truth is an undivided reliance on its inclusive powers; the test of conscious falsehood is the variety of the forms under which it presents itself, and its tendency towards employing whatever coercive means may be within its command, in order to procure the admission of what is unsusceptible of support from reason or persuasion. A dispassionate observer would feel himself more powerfully interested in favor of a man who, depending on the truth of his opinions, simply stated his reasons for entertaining them, than in that of his aggressor who, daringly avowing his unwillingness to answer them by argument, proceeded to repress the activity and break the spirit of their promulgator by that torture and imprisonment whose infliction he could command.

I hesitate not to affirm that the opinions which Mr. Eaton sustained when undergoing that mockery of a trial at which your Lordship presided appear to me more true and good than those of his accuser; but were they false as the visions of a Calvinist, it still would be the duty of those who love liberty and virtue to raise their voice indignantly against a reviving system of persecution, against the coercively repressing any opinion which, if false, needs but the opposition of truth; which if true, in spite of force must ultimately prevail.

Mr. Eaton asserted that the scriptures were from beginning to end a fable and imposture, that the Apostles were liars and deceivers. He denied the miracles, the resurrection, and ascension of Jesus Christ. He did so, and the Attorney General denied the propositions which he asserted and asserted those which he denied. What singular conclusion is deducible from this fact? None but that the Attorney General and Mr. Eaton sustained two opposite opinions. The Attorney General puts some obsolete and tyrannical laws in force against Mr. Eaton because he publishes a book tending to prove that certain supernatural events, which are supposed to have taken place eighteen centuries ago in a remote corner of the world, did not actually take place. But how are the truth or falsehood of the facts in dispute relevant to the merit or demerit attachable to the advocates of the two opinions? No man is accountable for his belief, because no man is capable of directing it. Mr. Eaton is therefore totally blameless. What are we to think of the justice of a sentence which punishes an individual against whom it is not even attempted to attach the slightest stain of criminality?

It is asserted that Mr. Eaton's opinions are calculated to subvert morality. How? What moral truth is spoken of with irreverence or ridicule in the book which he published? Morality, or the duty of a man and citizen, is founded on the relations which arise from the association of human beings, and which vary with the circumstances produced by the different states of this association. This duty in similar situations must be precisely the same in all ages and nations. The opinion contrary to this has arisen from a supposition that the will of God is the source or criterion of morality. It is plain that the utmost exertion of Omnipotence could not cause that to be virtuous which actually is vicious. An all-powerful Demon might indubitably annex punishments to virtue and rewards to vice, but could not by these means effect the slightest change in their abstract and immutable natures. Omnipotence could vary by a providential interposition the relations of human society; in this latter case, what before was virtuous would become vicious, according to the necessary and natural result of the alteration; but the abstract natures of the opposite principles would have sustained not the slightest change; for instance, the punishment with which society restrains the robber, the assassin, and the ravisher is just, laudable, and requisite. We admire and respect the institutions which curb those who would defeat the ends for which society was established; but should a precisely similar coercion be exercised against one who merely expressed his disbelief of a system admitted by those entrusted with the executive power, using at the same time no methods of promulgation but those afforded by reason, certainly this coercion would be eminently inhuman and immoral; and the supposition that any revelation from an unknown power avails to palliate a persecution so senseless, unprovoked, and indefensible is at once to destroy the barrier which reason places between vice and virtue, and leave to unprincipled fanaticism a plea whereby it may excuse every act of frenzy which its own wild passions and the inspirations of the Deity have engendered.

Moral qualities are such as only a human being can possess. To attribute them to the Spirit of the Universe, or to suppose that it is capable of altering them, is to degrade God into man and to annex to this incomprehensible being qualities incompatible with any *possible* definition of its nature. It may be here objected—ought not the Creator to possess the perfections of the creature? No. To attribute to God the moral qualities of man is to suppose him susceptible of passions which, arising out of corporeal organisation, it is plain that a pure spirit cannot possess. A bear is not perfect except he is rough, a tyger is not perfect if he be not voracious, an elephant is not perfect if otherwise than docile. How *deep* an argument must not that be which proves that the Deity is as rough as a bear, as voracious as a tyger, and as docile as an elephant! But even suppose with the vulgar that God is a venerable old man seated on a throne of clouds, his breast the theatre of various passions analogous to those of humanity, his will changeable and uncertain as that of an earthly king—still goodness and justice are qualities seldom nominally denied him, and it will be admitted that he disapproves of any action incompatible with those qualities. Persecution for opinion is unjust. With what consistency, then, can the worshippers of a Deity whose benevolence they boast embitter the existence of their fellow being because his ideas of that Deity are different from those which they entertain?—Alas! there is no consistency in those persecutors who worship a benevolent Deity; those who worship a Demon would alone act consonantly to these principles by imprisoning and torturing in his name.

Persecution is the only name applicable to punishment inflicted on an individual in consequence of his opinions. What end is persecution designed to answer? Can it convince him whom it injures? Can it prove to the people the falsehood of his opinions? It may make him a hypocrite and them cowards, but bad means can promote no good end. The unprejudiced mind looks with suspicion on a doctrine that needs the sustaining hand of power.

Socrates was poisoned because he dared to combat the degrading superstitions in which his countrymen were educated. Not long after his death, Athens recognized the injustice of his sentence; his accuser Melitus was condemned, and Socrates became a demigod.

Jesus Christ was crucified because he attempted to supersede the ritual of Moses with regulations more moral and humane—his very judge made public acknowledgment of his innocence, but a bigoted and ignorant mob demanded the deed of horror. Barabbas the murderer and traitor was released. The meek reformer Jesus was immolated to the sanguinary Deity of the Jews. Time rolled on, time changed the situations, and with them, the opinions of men.

The vulgar, ever in extremes, became persuaded the crucifixion of Jesus was a supernatural event, and testimonies of miracles, so frequent in unenlightened ages, were not wanting to prove that he was something divine. This belief, rolling through the lapse of ages, acquired force and extent, until the divinity of Jesus became a dogma, which to dispute was death, which to doubt was infamy.

Christianity is now the established religion; he who attempts to disprove it must behold murderers and traitors take precedence of him in public opinion, tho', if his genius be equal to his courage and assisted by a peculiar coalition of circumstances, future ages may exalt him to a divinity and persecute others in his name, as he was persecuted in the name of his predecessor in the homage of the world.

The same means that have supported every other popular belief have supported Christianity. War, imprisonment, murder, and falsehood; deeds of unexampled and incomparable atrocity have made it what it is. We derive from our ancestors a belief thus fostered and supported. We quarrel, persecute, and hate for its maintenance. Does not analogy favour the opinion that, as like other systems it has arisen and augmented, so like them it will decay and perish; that, as violence and falsehood, not reasoning and persuasion, have procured its admission among mankind, so, when enthusiasm has subsided and time, that infallible controverter of false opinions, has involved its pretended evidences in the darkness of antiquity, it will become obsolete, and that men will then laugh as heartily at grace, faith, redemption, and original sin as they now do at the metamorphoses of Jupiter, the miracles of Romish Saints, the efficacy of witchcraft, and the appearance of departed spirits?

Had the Christian religion commenced and continued by the mere force of reasoning and persuasion, by its self-evident excellence and fitness, the preceding analogy would be inadmissible. We should never speculate upon the future obsoleteness of a system perfectly conformable to nature and reason. It would endure as long as they endured, it would be a truth as indisputable as the light of the sun, the criminality of murder, and other facts, physical and moral, which, depending on our organization and relative situations, must remain acknowledged so long as man is man. It is an incontrovertible fact, the consideration of which ought to repress the hasty conclusions of credulity or moderate its obstinacy in maintaining them, that had the Jews not been a barbarous and fanatical race of men, had even the resolution of Pontius Pilate been equal to his candour, the Christian religion never could have prevailed; it could not even have existed. Man! the very existence of whose most cherished opinions depends from a thread so feeble, arises out of a source so equivocal, learn at least humility; own at least that it is possible for thyself also to have been seduced by education and circumstance into the admission of tenets destitute of rational proof, and the truth of which has not yet been satisfactorily demonstrated. Acknowledge at least that the falsehood of thy brother's opinions is no sufficient reason for his meriting thy hatred. What! because a fellow being disputes the reasonableness of thy faith, wilt thou punish him with torture and imprisonment? If persecution for religious opinions were admitted by the moralist, how wide a door would not be open by which convulsionists of every kind might make inroads on the peace of society! How many deeds of barbarism and blood would not receive a sanction! But I will demand if that man is not rather entitled to the respect than the discountenance of society, who, by disputing a received doctrine, either proves its falsehood and inutility, thereby aiming at the abolition of what is false and useless, or giving to its adherents an opportunity of establishing its excellence and truth. Surely this can be no crime. Surely the individual who devotes his time to fearless and unrestricted inquiry into the grand questions arising out of our moral nature ought rather to receive the patronage than encounter the vengeance of an enlightened legislature. I would have you to know, my Lord, that fetters of iron cannot bind or subdue the soul of virtue. From the damps and solitude of its dungeon it ascends, free and undaunted, whither thine, from the pompous seat of judgment, dare not soar. I do not warn you to beware lest your profession as a Christian should make you forget that you are a man; but I warn you against festinating that period which, under the present coercive system, is too rapidly maturing, when the seats of justice shall be the seats of venality and slavishness and the cells of Newgate become the abode of all that is honourable and true.

I mean not to compare Mr. Eaton with Socrates or Jesus; he is a man of blameless and respectable character; he is a citizen unimpeached with crime; if, therefore, his rights as a citizen and a man have been infringed, they have been infringed by illegal and immoral violence. But I will assert that should a second Jesus arise among men, should such a one as Socrates again enlighten the earth, lengthened imprisonment and infamous punishment (according to the regimen of persecution revived by your Lordship) would effect what hemlock and the cross have heretofore effected, and the stain on the national character, like that on Athens and Judea, would remain indelible but by the destruction of the history in which it is recorded. When the Christian Religion shall have faded from the earth, when its memory like that of Polytheism now shall remain, but remain only as the subject of ridicule and wonder, indignant posterity would attach immortal infamy to such an outrage; like the murder of Socrates, it would secure the execration of every age.

The horrible and wide wasting enormities which gleam like comets thro' the darkness of gothic and superstitious ages are regarded by the moralist as no more than the necessary effects of known causes; but when an enlightened age and nation signalizes itself by a deed, becoming none but barbarians and fanatics, Philosophy itself is even induced to doubt whether human nature will ever emerge from the pettishness and imbecility of its childhood. The system of persecution at whose new birth you, my Lord, are one of the presiding midwives, is not more impotent and wicked than inconsistent. The press is loaded with what are called (ironically I should conceive) *proofs* of the Christian religion; these books are replete with invective and calumny against Infidels; they presuppose that he who rejects Christianity must be utterly divested of reason and feeling. They advance the most unsupported assertions and take as first principles the most revolting dogmas. The inferences drawn from these assumed premises are imposingly logical and correct; but if a foundation is weak, no architect is needed to foretell the instability of the superstructure. If the truth of Christianity is not disputable, for what purpose are these books written? If they are sufficient to prove it, what further need of controversy? *If God has spoken, why is the universe not convinced?* [7] If the Christian Religion needs deeper learning, more painful investigation to establish its genuineness, wherefore attempt to accomplish that by force which the human mind can alone effect with satisfaction to itself? If, lastly, its truth *cannot* be demonstrated, wherefore impotently attempt to snatch from God the government of his creation and impiously assert that the Spirit of Benevolence has left that knowledge most essential to the well-being of man, the only one which since its promulgation has been the subject of unceasing cavil, the cause of irreconcileable hatred? Either the Christian Religion is true, or it is not. If true, it comes from God, and its

7 **If God . . . convinced?** from Holbach's *Système de la nature*

authenticity can admit of doubt and dispute no further than its Omnipotent Author is willing to allow; if true, it admits of rational proof and is capable of being placed equally beyond controversy, as the principles which have been established concerning matter and mind by Locke and Newton; and in proportion to the usefulness of the fact in dispute, so must it be supposed that a benevolent being is anxious to procure the diffusion of its knowledge on the earth. If false, surely no enlightened legislature would punish the reasoner who opposes a system so much the more fatal and pernicious as it is extensively admitted —so much the more productive of absurd and ruinous consequences as it is entwined by education, with the prejudices and affections of the human heart, in the shape of a popular belief.

Let us suppose that some half-witted philosopher should assert that the earth was the centre of the universe or that ideas could enter the human mind independently of sensation or reflection. This man would assert what is demonstrably incorrect; he would promulgate a false opinion. Yet would he therefore deserve pillory and imprisonment? By no means; probably few would discharge more correctly the duties of a citizen and a man. I admit that the case above stated is not precisely in point. The thinking part of the community has not received as indisputable the truth of Christianity as they have that of the Newtonian system. A very large portion of society, and that powerfully and extensively connected, derives its sole emolument from the belief of Christianity as a popular faith.

To torture and imprison the asserter of a dogma, however ridiculous and false, is highly barbarous and impolite. How then does not the cruelty of persecution become aggravated when it is directed against the opposer of an opinion *yet under dispute*, and which men of unrivalled acquirements, penetrating genius, and stainless virtue have spent, and at last sacrificed, their lives in combating.

The time is rapidly approaching—I hope, that you, my Lord, may live to behold its arrival—when the Mahometan, the Jew, the Christian, the Deist, and the Atheist will live together in one community, equally sharing the benefits which arise from its association, and united in the bonds of charity and brotherly love. My Lord, you have condemned an innocent man—no crime was imputed to him—and you sentenced him to torture and imprisonment. I have not addressed this letter to you with the hopes of convincing you that you have acted wrong. The most unprincipled and barbarous of men are not unprepared with sophisms to prove that they would have acted in no other manner and to shew that vice is virtue. But I raise my solitary voice to express my disapprobation, so far as it goes, of the cruel and unjust sentence you passed upon Mr. Eaton; to assert, so far as I am capable of influencing, those rights of humanity which you have wantonly and unlawfully infringed.

My Lord,
Yours, etc.

On the Punishment
of Death

A FRAGMENT

The first law which it becomes a Reformer to propose and support at the approach of a period of great political change is the abolition of the punishment of death.

It is sufficiently clear that revenge, retaliation, atonement, expiation are rules and motives so far from deserving a place in any enlightened system of political life, that they are the chief sources of a prodigious class of miseries in the domestic circles of society. It is clear that however the spirit of legislation may appear to frame institutions upon more philosophical maxims, it has hitherto, in those cases which are termed criminal, done little more than palliate the spirit by gratifying a portion of it, and afforded a compromise between that which is best—the inflicting of no evil upon a sensitive being without a decisively beneficial result in which he should at least participate— and that which is worst—that he should be put to torture for the amusement of those whom he may have injured or may seem to have injured.

Omitting these remoter considerations, let us inquire what *Death* is—that punishment which is applied as a measure of transgressions of indefinite shades of distinction, so soon as they shall have passed that degree and colour of enormity with which it is supposed no inferior infliction is commensurate.

And first, whether death is good or evil, a punishment or a reward, or whether it be wholly indifferent, no man can take upon himself to assert. That that within us which thinks and feels continues to think and feel after the dissolution of the body has been the almost universal opinion of mankind, and the accurate philosophy of what I may be permitted to term the modern Academy, by showing the prodigious depth and extent of our ignorance respecting the causes and nature of sensation, renders probable the affirmative of a proposition, the negative of which it is so difficult to conceive, and the popular arguments against which, derived from what is called the atomic system, are proved to be applicable only to the relation which one object bears to another, as apprehended by the mind, and not to existence itself, or the nature of that essence which is the medium and receptacle of objects.

The popular system of religion suggests the idea that the mind, after death, will be painfully or pleasurably affected according to its determinations during life. However ridiculous and pernicious we must admit the vulgar accessories of this creed to be, there is a certain analogy, not wholly absurd, between the consequences resulting to an individual during life from the virtuous or vicious, prudent or imprudent, conduct of his external actions, to those consequences which are conjectured to ensue from the discipline and order of his internal thoughts, as affecting his condition in a future state. They omit, indeed, to calculate upon the accidents of disease, and temperament, and organisation, and circumstance, together with the multitude of independent agencies which affect the opinions, the conduct, and the happiness of individuals, and produce determinations of the will and modify the judgment so as to produce effects the most opposite in natures considerably similar. These are those operations in the order of the whole of nature tending, we are prone to believe, to some definite mighty end to which the agencies of our peculiar nature are subordinate; nor is there any reason to suppose that in a future state they should become suddenly exempt from that subordination. The philosopher is unable to determine whether our existence in a previous state has affected our present condition and abstains from deciding whether our present condition will affect us in that which may be future. That, if we continue to exist, the manner of our existence will be such as no inferences nor conjectures afforded by a consideration of our earthly experience can elucidate, is sufficiently obvious. The opinion that the vital principle within us, in whatever mode it may continue to exist, must lose that consciousness of definite and individual being which now characterises it and become a unit in the vast sum of action and of thought which disposes and animates the universe, and is called God, seems to belong to that class of opinion which has been designated as indifferent.

To compel a person to know all that can be known by the dead concerning that which the living fear, hope, or forget; to plunge him into the pleasure or pain which there awaits him; to punish or reward him in a manner and in a degree incalculable and incomprehensible by us; to disrobe him at once from all that intertexture of good and evil with which Nature seems to have clothed every form of individual existence, is to inflict on him the doom of death.

A certain degree of pain and terror usually accompany the infliction of death. This degree is infinitely varied by the infinite variety in the temperament and opinions of the sufferers. As a measure of punishment, strictly so considered, and as an exhibition which, by its known effects on the sensibility of the sufferer, is intended to intimidate the spectators from incurring a similar liability, it is singularly inadequate.

Firstly, persons of energetic character, in whom, as in men who suffer for political crimes, there is a large mixture of enterprise, and fortitude, and disinterestedness, and the elements, though misguided and disarranged, by which the strength and happiness of a nation might have been cemented, die in such a manner as to make death appear not evil but good. The death of what is called a traitor, that is, a person who, from whatever motive, would abolish the government of the day, is as often a triumphant exhibition of suffering virtue as the warning of a culprit. The multitude, instead of departing with a panic-stricken approbation of the laws which exhibited such a spectacle, are inspired with pity, admiration, and sympathy; and the most generous among them feel an emulation to be the authors of such flattering emotions as they experience stirring in their bosoms. Impressed by what they see and feel, they make no distinction between the motives which incited the criminals to the actions for which they suffer, or the heroic courage with which they turned into good that which their judges awarded to them as evil, or the purpose itself of those actions, though that purpose may happen to be eminently pernicious. The laws in this case lose that sympathy which it ought to be their chief object to secure, and in a participation of which consists their chief strength in maintaining those sanctions by which the parts of the social union are bound together so as to produce, as nearly as possible, the ends for which it is instituted.

Secondly, persons of energetic character, in communities not modelled with philosophical skill to turn all the energies which they contain to the purposes of common good, are prone also to fall into the temptation of undertaking, and are peculiarly fitted for despising the perils attendant upon consummating, the most enormous crimes. Murder, rapes, extensive schemes of plunder are the actions of persons belonging to this class; and death is the penalty of conviction. But the coarseness of organisation peculiar to men capable of committing acts wholly selfish is usually found to be associated with a proportionate insensibility to fear or pain. Their sufferings communicate to those of the spectators who may be liable to the commission of similar crimes, a sense of the lightness of that event, when closely examined, which, at a distance, as uneducated persons are accustomed to do, probably they regarded with horror. But a great majority of the spectators are so bound up in the interests and the habits of social union that no temptation would be sufficiently strong to induce them to a commission of the enormities to which this penalty is assigned. The more powerful and the richer among them—and a numerous class of little tradesmen are richer and more powerful than those who are employed by them, and the employer, in general, bears this relation to the employed—regard their own wrongs as in some degree avenged and their own rights secured by this punishment, inflicted as the penalty of whatever crime. In cases of murder or mutilation, this feeling is almost universal. In those, therefore, whom this exhibition does not awaken to the sympathy which extenuates crime and discredits the law which restrains it, it produces feelings more directly at war with the genuine purposes of political society. It excites those emotions which it is the chief object of civilisation to extinguish for ever, and in the extinction of which alone there can be any hope of better institutions than those under which men now misgovern one another. Men feel that their revenge is gratified and that their security is established by the extinction and the sufferings of beings in most respects resembling themselves; and their daily occupations constraining them to a precise form in all their thoughts, they come to connect inseparably the idea of their own advantage with that of the death and torture of others. It is manifest that the object of sane polity is directly the reverse, and that laws founded upon reason should accustom the gross vulgar to associate their ideas of security and of interest with the reformation and the strict restraint, for that purpose alone, of those who might invade it.

The passion of revenge is originally nothing more than an habitual perception of the ideas of the sufferings of the person who inflicts an injury, as connected, as they are in a savage state or in such portions of society as are yet undisciplined to civilisation, with security that that injury will not be repeated in future. This feeling, engrafted upon superstition and confirmed by habit, at last loses sight of the only object for which it may be supposed to have been implanted and becomes a passion and a duty to be pursued and fulfilled, even to the destruction of those ends to which it originally tended. The other passions, both good and evil—Avarice, Remorse, Love, Patriotism —present a similar appearance; and to this principle of the mind over-shooting the mark at which it aims, we owe all that is eminently base or excellent in human nature; in providing for the nutriment or the extinction of which consists the true art of the legislator.[1]

1 The savage and the illiterate are but faintly aware of the distinction between the future and the past; they make actions belonging to periods so distinct, the subjects of similar feelings; they live only in the present, or in the past as it is present. It is in this that the philosopher excels one of the many; it is this which distinguishes the doctrine of philosophic necessity from fatalism; and that determination of the will, by which it is the active source of future events, from that liberty or indifference to which the abstract liability of irremediable actions is attached, according to the notions of the vulgar.

This is the source of the erroneous excesses of Remorse and

Nothing is more clear than that the infliction of punishment in general, in a degree which the reformation and the restraint of those who transgress the laws does not render indispensable, and none more than death, confirms all the inhuman and unsocial impulses of men. It is almost a proverbial remark that those nations in which the penal code has been particularly mild have been distinguished from all others by the rarity of crime. But the example is to be admitted to be equivocal. A more decisive argument is afforded by a consideration of the universal connection of ferocity of manners and a contempt of social ties, with the contempt of human life. Governments which derive their institutions from the existence of circumstances of barbarism and violence, with some rare exceptions perhaps, are bloody in proportion as they are despotic, and form the manners of their subjects to a sympathy with their own spirit.

The spectators who feel no abhorrence at a public execution, but rather a self-applauding superiority and a sense of gratified indignation, are surely excited to the most inauspicious emotions. The first reflection of such a one is the sense of his own internal and actual worth as preferable to that of the victim, whom circumstances have led to destruction. The meanest wretch is impressed with a sense of his own comparative merit. He is one of those on whom the tower of Siloam fell not—he is such a one as Jesus Christ found not in all Samaria, who, in his own soul, throws the first stone at the woman taken in adultery.[2] The popular religion of the country takes its designation from that illustrious person whose beautiful sentiment I have quoted. Any one who has stript from the doctrines of this person the veil of familiarity will perceive how adverse their spirit is to feelings of this nature.

Revenge, the one extending itself over the future and the other over the past, provinces in which their suggestions can only be the sources of evil. The purpose of a resolution to act more wisely and virtuously in future and the sense of a necessity of caution in repressing an enemy are the sources from which the enormous superstitions implied in the words cited have arisen. [Shelley's note] 2 **He is . . . adultery** New Testament references to feelings of self-righteousness or arrogance—Luke 13:4; Luke 7:1–9; John 8:3–11

An Address to the People on the Death of the Princess Charlotte

I. The Princess Charlotte[1] is dead. She no longer moves, nor thinks, nor feels. She is as inanimate as the clay with which she is about to mingle. It is a dreadful thing to know that she is a putrid corpse, who but a few days since was full of life and hope; a woman young, innocent, and beautiful, snatched from the bosom of domestic peace, and leaving that single vacancy which none can die and leave not.

II. Thus much the death of the Princess Charlotte has in common with the death of thousands. How many women die in childbed and leave their families of motherless children and their husbands to live on, blighted by the remembrance of that heavy loss? How many women of active and energetic virtues—mild, affectionate, and wise, whose life is as a chain of happiness and union, which once being broken, leaves those whom it bound to perish —have died and have been deplored with bitterness which is too deep for words? Some have perished in penury or

The full title page reads: "We Pity the Plumage, but Forget the Dying Bird"; *An Address to the People on the Death of the Princess Charlotte*, by The Hermit of Marlow. [The quotation is an adaptation of Paine's accusation against Edmund Burke in *The Rights of Man*] 1 daughter of the Prince Regent (later George IV); had been the one really popular and respected person in line for the throne; died in childbirth, Nov. 6, 1817

shame, and their orphan baby has survived, a prey to the scorn and neglect of strangers. Men have watched by the bedside of their expiring wives and have gone mad when the hideous death-rattle was heard within the throat, regardless of the rosy child sleeping in the lap of the unobservant nurse. The countenance of the physician had been read by the stare of this distracted husband till the legible despair sunk into his heart. All this has been and is. You walk with a merry heart through the streets of this great city and think not that such are the scenes acting all around you. You do not number in your thought the mothers who die in childbed. It is the most horrible of ruins. In sickness, in old age, in battle, death comes as to his own home; but in the season of joy and hope, when life should succeed to life and the assembled family expects one more, the youngest and the best beloved, that the wife, the mother—she for whom each member of the family was so dear to one another should die! Yet thousands of the poorest poor, whose misery is aggravated by what cannot be spoken now, suffer this. And have they no affections? Do not their hearts beat in their bosoms and the tears gush from their eyes? Are they not human flesh and blood? Yet none weep for them—none mourn for them—none when their coffins are carried to the grave (if indeed the parish furnishes a coffin for all) turn aside and moralize upon the sadness they have left behind.

III. The Athenians did well to celebrate with public mourning the death of those who had guided the republic with their valour and their understanding, or illustrated it with their genius. Men do well to mourn for the dead; it proves that we love something beside ourselves; and he must have a hard heart who can see his friend depart to rottenness and dust, and speed him without emotion on his voyage to "that bourne whence no traveller returns." [2] To lament for those who have benefited the state is a habit of piety yet more favourable to the cultivation of our best affections. When Milton died it had been well

2 **"that bourne . . . returns"** misquoted from Hamlet's soliloquy, *Hamlet*, III, 1, 79–80: "The undiscovered country, from whose bourn / No traveller returns"

that the universal English nation had been clothed in solemn black and that the muffled bells had tolled from town to town. The French nation should have enjoined a public mourning at the deaths of Rousseau and Voltaire. We cannot truly grieve for every one who dies beyond the circle of those especially dear to us; yet in the extinction of the objects of public love and admiration and gratitude, there is something, if we enjoy a liberal mind, which has departed from within that circle. It were well done also, that men should mourn for any public calamity which has befallen their country or the world, though it be not death. This helps to maintain that connexion between one man and another, and all men considered as a whole, which is the bond of social life. There should be public mourning when those events take place which make all good men mourn in their hearts; the rule of foreign or domestic tyrants, the abuse of public faith, the wresting of old and venerable laws to the murder of the innocent, the established insecurity of all those, the flower of the nation, who cherish an unconquerable enthusiasm for public good. Thus, if Horne Tooke[3] and Hardy[4] had been convicted of high treason, it had been good that there had been not only the sorrow and the indignation which would have filled all hearts but the external symbols of grief. When the French Republic was extinguished, the world ought to have mourned.

IV. But this appeal to the feelings of men should not be made lightly or in any manner that tends to waste on inadequate objects those fertilizing streams of sympathy which a public mourning should be the occasion of pouring forth. This solemnity should be used only to express a wide and intelligible calamity, and one which is felt to

3 **John Horne Tooke** (1736–1812) radical agitator for reform in England; imprisoned for collecting funds for relief of relatives of Americans "murdered by the King's troops at Lexington and Concord"; indicted for high treason but acquitted in 1794; elected to Parliament in 1801 but ejected after one session
4 **Thomas Hardy** (1752–1832) radical reformer arrested in 1794 for activity in London Correspondence Society for political reform; charged with treason but soon cleared of charges

be such by those who feel for their country and for mankind; its character ought to be universal, not particular.

V. The news of the death of the Princess Charlotte and of the execution of Brandreth, Ludlam, and Turner[5] arrived nearly at the same time. If beauty, youth, innocence, amiable manners, and the exercise of the domestic virtues could alone justify public sorrow when they are extinguished forever, this interesting Lady would well deserve that exhibition. She was the last and the best of her race. But there were thousands of others equally distinguished as she for private excellences who have been cut off in youth and hope. The accident of her birth neither made her life more virtuous nor her death more worthy of grief. For the public she had done nothing either good or evil; her education had rendered her incapable of either in a large and comprehensive sense. She was born a Princess, and those who are destined to rule mankind are dispensed with acquiring that wisdom and that experience which is necessary even to rule themselves. She was not like Lady Jane Grey, or Queen Elizabeth, a woman of profound and various learning. She had accomplished nothing and aspired to nothing, and could understand nothing respecting those great political questions which involve the happiness of those over whom she was destined to rule. Yet this should not be said in blame, but in compassion; let us speak no evil of the dead. Such is the misery, such the impotence of royalty. Princes are prevented from the cradle from becoming anything which may deserve that greatest of all rewards next to a good conscience, public admiration and regret.

VI. The execution of Brandreth, Ludlam, and Turner is an event of quite a different character from the death of the Princess Charlotte. These men were shut up in a horrible dungeon for many months, with the fear of a hideous death and of everlasting hell thrust before their eyes; and at last were brought to the scaffold and hung. They too had domestic affections and were remarkable for

5 **Jeremiah Brandreth, Isaac Ludlam, William Turner** three laborers apparently framed by the government and charged as dangerous revolutionaries; convicted and publicly executed

the exercise of private virtues. Perhaps their low station permitted the growth of those affections in a degree not consistent with a more exalted rank. They had sons, and brothers, and sisters, and fathers who loved them, it should seem, more than the Princess Charlotte could be loved by those whom the regulations of her rank had held in perpetual estrangement from her. Her husband was to her as father, mother, and brethren. Ludlam and Turner were men of mature years, and the affections were ripened and strengthened within them. What these sufferers felt shall not be said. But what must have been the long and various agony of their kindred may be inferred from Edward Turner, who, when he saw his brother dragged along upon the hurdle, shrieked horribly and fell in a fit, and was carried away like a corpse by two men. How fearful must have been their agony, sitting in solitude on that day when the tempestuous voice of horror from the crowd told them that the head so dear to them was severed from the body! Yes—they listened to the maddening shriek which burst from the multitude; they heard the rush of ten thousand terror-stricken feet, the groans and the hootings which told them that the mangled and distorted head was then lifted into the air. The sufferers were dead. What is death? Who dares to say that which will come after the grave? [6] Brandreth was calm and evidently believed that the consequences of our errors were limited by that tremendous barrier. Ludlam and Turner were full of fears lest God should plunge them in everlasting fire. Mr. Pickering, the clergyman, was evidently anxious that Brandreth should not by a false confidence lose the single opportunity of reconciling himself with the Ruler of the future world. None knew what death was, or could know. Yet these men were presumptuously thrust into that unfathomable gulf by other men who knew as little and who reckoned not the present or the future sufferings of their victims. Nothing is more horrible than that man should for any cause shed the life of man. For all other calamities there is a remedy or a consolation. When that Power through which we live ceases to maintain the life

6 "Your death has eyes in his head—mine is not painted so."
Cymbeline. [Shelley's note]

which it has conferred, then is grief and agony and the burthen which must be borne; such sorrow improves the heart. But when man sheds the blood of man, revenge, and hatred, and a long train of executions, and assassinations, and proscriptions is perpetuated to remotest time.

VII. Such are the particular and some of the general considerations depending on the death of these men. But however deplorable, if it were a mere private or customary grief, the public, as the public, should not mourn. But it is more than this. The events which led to the death of those unfortunate men are a public calamity. I will not impute blame to the jury who pronounced them guilty of high treason; perhaps the law requires that such should be the denomination of their offence. Some restraint ought indeed to be imposed on those thoughtless men who imagine they can find in violence a remedy for violence, even if their oppressors had tempted them to this occasion of their ruin. They are instruments of evil, not so guilty as the hands that wielded them, but fit to inspire caution. But their death by hanging and beheading, and the circumstances of which it is the characteristic and the consequence, constitute a calamity such as the English nation ought to mourn with an unassuageable grief.

VIII. Kings and their ministers have in every age been distinguished from other men by a thirst for expenditure and bloodshed. There existed in this country, until the American war, a check, sufficiently feeble and pliant indeed, to this desolating propensity. Until America proclaimed itself a republic, England was perhaps the freest and most glorious nation subsisting on the surface of the earth. It was not what is to the full desirable that a nation should be, but all that it can be when it does not govern itself. The consequences, however, of that fundamental defect soon became evident. The government which the imperfect constitution of our representative assembly threw into the hands of a few aristocrats, improved the method of anticipating the taxes by loans, invented by the ministers of William III, until an enormous debt had been created. In the war against the republic of France this policy was followed up, until now the *mere interest* of the public debt amounts to more than twice as much as the lavish expenditure of the public treasure for maintaining the standing army, and the royal family, and the pensioners, and the placemen. The effect of this debt is to produce such an unequal distribution of the means of living as saps the foundation of social union and civilized life. It creates a double aristocracy, instead of one which was sufficiently burthensome before, and gives twice as many people the liberty of living in luxury and idleness on the produce of the industrious and the poor. And it does not give them this because they are more wise and meritorious than the rest, or because their leisure is spent in schemes of public good, or in those exercises of the intellect and the imagination whose creations ennoble or adorn a country. They are not like the old aristocracy men of pride and honour, *sans peur et sans tache*,[7] but petty piddling slaves who have gained a right to the title of public creditors, either by gambling in the funds,[8] or by subserviency to government, or some other villainous trade. They are not the "Corinthian capital of polished society," but the petty and creeping weeds which deface the rich tracery of its sculpture. The effect of this system is that the day labourer gains no more now by working sixteen hours a day than he gained before by working eight. I put the thing in its simplest and most intelligible shape. The labourer, he that tills the ground and manufactures cloth, is the man who has to provide, out of what he would bring home to his wife and children, for the luxuries and comforts of those whose claims are represented by an annuity of forty-four millions a year levied upon the English nation. Before, he supported the army and the pensioners, and the royal family, and the landholders; and this is a hard necessity to which it was well that he should submit. Many and various are the mischiefs flowing from oppression, but this is the representative of them all; namely, that one man is forced to labour for another in a degree not only not necessary to the support of the subsisting distinctions among mankind, but so as by the excess of the injustice to endanger the very foundations of all that is valuable in social order, and

7 "without fear and without stain"   8 **funds** in England, public securities or national stocks

to provoke that anarchy which is at once the enemy of freedom and the child and the chastiser of misrule. The nation, tottering on the brink of two chasms, began to be weary of a continuance of such dangers and degradations and the miseries which are the consequence of them; the public voice loudly demanded a free representation of the people. It began to be felt that no other constituted body of men could meet the difficulties which impend. Nothing but the nation itself dares to touch the question as to whether there is any remedy or no to the annual payment of forty-four millions a year, beyond the necessary expenses of state, forever and forever. A nobler spirit also went abroad, and the love of liberty, and patriotism, and the self-respect attendant on those glorious emotions, revived in the bosoms of men. The government had a desperate game to play.

IX. In the manufacturing districts of England discontent and disaffection had prevailed for many years; this was the consequence of that system of double aristocracy produced by the causes before mentioned. The manufacturers,[9] the helots of luxury, are left by this system famished, without affections, without health, without leisure or opportunity for such instruction as might counteract those habits of turbulence and dissipation produced by the precariousness and insecurity of poverty. Here was a ready field for any adventurer who should wish for whatever purpose to incite a few ignorant men to acts of illegal outrage. So soon as it was plainly seen that the demands of the people for a free representation must be conceded if some intimidation and prejudice were not conjured up, a conspiracy of the most horrible atrocity was laid in train. It is impossible to know how far the higher members of the government are involved in the guilt of their infernal agents. It is impossible to know how numerous or how active they have been, or by what false hopes they are yet inflaming the untutored multitude to put their necks under the axe and into the halter. But thus much is known, that so soon as the whole nation lifted up its voice for parliamentary reform, spies were sent forth. These were selected

9 **manufacturers** factory laborers, or laboring class as a whole

from the most worthless and infamous of mankind and dispersed among the multitude of famished and illiterate labourers. It was their business if they found no discontent to create it. It was their business to find victims, no matter whether right or wrong. It was their business to produce upon the public an impression that, if any attempt to attain national freedom or to diminish the burthens of debt and taxation under which we groan were successful, the starving multitude would rush in and confound all orders and distinctions, and institutions and laws, in common ruin. The inference with which they were required to arm the ministers was that despotic power ought to be eternal. To produce this salutary impression, they betrayed some innocent and unsuspecting rustics into a crime whose penalty is a hideous death. A few hungry and ignorant manufacturers, seduced by the splendid promises of these remorseless blood-conspirators, collected together in what is called rebellion against the state. All was prepared, and the eighteen dragoons assembled in readiness, no doubt, conducted their astonished victims to that dungeon which they left only to be mangled by the executioner's hand. The cruel instigators of their ruin retired to enjoy the great revenues which they had earned by a life of villainy. The public voice was overpowered by the timid and the selfish, who threw the weight of fear into the scale of public opinion, and parliament confided anew to the executive government those extraordinary powers which may never be laid down, or which may be laid down in blood, or which the regularly constituted assembly of the nation must wrest out of their hands. Our alternatives are a despotism, a revolution, or reform.[10]

X. On the 7th of November, Brandreth, Turner, and Ludlam ascended the scaffold. We feel for Brandreth the less, because it seems he killed a man. But recollect who instigated him to the proceedings which led to murder. On the word of a dying man, Brandreth tells us, that "OLIVER *brought him to this*"—that, "*but for* OLIVER *he would not have been there.*" See, too, Ludlam and

10 **Our . . . reform** from the liberal point of view, there is no alternative to reform

Turner, with their sons and brothers and sisters, how they kneel together in a dreadful agony of prayer. Hell is before their eyes, and they shudder and feel sick with fear lest some unrepented or some wilful sin should seal their doom in everlasting fire. With that dreadful penalty before their eyes—with that tremendous sanction for the truth of all he spoke, Turner exclaimed loudly and distinctly, *while the executioner was putting the rope round his neck,* "THIS IS ALL OLIVER AND THE GOVERNMENT." What more he might have said we know not, because the chaplain prevented any further observations. Troops of horse, with keen and glittering swords, hemmed in the multitudes collected to witness this abominable exhibition. "When the stroke of the axe was heard, there was a burst of horror from the crowd.[11] The instant the head was exhibited, there was a tremendous shriek set up, and the multitude ran violently in all directions, as if under the impulse of sudden frenzy. Those who resumed their stations, groaned and hooted." It is a national calamity that we endure men to rule over us who sanction for whatever ends a conspiracy which is to arrive at its purpose through such a frightful pouring forth of human blood and agony. But when that purpose is to trample upon our rights and liberties forever, to present to us the alternatives of anarchy and oppression, and triumph when the astonished nation accepts the latter at their hands, to maintain a vast standing army, and add year by year to a public debt, which, already, they know, cannot be discharged, and which, when the delusion that supports it fails, will produce as much misery and confusion through all classes of society as it has continued to produce of famine and degradation to the undefended poor; to imprison and calumniate those who may offend them, at will; when this, if not the purpose, is the effect of that conspiracy, how ought we not to mourn?

XI. Mourn then People of England. Clothe yourselves in solemn black. Let the bells be tolled. Think of mortality and change. Shroud yourselves in solitude and the gloom of sacred sorrow. Spare no symbol of universal grief. Weep

11 These expressions are taken from *The Examiner,* Sunday, Nov. 9th. [Shelley's note]

—mourn—lament. Fill the great City—fill the boundless fields with lamentation and the echo of groans. A beautiful Princess is dead: she who should have been the Queen of her beloved nation and whose posterity should have ruled it for ever. She loved the domestic affections and cherished arts which adorn and valour which defends. She was amiable and would have become wise, but she was young, and in the flower of youth the despoiler came. LIBERTY is dead. Slave! I charge thee disturb not the depth and solemnity of our grief by any meaner sorrow. If One has died who was like her that should have ruled over this land, like Liberty, young, innocent, and lovely, know that the power through which that one perished was God, and that it was a private grief. But *man* has murdered Liberty, and whilst the life was ebbing from its wound, there descended on the heads and on the hearts of every human thing the sympathy of an universal blast and curse. Fetters heavier than iron weigh upon us, because they bind our souls. We move about in a dungeon more pestilential than damp and narrow walls, because the earth is its floor and the heavens are its roof. Let us follow the corpse of British Liberty slowly and reverentially to its tomb; and if some glorious Phantom should appear and make its throne of broken swords and sceptres and royal crowns trampled in the dust, let us say that the Spirit of Liberty has arisen from its grave and left all that was gross and mortal there, and kneel down and worship it as our Queen.

from Essay on Christianity

. . . Jesus Christ opposed with earnest eloquence the panic fears and hateful superstitions which have enslaved mankind for ages. Nations had risen against nations employing the subtilest devices of mechanism and mind to waste and excruciate and overthrow. The great community of mankind had been subdivided into ten thousand communities each organized for the ruin of the other. Wheel within wheel the vast machine was instinct with the restless spirit of desolation. Pain has been inflicted, therefore pain should be inflicted in return. Retaliation is the only remedy which can be applied to violence because it teaches the injurer the true nature of his own conduct and operates as a warning against its repetition. Nor must the same measure of calamity be returned as was received. If a man borrows a certain sum from me, he is bound to repay that sum. Shall no more be required from the enemy who destroys my reputation or ravages my fields? It is just that he should suffer ten times the loss which he has inflicted that the legitimate consequences of his deed may never be obliterated from his remembrance and that others may clearly discern and feel the danger of invading the peace of human society. Such reasonings and the impetuous feelings arising from them have armed nation against nation, family against family, man against man. An Athenian soldier in the Ionian army which had assembled for the purpose of vindicating the liberty of the Asiatic Greeks accidentally set fire to Sardis. The city being composed of combustible materials was burned to the ground. The Persians believed that this circumstance of aggression made it their duty to retaliate on Athens. They assembled successive expeditions on the most extensive scale. Every nation of the East was united to ruin the Græcian States. Athens was burned to the ground, the whole territory laid waste, and every living thing which it [was] containing. After suffering and inflicting incalculable mischiefs, they desisted from their purpose only when they became impotent to effect it. The desire of revenge for the aggression of Persia outlived among the Greeks that love of liberty which had been their most glorious distinction among the nations of mankind, and Alexander became the instrument of its completion. The mischiefs attendant on this consummation of fruitless ruin are too manifold and too tremendous to be related. If all the thought which had been expended on the construction of engines of agony and death, the modes of aggression and defence, the raising of armies, and the acquirement of those arts of tyranny and falsehood without which mixed multitudes deluded and goaded to mutual ruin could neither be led nor governed, had been employed to promote the true welfare, and extend the real empire of man how different would have been the present situation of human society! How different the state of knowledge on physical and moral science, on which the power and happiness of mankind essentially depend! What nation has the example of the desolation of Attica by Mardonius and Xerxes, or the extinction of the Persian empire by Alexander of Macedon restrained from outrage? Was not the pretext of this latter system of spoliation derived immediately from the former? Had revenge in this instance any other effect than to increase instead of diminishing the mass of malice and evil already existing in the world? [1]

The emptiness and folly of retaliation is apparent from every example which can be brought forward. Not only Jesus Christ, but the most eminent professors of every sect of philosophy have reasoned against this futile superstition. Legislation is in one point of view to be considered as an attempt to provide against the excesses of this deplorable mistake. It professes to assign the penalty of all private injuries, and denies to individuals the right of vindicating their proper cause. This end is certainly not attained without some accommodation to the propensities

[1] **If all the thought . . . world** a passage later echoed by George Bernard Shaw in his Preface to *Androcles and the Lion*

which it desires to destroy. Still, it professes to recognize no principle but the production of the greatest eventual good with the least immediate injury, and to regard the torture or the death of any human being as unjust, of whatever mischief he may have been the author, so long as the result shall not more than compensate for the immediate pain. Such are the only justifiable principles and such is the [true] reason of law.[2]

Mankind, transmitting from generation to generation the horrible legacy of accumulated vengeances and pursuing with the feelings of duty the misery of their fellow beings, have not failed to attribute to the universal cause a character analogous with their own. The image of this invisible mysterious being is more or less excellent and perfect, resembles more or less its original and object, in proportion to the perfectness of the mind on which it is impressed. Thus the nation which has arrived at the highest step in the scale of moral progression will believe most purely in that God the knowledge of whose real attributes [has] been considered as the firmest basis of the true religion. The reason of the belief of each individual also will be so far regulated by his conceptions of what is good. Thus, the conceptions which any nation or individual entertains of the God of its popular worship may be inferred from their own actions and opinions which are the subjects of their approbation among their fellow-men. Jesus Christ instructed his disciples to be perfect as their father in Heaven is perfect, declaring at the same time his belief that human perfection requires the refraining from revenge or retribution in any of its various shapes. The perfection of the human and the divine character is thus asserted to be the same; man by resembling God fulfils most accurately the tendencies of his nature, and God comprehends within itself all that constitutes human perfection. Thus God is a model thro[ugh] which the excellence of man is to be estimated, whilst the *abstract* perfection of the human character is the type of the *actual* perfection of the divine. It is not to [be] believed that a person of such comprehensive views

2 **law** this word is followed by a blank space in the manuscript

as Jesus Christ could have fallen into so manifest a contradiction as to assert that men would be tortured after death
by that being whose character is held up as a model to
human kind because he is incapable of malevolence or
revenge. All the arguments which have been brought forward to justify retribution fail when retribution is destined
neither to operate as an example to other agents nor to the
offender himself. How feeble such reasoning is to be considered has been already shewn; but it is the character of
an evil dæmon to consign the beings whom he has endowed with sensation to improfitable anguish. The peculiar
circumstances attendant on the conception of God casting
sinners to burn in Hell forever combine to render that conception the most perfect specimen of the greatest imagina-
ble crime. Jesus Christ represented God as the principle
of all good, the source of all happiness, the wise and
benevolent creator and preserver of all living things. But
the interpreters of his doctrine have confounded the good
and the evil principle. They observed the emanations of
their universal natures to be inextricably intangled in the
world, and trembling before the power of the cause of all
things, addressed to it such flattery as is acceptable to the
ministers of human tyranny, attributing love and wisdom
to those energies which they felt to be exerted indiffer-
ently for the purposes of benefit and calamity. Jesus
Christ expressly asserts that distinction between the good
and evil principle which it has been the practice of all
theologians to confound. How far his doctrines, or their
interpretation, may be true, it would scarcely have been
worthwhile to enquire, if the one did not afford an example and an incentive to the attainment of true virtue whilst
the other holds out a sanction and apology for every
species of mean and cruel vice.

In proportion as mankind becomes wise, yes, in exact
proportion to that wisdom should be the extinction of the
unequal system under which they now subsist. Government
is in fact the mere badge of their depravity. They are so
little aware of the inestimable benefits of mutual love as to
indulge without thought and almost without motive in
the worst excesses of selfishness and malice. Hence without
graduating human society into a scale of empire and sub-

jection, its very existence has become impossible. It is necessary that universal benevolence should supersede the regulations of precedent and prescription before these regulations can safely be abolished. Meanwhile their very subsistence depends on the system of injustice and violence which they have been devised to palliate. They suppose men endowed with the power of deliberating and determining for their equals; whilst these men as frail and as ignorant as the multitude whom they rule, possess, as a practical consequence of this power, the right which they of necessity exercise to pervert together with their own the physical and moral and intellectual nature of all mankind. It is the object of wisdom to equalize the distinctions on which this power depends; by exhibiting in their proper worthlessness the objects, a contention concerning which renders its existence a necessary evil. The evil in fact is virtually abolished wherever *justice* is practised, and it is abolished in precise proportion to the prevalence of true virtue. The whole frame of human things is infected by the insidious poison. Hence it is that man is blind in his understanding, corrupt in his moral sense, and diseased in his physical functions. The wisest and most sublime of the ancient poets saw this truth, and embodied their conception of its value in retrospect to the earliest ages of mankind. They represented equality as the reign of Saturn and taught that mankind had gradually degenerated from the virtue which enabled them to enjoy or maintain this happy state. Their doctrine was philosophically false. Later and more correct observations have instructed us that uncivilized man is the most pernicious and miserable of beings, and that the violence and injustice which are the genuine indications of real inequality obtain in the society of these beings without mixture and without palliation. Their imaginations of a happier state of human society were referred indeed to the [Saturnian (?)] period; they ministered indeed to thoughts of despondency and sorrow. But they were the children of airy hope, the prophets and parents of mysterious futurity. Man was once as a wild beast, he has become a moralist a metaphysician a poet and an astronomer; Lucretius or Virgil might have referred the comparison to themselves; and as a proof of this progress of the nature of man, challenged a comparison with the cannibals of Scythia.[3] The experience of the ages which have intervened between the present period and that in which Jesus Christ taught tends to prove his doctrine and to illustrate theirs. There is more equality, because there is more justice among mankind and there is more justice because there is more universal knowledge. . . .

3 Jesus Christ foresaw what these poets retrospectively imagined. [Shelley's note]

The Moral Teaching
of Jesus Christ

The preachers of the Christian religion urge the morality of Jesus Christ as being in itself miraculous and
stamped with the impression of divinity. Mahomet advanced the same pretensions respecting the composition
of the Koran and, if we consider the numbers of his followers, with greater success. But these gentlemen condemn
themselves, for in their admiration they prefer the com-
ment to the text. Read the words themselves of this extraordinary person, and weigh their import well. The doctrines
indeed, in my judgment, are excellent and strike at the root
of moral evil. If acted upon, no political or religious institution could subsist a moment. Every man would be his own
magistrate and priest; the change so long desired would
have attained its consummation, and man exempt from
the external evils of his own choice would be left free to
struggle with the physical evils which exist in spite of
him. But these are the very doctrines which, in another
shape, the most violent asserters of Christianity denounce
as impious and seditious; who are such earnest champions
for social and political disqualification as they? This alone
would be a demonstration of the falsehood of Christianity,
that the religion so called is the strongest ally and bulwark
of that system of successful force and fraud and of the
selfish passions from which it has derived its origin and
permanence, against which Jesus Christ declared the most
uncompromising war and the extinction of which appears
to have been the great motive of his life. We are called
upon to believe in the divinity of a doctrine the effect of

A fragmentary essay which Shelley left in rough-draft form

which has been to establish more firmly than [that] which it was promulgated to destroy, and that they who invite us to . . . our reason with envious priests and tyrannical princes, whose [existence] is an everlasting answer to the pretensions of Christianity. Doctrines of reform were never carried to so great a length as by Jesus Christ. The republic of Plato and the Political Justice of Godwin are probable and practical systems in the comparison.

The doctrines of Jesus Christ though excellent are not new. The immortality of the soul was already a dogma, familiar from all antiquity to every nation of the earth except the Jews. Plato said all that could be said on this subject; and whoever had aspired to excel this mighty mind ought to have sought their information from undoubted sources. Jesus claimed no pretension of the kind, and the Christian knows as little as did the Pagan of the foundation of this notion. The idea of forgiveness of injuries, the error of revenge, and the immorality and inutility of punishment considered as punishment (for these correlative doctrines) are stated by Plato in the first book of the republic; and . . .

A Proposal for Putting
Reform to the Vote
Throughout the Kingdom

A great question is now agitating in this nation, which no man or party of men is competent to decide; indeed there are no materials of evidence which can afford a foresight of the result. Yet on its issue depends whether we are to be slaves or free men.

It is needless to recapitulate all that has been said about *Reform*. Every one is agreed that the House of Commons is not a representation of the people. The only theoretical question that remains is whether the people ought to legislate for themselves or be governed by laws and impoverished by taxes originating in the edicts of an assembly which represents somewhat less than a thousandth part of the intire community. I think they ought not to be so taxed and governed. An hospital for lunatics is the only theatre where we can conceive so mournful a comedy to be exhibited as this mighty nation now exhibits: a single person bullying and swindling a thousand of his comrades out of all they possessed in the world, and then trampling and spitting upon them, though he were the most contemptible and degraded of mankind, and they had strength in their arms and courage in their hearts. Such a parable realized in political society is a spectacle worthy of the utmost indignation and abhorrence.

The prerogatives of Parliament constitute a sovereignty which is exercised in contempt of the People, and it is in strict consistency with the laws of human nature that it should have been exercised for the People's misery and ruin. Those whom they despise, men instinctively seek to render slavish and wretched, that their scorn may be secure. It is the object of the Reformers to restore the People to a sovereignty thus held in their contempt. It is my object, or I would be silent now.

Servitude is sometimes voluntary. Perhaps the People choose to be enslaved; perhaps it is their will to be degraded and ignorant and famished; perhaps custom is their only God, and they, its fanatic worshippers, will shiver in frost and waste in famine rather than deny that idol; perhaps the majority of this nation decree that they will not be represented in Parliament, that they will not deprive of power those who have reduced them to the miserable condition in which they now exist. It is *their* will—it is their own concern. If such be their decision, the champions of the rights and the mourners over the errors and calamities of man must retire to their homes in silence until accumulated sufferings shall have produced the effect of reason.

The question now at issue is whether the majority of the adult individuals of the United Kingdom of Great Britain and Ireland desire or no a complete representation in the Legislative Assembly.

I have no doubt that such is their will, and I believe this is the opinion of most persons conversant with the state of the public feeling. But the fact ought to be formally ascertained before we proceed. If the majority of the adult population should solemnly state their desire to be that the representatives whom they might appoint should constitute the Commons House of Parliament, there is an end to the dispute. Parliament would then be required, not petitioned, to prepare some effectual plan for carrying the general will into effect; and if Parliament should then refuse, the consequences of the contest that might ensue would rest on its presumption and temerity. Parliament would have rebelled against the People then.

If the majority of the adult population shall, when seriously called upon for their opinion, determine on grounds however erroneous that the experiment of innovation by Reform in Parliament is an evil of greater magnitude than the consequences of misgovernment to which Parliament has afforded a constitutional sanction, then it becomes us to be silent; and we should be guilty of the great crime which I have conditionally imputed to the House of Commons, if after unequivocal evidence that it was the national will to acquiesce in the existing system we should, by partial assemblies of the multitude, or by any party acts, excite the minority to disturb this decision.

The first step towards Reform is to ascertain this point. For which purpose I think the following plan would be effectual:

That a Meeting should be appointed to be held at the *Crown and Anchor Tavern* on the   of   , to take into consideration the most effectual measures for ascertaining whether or no a Reform in Parliament is the will of the majority of the individuals of the British Nation.

That the most eloquent, and the most virtuous, and the most venerable among the Friends of Liberty should employ their authority and intellect to persuade men to lay aside all animosity and even discussion respecting the topics on which they are disunited, and by the love which they bear to their suffering country conjure them to contribute all their energies to set this great question at rest— whether the nation desires a Reform in Parliament or no?

That the friends of Reform, residing in any part of the country, be earnestly entreated to lend perhaps their last and the decisive effort to set their hopes and fears at rest; that those who can should go to London, and those who cannot, but who yet feel that the aid of their talents might be beneficial, should address a letter to the Chairman of the Meeting, explaining their sentiments: let these letters be read aloud, let all things be transacted in the face of day. Let Resolutions, of an import similar to those that follow, be proposed.

1. That those who think that it is the duty of the People of this nation to exact such a Reform in the Commons House of Parliament as should make that House a complete representation of their will, and that the People have a right to perform this duty, assemble here for the purpose of collecting evidence as to how far it is the will of the majority of the People to acquit themselves of this duty and to exercise this right.

2. That the population of Great Britain and Ireland

be divided into three hundred distinct portions, each to contain an equal number of inhabitants, and three hundred persons be commissioned, each personally to visit every individual within the district named in his commission, and to enquire whether or no that individual is willing to sign the declaration contained in the third Resolution, requesting him to annex to his signature any explanation or exposure of his sentiments which he might choose to place on record. That the following Declaration be proposed for signature:

3. That the House of Commons does not represent the will of the People of the British Nation; we the undersigned therefore declare, and publish, and our signatures annexed shall be evidence of our firm and solemn conviction that the liberty, the happiness, and the majesty of the great nation to which it is our boast to belong have been brought into danger and suffered to decay through the corrupt and inadequate manner in which Members are chosen to sit in the Commons House of Parliament; we hereby express, before God and our country, a deliberate and unbiassed persuasion that it is our duty, if we shall be found in the minority in this great question, incessantly to petition; if among the majority, to require and exact that that House should originate such measures of Reform as would render its Members the actual Representatives of the Nation.

4. That this Meeting shall be held day after day until it determines on the whole detail of the plan for collecting evidence as to the will of the nation on the subject of a Reform in Parliament.

5. That this Meeting disclaims any design, however remote, of lending their sanction to the revolutionary and disorganizing schemes which have been most falsely imputed to the Friends of Reform, and declares that its object is purely constitutional.

6. That a subscription be set on foot to defray the expenses of this Plan.

In the foregoing proposal of Resolutions, to be submitted to a National Meeting of the Friends of Reform, I have purposely avoided detail. If it shall prove that I have in any degree afforded a hint to men who have earned and established their popularity by personal sacrifices and intellectual eminence such as I have not the presumption to rival, let it belong to them to pursue and develop all suggestions relating to the great cause of liberty which has been nurtured (I am scarcely conscious of a metaphor) with their very sweat, and blood, and tears; some have tended it in dungeons, others have cherished it in famine, all have been constant to it amidst persecution and calumny, and in the face of the sanctions of power—so accomplish what ye have begun.

I shall mention therefore only one point relating to the practical part of my Proposal. Considerable expenses, according to my present conception, would be necessarily incurred; funds should be created by subscription to meet these demands. I have an income of a thousand a year, on which I support my wife and children in decent comfort and from which I satisfy certain large claims of general justice. Should any plan resembling that which I have proposed be determined on by you, I will give £100, being a tenth part of one year's income, towards its object; and I will not deem so proudly of myself as to believe that I shall stand alone in this respect when any rational and consistent scheme for the public benefit shall have received the sanction of those great and good men who have devoted themselves for its preservation.

A certain degree of coalition among the sincere Friends of Reform, in whatever shape, is indispensable to the success of this proposal. The friends of Universal or of Limited Suffrage, of Annual or Triennial Parliaments, ought to settle these subjects on which they disagree when it is known whether the nation desires that measure on which they are all agreed. It is trivial to discuss what species of Reform shall have place when it yet remains a question whether there will be any Reform or no.

Meanwhile, nothing remains for me but to state explicitly my sentiments on this subject of Reform. The statement is indeed quite foreign to the merits of the Proposal in itself, and I should have suppressed it until called upon to subscribe such a requisition as I have suggested if the question which it is natural to ask, as to what are the sentiments of the person who originates the scheme, could have received in any other manner a more simple and direct reply. It appears to me that Annual Parliaments ought to be adopted as an immediate measure, as one which strongly tends to preserve the liberty and happiness of the nation; it would enable men to cultivate those energies on which the performance of the political duties belonging to the citizen of a free state, as the rightful guardian of its prosperity, essentially depends; it would familiarize men with liberty by disciplining them to an habitual acquaintance with its forms. Political institution is undoubtedly susceptible of such improvements as no rational person can consider possible, so long as the present degraded condition to which the vital imperfections in the existing system of government has reduced the vast multitude of men shall subsist. The securest method of arriving at such beneficial innovations is to proceed gradually and with caution; or in the place of that order and freedom which the Friends of Reform assert to be violated now, anarchy and despotism will follow. Annual Parliaments have my entire assent. I will not state those general reasonings in their favour which Mr. Cobbett[1] and other writers have already made familiar to the public mind.

With respect to Universal Suffrage, I confess I consider its adoption, in the present unprepared state of public knowledge and feeling, a measure fraught with peril. I think that none but those who register their names as paying a certain small sum in *direct taxes* ought, at present, to send Members to Parliament. The consequences of the immediate extension of the elective franchise to every male adult would be to place power in the hands of men who have been rendered brutal and torpid and ferocious by ages of slavery. It is to suppose that the qualities belonging to a demagogue are such as are sufficient to endow a legislator. I allow Major Cartwright's[2] arguments to be unanswerable; abstractedly it is the right of every human being to have a share in the government. But Mr. Paine's arguments[3] are also unanswerable; a pure republic may be

1 **William Cobbett** (1763–1835) the English journalist whose theories varied from conservative to radical   2 **John Cartwright** (1740–1824) favored the cause of American independence and early advocated reform of Parliament; elder brother of the inventor of the power loom, Edward Cartwright   3 **Mr. Paine's arguments** those in the writings of Thomas Paine (1737–1809),

shewn, by inferences the most obvious and irresistible, to be that system of social order the fittest to produce the happiness and promote the genuine eminence of man. Yet nothing can less consist with reason or afford smaller hopes of any beneficial issue than the plan which should abolish the regal and the aristocratical branches of our constitution before the public mind, through many gradations of improvement, shall have arrived at the maturity which can disregard these symbols of its childhood.

---

self-proclaimed citizen of the world, who urged radical means, including violent revolution, of overthrowing tyrannical systems

A Philosophical View
of Reform

[Foreword]

Those who imagine that their personal interest is directly or indirectly concerned in maintaining the power in which they are clothed by the existing institutions of English Government do not acknowledge the necessity of a material change in those institutions. . . . With this exception, there is no inhabitant of the British Empire of mature age and perfect understanding not fully persuaded of the necessity of Reform. Let us believe not only that [it] is necessary because it is just and ought to be, but necessary because it is inevitable and must be.

[Outline]

1st. Sentiment of the Necessity of change.
2nd. Practicability and Utility of such a change.
3rd. State of Parties as regards it.
4th. Probable mode—Desirable mode.

Chapter I

Introduction

From the dissolution of the Roman Empire, that vast and successful scheme for the enslaving [of] the most civilized portion of mankind, to the epoch of the present year, have succeeded a series of schemes on a smaller scale, operating to the same effect. Names borrowed from the life and opinions of Jesus Christ were employed as symbols of domination and imposture, and a system of liberty and equality (for such was the system preached by that great Reformer) was perverted to support oppression. Not his doctrines, for they are too simple and direct to be susceptible of such perversion—but the mere names. Such was the origin of the Catholic Church, which together with the several dynasties then beginning to consolidate themselves in Europe, means, being interpreted, a plan according to which the cunning and selfish few have employed the fears and hopes of the ignorant many to the establishment of their own power and the destruction of the real interests of all.

The Republics and municipal Governments of Italy opposed for some time a systematic and effectual resistance to the all-surrounding tyranny. The Lombard League defeated the armies of the despot in open field, and until Florence was betrayed to those flattered traitors [and] polished tyrants, the Medici, Freedom had one citadel wherein it could find refuge from a world which was its enemy. Florence long balanced, divided, and weakened the strength of the Empire and the Popedom. To this cause, if to anything, was due the undisputed superiority of Italy in literature and the arts over all its contemporary nations, that union of energy and of beauty which distinguish[es] from all other poets the writings of Dante, that restlessness of fervid power which expressed itself in painting and sculpture, and in daring architectural forms, and from which, and conjointly from the creations of Athens, its predecessor and its image, Raphael and Michel Angelo drew the inspiration which created those forms and colours now the astonishment of the world. The father of our own literature, Chaucer, wrought from the simple and powerful language of a nursling of this Republic the basis of our own literature. And thus we owe, among other causes, the exact condition belonging to [our own] intellectual existence to the generous disdain of submission which burned in the bosoms of men who filled a distant generation and inhabited another land.

When this resistance was overpowered (as what resistance to fraud and [tyranny] has not been overpowered?), another was even then maturing. The progress of philosophy and civilization which ended in that imperfect emancipation of mankind from the yoke of priests and kings, called the Reformation, had already commenced. Exasperated by their long sufferings, inflamed by the spark of that superstition from the flames of which they were emerging, the poor rose against their natural enemies, the rich, and repaid with bloody interest the tyranny of ages. One of the signs of the times was that the oppressed peasantry rose like the negro slaves of West Indian Plantations and murdered their tyrants when they were unaware. For so dear is power that the tyrants themselves neither then, nor now, nor ever, left or leave a path to freedom but through their own blood. The contest then waged under the names of religion which have seldom been any more [than] the popular and visible symbols which express the degree of power in some shape or other asserted by one party and disclaimed by the other, ended; and the result, though partial and imperfect, is perhaps the most animating that the philanthropist can contemplate in the history of man. The Republic of Holland, which has been so long an armoury of the arrows of learning by which superstition has been wounded even to death, was established by this contest. What though the name of Republic—and by whom but by conscience-stricken tyrants could it be extinguished—is no more? The Republics of Switzerland derived from this event their consolidation and their union. From England then first began to pass away the stain of conquest. The exposition of a certain portion of religious imposture drew with it an enquiry into political imposture and was attended with an extraordinary exertion of the energies of intellectual power. Shakespeare and Lord Bacon and the great writers of the age of Elizabeth and James the 1st were at once the effects of the new spirit in men's minds and the causes of its more complete developement. By rapid gradation the nation was conducted to the temporary abolition of aristocracy and episcopacy, and [to] the mighty example which, "in teaching nations how to live," England afforded to the world—of bringing to public justice one of those chiefs of a conspiracy of privileged murderers and robbers whose impunity has been the consecration of crime.[1]

After the selfish passions and compromising interests of men had enlisted themselves to produce and establish the Restoration of Charles the 2nd, the unequal combat was renewed under the reign of his successor,[2] and that compromise between the unextinguishable spirit of Liberty and the ever watchful spirit of fraud and tyranny called the Revolution had place. On this occasion monarchy and aristocracy and episcopacy were at once established and limited by law. Unfortunately they lost no more in extent of power than they gained in security of possession. Meanwhile those by whom they were established acknowledged and declared that the will of the People was the source from which these powers, in this instance, derived the right to subsist.[3] A man has no right to be a King or a Lord or a Bishop but so long as it is for the benefit of the People and so long as the People judge that it is for their benefit that he should impersonate that character. The solemn establishment of this maxim as the basis of our constitutional law, more than any beneficial and energetic application of it to the circumstances of this æra of its promulgation, was the fruit of that vaunted event. Correlative with this series of events in England was the commencement of a new epoch in the history of the progress of civilization and society.

That superstition which has disguised itself under the name of the religion of Jesus subsisted under all its forms, even where it had been separated from those things especially considered as abuses by the multitude, in the shape of intolerant and oppressive hierarchies. Catholics massacred Protestants and Protestants proscribed Catholics, and extermination was the sanction of each faith within the limits of the power of its professors. The New Testament is in everyone's hand, and the few who ever read it with the simple sincerity of an unbiassed judgement may perceive how distinct from the opinions of any of those

1 **mighty example . . . crime** the execution, in 1649, of Charles I 2 James II (1685–1688) 3 **Meanwhile . . . subsist** especially expounded in John Locke's *Treatises of Government* (1690)

professing themselves establishers[4] were the doctrines and the actions of Jesus Christ. At the period of the Reformation this test was applied, and this judgement formed, of the then existing hierarchy, and the same compromise was then made between the spirit of truth and the spirit of imposture after [the] struggle which ploughed up the area of the human mind, as was made in the particular instance of England between the spirit of freedom and the spirit of tyranny at that event called the Revolution.[5] In both instances the maxims so solemnly recorded remain as trophies of our difficult and incomplete victory, planted in the enemies' land. *The will of the People to change their government is an acknowledged right in the Constitution of England.* The protesting against religious dogmas which present themselves to his mind as false is the inalienable prerogative of every human being.

The new epoch was marked by the commencement of deeper enquiries into the forms of human nature than are compatible with an unreserved belief in any of those popular mistakes upon which popular systems of faith with respect to the cause and agencies of the universe, with all their superstructure of political and religious tyranny, are built. Lord Bacon, Spinoza, Hobbes, Bayle, Montaigne, regulated the reasoning powers, criticized the past history, exposed the errors by illustrating their causes and their connexion, and anatomized the inmost nature of social man. Then, with a less interval of time than of genius, followed [Locke] and the philosophers of his exact and intelligible but superficial school. Their illustrations of some of the minor consequences of the doctrines established by the sublime genius of their predecessors were correct, popular, simple, and energetic. Above all, they indicated inferences the most incompatible with the popular religions and the established governments of Europe. [Philosophy went forth into the inchanted forest of the demons of worldly power, as the pioneer of the overgrowth of ages.] [6] Berkeley and Hume, [and] Hartley [at

4 **establishers**　founders of denominations and sects　5 **Revolution**　that of 1688　6 **[Philosophy . . . ages]**　bracketed passages, in various stages of completion or cancellation, are frequent in the fragmentary manuscript. Those bracketed passages whose

a] later age, following the traces of these inductions, have clearly established the certainty of our ignorance with respect to those obscure questions which under the name of religious truths have been the watchwords of contention and the symbols of unjust power ever since they were distorted by the narrow passions of the immediate followers of Jesus from that meaning to which philosophers are even now restoring them. A crowd of writers in France seized upon the most popular portions of the new philosophy which conducted to inferences at war with the dreadful oppressions under which the country groaned, made familiar to mankind the fals[e]hood of their religious mediators and political oppressors. Considered as philosophers their error seems to have consisted chiefly of a limitedness of view; they told the truth, but not the whole truth. This might have arisen from the terrible sufferings of their countrymen inviting them rather to apply a portion of what had already been discovered to their immediate relief, than to pursue one interest, the abstractions of thought, as the great philosophers who preceded them had done, for the sake of a future and more universal advantage. Whilst that philosophy which, burying itself in the obscure part of our nature, regards the truth and fals[e]hood of dogmas relating to the cause of the universe and the nature and manner of man's relation with it, was thus stripping Power of its darkest mask, Political Philosophy, or that which considers the relations of man as a social being, was assuming a precise form. This philosophy indeed sprang from and maintained a connexion with that other as its parent. What would Swift and Bolingbroke and Sidney and Locke and Montesquieu, or even Rousseau, not to speak of political philosophers of our own age, Godwin and Bentham, have been but for Lord Bacon, Montaigne, and Spinoza, and the other great luminaries of the preceding epoch? Something excellent and eminent, no doubt, the least of these would have been, but something different from and inferior to what they are. A series of these writers illustrated with more or less success the principles of human nature as applied to man in political

contribution and intended placement seem indefinite are omitted in this edition society. A thirst for accommodating the existing forms according to which mankind are found divided to those rules of freedom and equality which are thus discovered as being the elementary principles according to which the happiness resulting from the social union ought to be produced and distributed, was kindled by these inquiries. Contemporary with this condition of the intellect all the powers of man seemed, though in most cases under forms highly inauspicious, to develop themselves with uncommon energy. The mechanical sciences attained to a degree of perfection which, though obscurely foreseen by Lord Bacon, it had been accounted madness to have prophesied in a preceding age. Commerce was pursued with a perpetually increasing vigour, and the same area of the Earth was perpetually compelled to furnish more and more subsistence. The means and sources of knowledge were thus increased together with knowledge itself, and the instruments of knowledge. The benefit of this increase of the powers of man became, in consequence of the inartificial forms into which society came to be distributed, an instrument of his additional evil. The capabilities of happiness were increased, and applied to the augmentation of misery. Modern society is thus a[n] engine assumed to be for useful purposes, whose force is by a system of subtle mechanism augmented to the highest pitch, but which, instead of grinding corn or raising water acts against itself and is perpetually wearing away or breaking to pieces the wheels of which it is composed. The result of the labours of the political philosophers has been the establishment of the principle of Utility as the substance, and liberty and equality as the forms according to which the concerns of human life ought to be administered. By this test the various institutions regulating political society have been tried and, as the undigested growth of the private passions, errors, and interests of barbarians and oppressors, have been condemned. And many new theories, more or less perfect, but all superior to the mass of evil which they would supplant, have been given to the world.

The system of government in the United States of America was the first practical illustration of the new philosophy. Sufficiently remote, it will be confessed, from the accuracy of ideal excellence is that representative system which will soon cover the extent of that vast Continent.

But it is scarcely less remote from the insolent and con-
taminating tyrannies under which, with some limitation of
these terms as regards England, Europe groaned at the period of the successful rebellion of America. America holds
forth the victorious example of an immensely populous,
and as far as the external arts of life are concerned, a
highly civilized community administered according to
republican forms. It has no king, that is it has no officer
to whom wealth and from whom corruption flows. It has
no hereditary oligarchy, that is it acknowledges no order
of men privileged to cheat and insult the rest of the members of the state, and who inherit a right of legislating and
judging which the principles of human nature compel
them to exercise to their own profit and to the detriment
of those not included within their peculiar class. It has no
established Church, that is it has no system of opinions
respecting the abstrusest questions which can be topics of
human thought, founded in an age of error and fanaticism,
and opposed by law to all other opinions, defended by
prosecutions, and sanctioned by enormous bounties given
to idle priests and forced thro' the unwilling hands of those
who have an interest in the cultivation and improvement of
the soil. It has no false representation, whose consequences
are captivity, confiscation, infamy and ruin, but a true representation. The will of the many is represented by the few
in the assemblies of legislation and by the officers of the
executive entrusted with the administration of the executive power almost as directly as the will of one person can
be represented by the will of another. [This is not the place
for dilating upon the inexpressible advantages (if such
advantages require any manifestation) of a self-governing
Society, or one which approaches it in the degree of the
Republic of the United States.] Lastly, it has an institution
by which it is honourably distinguished from all other
governments which ever existed. It constitutionally acknowledges the progress of human improvement and is framed
under the limitation of the probability of more simple
views of political science being rendered applicable to
human life. There is a law by which the constitution is
reserved for revision every ten years.[7] Every other set of

7 There . . . years Shelley's error; this idea was proposed to
the Constitutional Convention but not adopted

men who have assumed the office of legislation and framing institutions for future ages, with far less right to such an assumption than the founders of the American Republic, assumed that their work was the wisest and the best that could possibly have been produced. These illustrious men[8] looked upon the past history of their species and saw that it was the history of his mistakes and his sufferings arising from his mistakes; they observed the superiority of their own work to all the works which had preceded it, and they judged it probable that other political institutions would be discovered bearing the same relation to those which they had established which they bear to those which have preceded them. They provided therefore for the application of these contingent discoveries to the social state without the violence and misery attendant upon such change in less modest and more imperfect governments. The United States, as we would have expected from theoretical deduction, affords an example, compared with the old governments of Europe and Asia, of a free, happy, and strong people. Nor let it be said that they owe their superiority rather to the situation than to their government. Give them a king, and let that king waste in luxury, riot, and bribery the same sum which now serves for the entire expenses of their government. Give them an aristocracy, and let that aristocracy legislate for the people. Give them a priesthood, and let them bribe with a tenth of the produce of the soil a certain set of men to say a certain set of words. Pledge the larger part of them by financial subterfuges to pay the half of their property or earnings to another portion, and let the proportion of those who enjoy the fruits of the toil of others without toiling themselves be three instead of one. Give them a Court of Chancery[9] and let the property, the liberty and the interest in the dearest concerns of life, the exercise of the most sacred rights of a social being depend upon the will of one of the most servile creature[s] of that kingly and oligarchical and priestly power to which every man in proportion as he is of an enquiring and philosophical mind and of a sincere

8 **These illustrious men** framers of the U.S. Constitution
9 **Court of Chancery** in England, the court presided over by the lord chancellor

and honourable disposition is a natural, a necessary enemy. Give them, as you must if you give them these things, a great standing army to cut down the people if they murmur. If any American should see these words, his blood would run cold at the imagination of such a change. He well knows that the prosperity and happiness of the United States if subjected to such institutions [would] be no more.[10]

The just and successful Revolt of America corresponded with a state of public opinion in Europe of which it was the first result. The French Revolution was the second. The oppressors of mankind had enjoyed (O that we could say suffered) a long and undisturbed reign in France, and to the pining famine, the shelterless destitution of the inhabitants of that country had been added and heaped up insult harder to endure than misery. For the feudal system (the immediate causes and conditions of its institution having become obliterated) had degenerated into an instrument not only of oppression but of contumely, and both were unsparingly inflicted. Blind in the possession of strength, drunken as with the intoxication of ancestral greatness, the rulers perceived not that increase of knowledge in their subjects which made its exercise insecure. They called soldiers to hew down the people when their power was already past. The tyrants were, as usual, the aggressors. Then the oppressed, having been rendered brutal, ignorant, servile, and bloody by long slavery, having had the intellectual thirst, excited in them by the progress of civilization, satiated from fountains of literature poisoned by the spirit and the form of monarchy, arose and took a dreadful revenge on their oppressors. Their desire to wreak revenge, to this extent, in itself a mistake, a crime, a calamity, arose from the same source as their other miseries and errors, and affords an additional proof of the necessity of that long-delayed change which it accompanied and disgraced. If a just and necessary revolution could have been accomplished with as little expense of happiness and order in a country governed by despotic as [in] one

10 **The system . . . . no more** a paragraph in which Shelley presents the U.S. as an example of a society dedicated to the ending of all tyranny

governed by free laws, equal liberty and justice would lose their chief recommendations and tyranny be divested of its most revolting attributes. Tyranny entrenches itself within the existing interests of the most refined citizens of a nation and says 'If you dare trample upon these, be free.' Though this terrible condition shall not be evaded, the world is no longer in a temper to decline the challenge.

The French were what their literature is (excluding Montaigne and Rousseau, and some few leaders of the . . .) weak, superficial, vain, with little imagination, and with passions as well as judgements cleaving to the external form of things. Not that [they] are organically different from the inhabitants of the nations who have become . . . or rather not that their organical differences, whatever they may amount to, incapacitate them from arriving at the exercise of the highest powers to be attained by man. Their institutions made them what they were. Slavery and superstition, contumely and the tame endurance of contumely, and the habits engendered from generation to generation out of this transmitted inheritance of wrong, created this thing which has extinguished what has been called the likeness of God in man. The Revolution in France overthrew the hierarchy, the aristocracy and the monarchy, and the whole of that peculiarly insolent and oppressive system on which they were based. But as it only partially extinguished those passions which are the spirit of these forms, a reaction took place which has restored in a certain limited degree the old system. In a degree, indeed, exceedingly limited and stript of all its antient terrors. The hope of the Monarchy of France, with his teeth drawn and his claws pared, was its maintaining the formal likeness of most imperfect and insecure dominion. The usurpation of Bonaparte and then the Restoration of the Bourbons were the shapes in which this reaction clothed itself, and the heart of every lover of liberty was struck as with palsy by the succession of these events. But reversing the proverbial expression of Shakespeare, it may be the good which the Revolutionists did lives after them, their ills are interred with their bones.[11] But the military project of government of the great tyrant having failed, and there

11 **But . . . bones** *Julius Caesar*, III, 2, 81–82

being even no attempt—and, if there were any attempt,
there being not the remotest possibility of re-establishing
the enormous system of tyranny abolished by the Revolution, France is, as it were, regenerated. Its legislative assemblies are in a certain limited degree representations of
the popular will, and the executive power is hemmed in by
jealous laws. France occupies in this respect the same situation as was occupied by England at the restoration of
Charles the 2nd. It has undergone a revolution (unlike in
the violence and calamities which attended it, because
unlike in the abuses which it was excited to put down)
which may be paralleled with that in our own country
which ended in the death of Charles the 1st. The authors
of both Revolutions proposed a greater and more glorious
object than the degraded passions of their countrymen permitted them to attain. But in both cases abuses were
abolished which never since have dared to show their face.
There remains in the natural order of human things that
the tyranny and perfidy of the reigns of Charles the 2nd
and James the 2nd (for these were less the result of the
disposition of particular men than the vices which would
have been engendered in any but an extraordinary man by
the natural necessities of their situation), perhaps under a
milder form and within a shorter period should produce the
institution of a Government in France which may bear the
same relation to the state of political knowledge existing
at the present day, as the Revolution under William the
3rd bore to the state of political knowledge existing at that
period.

Germany, which is, among the great nations of Europe,
one of the latest civilized, with the exception of Russia,
is rising with the fervour of a vigorous youth to the assertion of those rights for which it has that desire arising
from knowledge, the surest pledge of victory. The deep passion and the bold and Æschylean vigour of the imagery
of their poetry; the enthusiasm, however distorted, of their
religious sentiments; the flexibility and comprehensiveness
of their language which is a many-sided mirror of every
changing thought, their severe, bold, and liberal spirit of
criticism; their subtle and deep philosophy, however
erroneous[ly] and illogical[ly] mingling fervid intuitions
into truth with obscure error (for the period of just distinc-

tion is yet to come), and their taste and power in the plastic arts, prove that they are a great People. And every great people either has been or is or will be free. The panic-stricken tyrants of that country promised to their subjects that their governments should be administered according to republican forms, they retaining merely the right of hereditary chief magistracy in their families. This promise, made in danger, the oppressors dream that they can break in security. And everything in consequence wears in Germany the aspect of rapidly maturing revolution.[12]

In Spain and in the dependencies of Spain good and evil in the forms of Despair and Tyranny are struggling foot to foot. That great people have been delivered bound hand and foot to be trampled upon and insulted by a traitorous and sanguinary tyrant, a wretch who makes credible all that might have been doubted in the history of Nero, Christiern,[13] Muley Ismael[14] or Ezzelin[15]—the persons who have thus delivered them were that hypocritical knot of conspiring tyrants, who proceeded upon the credit they gained by putting down the only tyrant among them who was not a hypocrite, to undertake the administration of those *arrondissements* of consecrated injustice and violence which they deliver to those who the nearest resemble them under the name of the "kingdoms of the earth." This action signed a sentence of death, confiscation, exile, or captivity against every philosopher and patriot in Spain. The tyrant Ferdinand, he whose name is changed into a proverb of execration, found natural allies in all the priests and a few of the most dishonourable military chiefs of that devoted country. And the consequences of military despotism and the black, stagnant, venomous hatred which priests in common with eunuchs seek every opportunity to wreak upon the portion of mankind exempt from their own unmanly disqualifications is slavery. And what is slavery—in its mildest form hideous, and, so long as one amiable or great attribute survives in its victims,

12 **everything . . . revolution** forecast of Germany's minor revolution of 1848   13 Sweden's Christian II, who gave order for Massacre of Stockholm (1520)   14 emperor of Morocco (1673–1727), notorious for putting his son to slow death   15 tyrannical thirteenth-century Lord of Padua

rankling and intolerable, but in its darkest shape [as] it now exhibits itself in Spain, it is the presence of all and more than all the evils for the sake of an exemption from which mankind submit to the mighty calamity of government. It is a system of insecurity of property and of person, of prostration of conscience and understanding, of famine heaped upon the greater number and contumely heaped upon all, defended by unspeakable tortures employed not merely as punishments but as precautions, by want, death, and captivity, and the application to political purposes of the execrated and enormous instruments of religious cruelty. Those men of understanding, integrity, and courage who rescued their country from one tyrant are exiled from it by his successor and his enemy and their legitimate king. Tyrants, however they may squabble among themselves, have common friends and foes. The taxes are levied at the point of the sword. Armed insurgents occupy all the defensible mountains of the country. The dungeons are peopled thickly, and persons of every sex and age have the fibres of their frame torn by subtle torments. Boiling water (such is an article in the last news from Spain) is poured upon the legs of a noble Spanish Lady newly delivered, slowly and cautiously that she may confess what she knows of a conspiracy against the tyrant, and she dies, as constant as the slave Epicharis, imprecating curses upon her torturers and passionately calling upon her children. These events, in the present condition of the understanding and sentiment of mankind, are the rapidly passing shadows which forerun successful insurrection, the ominous comets of our republican poet perplexing great monarchs with fear of change.[16] Spain, having passed through an ordeal severe in proportion to the wrongs and errors which it is kindled to erase, must of necessity be renovated. [The country which] produced Calderon and Cervantes, what else did it but breathe, thro[ugh] the tumult of the despotism and superstition which invested them, the prophecy of a glorious consummation?

The independents of South America are as it were already free. Great Republics are about to consolidate

16 **ominous . . . change** reference to Milton's "With fear of change Perplexing Monarchs," *Paradise Lost*, l. 597–598

themselves in a portion of the globe sufficiently vast and fertile to nourish more human beings than at present occupy, with the exception perhaps of China, the remainder of the inhabited earth. Some indefinite arrears of misery and blood remain to be paid to the Moloch of oppression. These, to the last drop and groan it will implacably exact. But not the less are [they] inevitably enfranchised. The Great Monarchies of Asia cannot, let us confidently hope, remain unshaken by the earthquake which shatters to dust the "mountainous strongholds" of the tryants of the western world.

Revolutions in the political and religious state of the Indian peninsula seem to be accomplishing, and it cannot be doubted but the zeal of the missionaries of what is called the Christian faith will produce beneficial innovation there, even by the application of dogmas and forms of what is here an outworn incumbrance. The Indians have been enslaved and cramped in the most severe and paralysing forms which were ever devised by man; some of this new enthusiasm ought to be kindled among them to consume it and leave them free, and even if the doctrines of Jesus do not penetrate through the darkness of that which those who profess to be his followers call Christianity, there will yet be a number of social forms modelled upon those European feelings from which it has taken its colour substituted to those according to which they are at present cramped, and from which, when the time for complete emancipation shall arrive, their disengagement may be less difficult, and under which their progress to it may be the less imperceptibly slow. Many native Indians have acquired, it is said, a competent knowledge in the arts and philosophy of Europe, and Locke and Hume and Rousseau are familiarly talked of in Brahminical society. But the thing to be sought is that they should, as they would if they were free, attain to a system of arts and literature of their own. Of Persia we know little but that it has been the theatre of sanguinary contests for power and that it is now at peace. The Persians appear to be from organization a beautiful, refined, and impassioned people and would probably soon be infected by the contagion of good. The Jews, that wonderful people which has preserved so long the symbols of their union, may reassume their ancestral seats, and. . . . The Turkish Empire is in its last stage of ruin, and it cannot be doubted but that the time is approaching when the deserts of Asia Minor and of Greece will be colonized by the overflowing population of countries less enslaved and debased, and that the climate and the scenery which was the birthplace of all that is wise and beautiful will not remain forever the spoil of wild beasts and unlettered Tartars. In Syria and Arabia the spirit of human intellect has roused a sect of people called Wahabees,[17] who maintain the Unity of God and the equality of man, and their enthusiasm must go on "conquering and to conquer" even if it must be repressed in its present shape. Egypt having but a nominal dependence upon Constantinople is under the government of Ottoman Bey,[18] a person of enlightened views who is introducing European literature and arts, and is thus beginning that change which Time, the great innovator, will accomplish in that degraded country; [and] by the same means its sublime enduring monuments may excite lofty emotions in the hearts of the posterity of those who now contemplate them without admiration.

Lastly, in the West Indian islands, first from the disinterested yet necessarily cautious measures of the English Nation, and then from the infection of the spirit of Liberty in France, the deepest stain upon civilized man is fading away. Two nations of free negroes are already established; one, in pernicious mockery of the usurpation over France, an empire, the other a republic—both animating yet terrific spectacles to those who inherit around them the degradation of slavery and the peril of dominion.[19]

Such is a slight sketch of the general condition of the

17 followers of Abdul-Wahhab (1691–1787), reformers seeking to restore a primitive form of Mohammedanism; powerful in all of Arabia until 1818; revival of power about 1910 18 This person sent his nephew to Lucca to study European learnings, and when his nephew asked with reference to some branch of study at enmity with Mahometanism whether he was permitted to engage in it, he replied, "You are at liberty to do anything which will not injure another." [Shelley's note] 19 **Two . . . dominion** reference to the liberating leadership of the Haitian general Toussaint L'Ouverture (1743–1803), the subject of Wordsworth's well-known sonnet

human race to which they have been conducted after the obliteration of the Greek republics by the successful external tyranny of Rome—its internal liberty having been first abolished—and by those miseries and superstitions consequent upon this event which compelled the human race to begin anew its difficult and obscure career of producing, to the forms of society, the greatest portion of good.

Meanwhile England, the particular object for the sake of which these general considerations have been stated on the present occasion, has arrived, like the nations which surround it, at a crisis in its destiny. The literature of England, an energetic development of which has ever followed or preceded a great and free development of the national will, has arisen, as it were, from a new birth. In spite of that low-thoughted envy which would undervalue, thro[ugh] a fear of comparison with its own insignificance, the eminence of contemporary merit, it is *felt by the British* [that] ours is in intellectual achievements a *memorable age*, and we live among such philosophers and poets as surpass beyond comparison any who have appeared in our nation since its last struggle for liberty.[20] For the most unfailing herald, or companion, or follower of an universal employment of the sentiments of a nation to the production of beneficial change is poetry, meaning by poetry an intense and impassioned power of communicating intense and impassioned impressions respecting man and nature. The persons in whom this power takes its abode may often, as far as regards many portions of their nature, have little tendency [to] the spirit of good of which it is the minister. But although they may deny and abjure, they are yet compelled to serve that which is seated on the throne of their own soul. And whatever systems they may [have] professed by support, they actually advance the interests of Liberty. It is impossible to read the productions of our most celebrated writers, whatever may be their system relating to thought or expression, without being startled by the electric life which there is in their words. They measure the circumference or sound the depths of human nature with a comprehensive and all-penetrating spirit at which they are

20 **its . . . liberty** renaissance and its aftermath

themselves perhaps most sincerely astonished, for it [is] less their own spirit than the spirit of their age. They are the priests of an unapprehended inspiration, the mirrors of gigantic shadows which futurity casts upon the present; the words which express what they conceive not; the trumpet which sings to battle and feels not what it inspires; the influence which is moved not but moves. Poets and philosophers are the unacknowledged legislators of the world.[21]

But, omitting these more abstracted considerations, has there not been and is there not in England a desire of change arising from the profound sentiment of the exceeding inefficiency of the existing institutions to provide for the physical and intellectual happiness of the people? It is proposed in this work (1) to state and examine the present condition of this desire, (2) to elucidate its causes and its object, (3) to then show the practicability and utility, nay the necessity of change, (4) to examine the state of parties as regards it, and (5) to state the probable, the possible, and the desirable mode in which it should be accomplished.

Chapter II

On the Sentiment of the Necessity of Change

Two circumstances arrest the attention of those who turn their regard to the present political condition of the English nation—first, that there is an almost universal sentiment of the approach of some change to be wrought in the institutions of the government, and secondly, the necessity and desirableness of such a change. From the first of these propositions, it being matter of fact, no person addressing the public can dissent. The latter, from a general belief in which the former flows and on which it depends, is matter of opinion, but [one] which to the mind of

21 **Meanwhile . . . . world** this paragraph was later used almost verbatim in final paragraph of A *Defence of Poetry*

all, excepting those interested in maintaining the contrary is a doctrine so clearly established that even they, admitting that great abuses exist, are compelled to impugn it by insisting upon the specious topic that popular violence, by which they alone could be remedied, would be more injurious than the continuance of these abuses. But as those who argue thus derive for the most part great advantage and convenience from the continuance of these abuses, their estimation of the mischiefs of uprisings [&] popular violence as compared with the mischiefs of tyrannical and fraudulent forms of government are likely, from the known principles of human nature,[22] to be exaggerated. Such an estimate comes to with a worse grace from them who, if they would in opposition to their own unjust advantage take the lead in reform, might spare the nation from

22 According to the principles of human nature as modified by the existing opinions and institutions of society, a man loves himself with an overweaning love. The generous emotions of disinterested affection which the records of human nature and our experience teach us that the human heart is highly susceptible of are confined within the narrow circle of our kindred and friends. And therefore there is a class' of men considerable from talents, influence, and station who of necessity are enemies to Reform.

For Reform would benefit the nation at their expense instead of suffering them to benefit themselves at the expense of the nation. If a reform however mild were to take place, they must submit to a diminution of those luxuries and vanities in the idolatry of which they have been trained. Not only they, but what in most cases would be esteemed a harder necessity, their wives and children and dependents, must be comprehended in the same restrictions. That degree of pain which however it is to be regretted, is necessarily attached to the relinquishment of the habits of particular persons at war with the general permanent advantage, must be inflicted by the mildest reform. It is not alleged that every person whose interest is directly or indirectly concerned in the maintaining things as they are, is therefore necessarily interested. There are individuals who can be just judges even against themselves, and by study and self-examination have established a severe tribunal within themselves to which these principles which demand the advantages of the greater number are admitted to appeal. With some it assumes the mark of fear, with others that of hope—with all it is expectation. [Shelley's note]

the inconveniences of the temporary dominion of the poor who, by means of that degraded condition which their insurrection would be designed to ameliorate, are sufficiently incapable of discerning their own genuine and permanent advantage, tho surely less incapable than those whose interests consist in proposing to themselves an object perfectly opposite [to] and wholly incompatible with that advantage: all public functionaries who are overpaid either in money or in power for their public services, beginning with the person invested with the royal authority, and ending with the turnkey who extorts his last shilling from his starving prisoner; all members of the House of Lords who tremble lest the annihilation of their borough interest might not involve the risk of their hereditary legislative power and of those distinctions which considered in a pecuniary point of view are injurious to those beyond the pale of their caste in proportion as they are beneficial to those within; an immense majority of the assembly called the House of Commons, who would be reduced, if they desired to administer public business, to consult the interest of their electors and conform themselves. The functionaries who know that their claims to several millions yearly of the produce of the soil for the service of certain dogmas, which if necessary other men would enforce as effectually for as many thousands, would undergo a very severe examination [in the event of a general Reform]. These persons propose to us the dilemma of submitting to a despotism which is notoriously gathering like an avalanche year by year, or taking the risk of something which it must be confessed bears the aspect of revolution. To this alternative we are reduced by the selfishness[23] of those who taunt us with it. And the history of the world teaches us not to hesitate an instant in the decision, if indeed the power of decision be not already past.

23 It is of no avail that they call this selfishness principle or that they are self-deluded by the same sophism with which they would deceive others. To attach another name to the same idea to which those principles which demand the advantage of the greater number are admitted to appeal may puzzle the hearer but can in no manner change the import of it. But these, even should they be few, would be few among the many. [Shelley's note]

The establishment of King William III on the throne of England has already been referred to as a compromise between liberty and despotism. The Parliament of which that event was the act had ceased to be, in an emphatic sense, a representation of the people. The Long Parliament, questionless, was the organ of the will of all classes of people in England since it effected the complete revolution in a tyranny consecrated by time. But since its meeting and since its dissolution a great change had taken place in England. Feudal manners and institutions having become obliterated, monopolies and patents having been abolished, property and personal liberty having been rendered secure, the nation advanced rapidly towards the acquirement of the elements of national prosperity. Population increased, a greater number of hands were employed in the labours of agriculture and commerce, towns arose where villages had been, and the proportion borne by those whose labour produces the materials of subsistence and enjoyment to those who claim for themselves a superfluity of these materials began to increase indefinitely. A fourth class therefore appeared in the nation, the unrepresented multitude. Nor was it so much that villages which sent no members to Parliament became great cities, and that towns which had been considerable enough to send members dwindled from local circumstances into villages. This cause no doubt contributed to the general effect of rendering the Commons' House a less complete representation of the people. Yet had this been all, though it had ceased to be a legal and actual it might still have been a virtual Representation of the People. But the nation universally became multiplied into a denomination which had no constitutional presence in the state. This denomination had not existed before, or had existed only to a degree in which its interests were sensibly interwoven with that of those who enjoyed a constitutional presence. Thus, the proportion borne by the Englishmen who possessed [the] faculty of suffrage to those who were excluded from that faculty at the several periods of 1641 and 1688 had changed by the operation of these causes from 1 to 8 to 1 to 20. The rapid and effectual progress by which it changed from 1 to 20 to one to many hundreds in the interval between 1688 and 1819 is a process, to those familiar with the history of the political economy of that period, which is rendered by these principles sufficiently intelligible. The number therefore of those who have influence on the government, even if numerically the same as at the former period, was relatively different. And a sufficiently just measure is afforded of the degree in which a country is enslaved or free, by the consideration of the relative number of individuals who are admitted to the exercise of political rights. Meanwhile another cause was operating of a deeper and more extensive nature. The *class* who compose the Lords must, by the advantage of their situation as the great landed proprietors, possess a considerable influence over nomination to the Commons. This influence, from an original imperfection in the equal distribution of suffrage, was always enormous, but it is only since it has been combined with the cause before stated that it has appeared to be fraught with consequences incompatible with public liberty. In 1641 this influence was almost wholly [inoperative to] pervert the counsels of the nation from its own advantage. But at that epoch the enormous tyranny of the agents of the royal power weighed equally upon all denominations of men, and united all counsels to extinguish it; add to which the nation was, as stated before, in a very considerable degree fairly represented in Parliament. [The] common danger which was the bond of union between the aristocracy and the people having been destroyed, the former systematized their influence through the permanence of hereditary right, whilst the latter were losing power by the inflexibility of the institutions which forbade a just accommodation to their numerical increase. After the operations of these causes had commenced, the accession of William III placed a seal upon forty years of Revolution.

The government of this country at the period of 1688 was regal, tempered by aristocracy, for what conditions of democracy attach to an assembly one portion of which [was] imperfectly nominated by less than a twentieth part of the people, and another perfectly nominated by the nobles? For the nobility, having by the assistance of the people imposed close limitations upon the royal power, finding that power to be its natural ally and the people (for the people from the increase of their numbers ac-

quired greater and more important rights whilst the organ
through which those rights might be asserted grew feebler
in proportion to the increase of the cause of those rights
and of their importance) its natural enemy, made the
Crown the mask and pretence of their own authority. At
this period began that despotism of the oligarchy of party,
and under colour of administering the executive power
lodged in the king, represented in truth the interests of
the rich. When it is said by political reasoners, speaking of
the interval between 1688 and the present time, that the
royal power progressively increased, they use an expression
which suggests a very imperfect and partial idea. The
power which has increased is that entrusted with the administration of affairs, composed of men responsible to the
aristocratic assemblies or to the reigning party in those
assemblies, which represents those orders of the nation
which are privileged and will retain power as long as it
pleases them and must be divested of power as soon as it
ceases to please them. The power which has increased
therefore is the [pow]er of the rich. The name and office
of king is merely the mask of this power and is a kind of
stalking-horse used to conceal these "catchers of men,"
whilst they lay their nets. Monarchy is only the string
which ties the robber's bundle. Though less contumelious
and abhorrent from the dignity of human nature than an
absolute monarchy, an oligarchy of this nature exacts more
of suffering from the people because it reigns both by the
opinion generated by imposture and the force which that
opinion places within its grasp.

At the epoch adverted to, the device of public credit
was first systematically applied as an instrument of government. It was employed at the accession of William III less
as a resource for meeting the financial exigencies of the
state than as a bond to connect those in the possession of
property with those who had, by taking advantage of an
accident of party, acceded to power. In the interval elapsed
since that period it has accurately fulfilled the intention
of its establishment and has continued to add strength to
the government even until the present crisis. Now this
device is one of those execrable contrivances of misrule
which overbalance the materials of common advantage
produced by the progress of civilization and increase the

number of those who are idle in proportion to those who work, while it increases, through the factitious wants of those indolent, privileged persons, the quantity of work to be done. The rich, no longer being able to rule by force, have invented this scheme that they may rule by fraud.

The most despotic governments of antiquity were strangers to this invention, which is a compendious method of extorting from the people far more than prætorian guards, and arbitrary tribunals, and excise officers created judges in the last resort could ever wring. Neither the Persian monarchy nor the Roman empire, where the will of one person was acknowledged as unappealable law, ever extorted a twentieth part the proportion now extorted from the property and labour of the inhabitants of Great Britain. The precious metals have been from the earliest records of civilization employed as the signs of labour and the titles to an unequal distribution of its produce. The [Government of] a country is necessarily entrusted with the affixing to certain portions of these metals a stamp, by which to mark their genuineness; no other is considered as current coin, nor can be a legal tender. The reason of this is that no alloyed coin should pass current, and thereby depreciate the genuine, and by augmenting the price of the articles which are the produce of labor defraud the holders of that which is genuine of the advantages legally belonging to them. If the Government itself abuses the trust reposed in it to debase the coin, in order that it may derive advantage from the unlimited multiplication of the mark entitling the holder to command the labour and property of others, the gradations by which it sinks, as labour rises, to the level of their comparative values, produces public confusion and misery. The foreign exchange meanwhile instructs the Government how temporary was its resource. This mode of making the distribution of the sign of labour a source of private aggrandisement, at the expense of public confusion and loss, was not wholly unknown to the nations of antiquity.

But the modern scheme of public credit is a far subtler and more complicated contrivance of misrule. All great transactions of personal property in England are managed by signs, and that is by the authority of the possessor expressed upon paper, thus representing in a compendious form his right to so much gold, which represents his right to so much labour. A man may write on a piece of paper what he pleases; he may say he is worth a thousand when he is not worth a hundred pounds. If he can make others believe this, he has credit for the sum to which his name is attached. And so long as this credit lasts, he can enjoy all the advantages which would arise out of the actual possession of the sum he is believed to possess. He can lend two hundred to this man and three to that other, and his bills, among those who believe that he possesses this sum, pass like money. Of course in the same proportion as bills of this sort, beyond the actual goods or gold and silver possessed by the drawer, pass current, they defraud those who have gold and silver and goods of the advantages legally attached to the possession of them, and they defraud the labourer and artizan of the advantage attached to increasing the nominal price of labour, and such a participation in them as their industry *might* command, whilst they render wages fluctuating and add to the toil of the cultivator and manufacturer.

The existing government of England in substituting a currency of paper [for] one of gold has had no need to depreciate the currency by alloying the coin of the country; they have merely fabricated pieces of paper on which they promise to pay a certain sum. The holders of these papers came for payment in some representation of property universally exchangeable. They then declared that the persons who held the office for that payment could not be forced by law to pay. They declared subsequently that these pieces of paper were the legal coin of the country. Of this nature are all such transactions of companies and banks as consist in the circulation of promissory notes to a greater amount than the actual property possessed by those whose names they bear. They have the effect of augmenting the prices of provision and of benefiting at the expense of the community the speculators in this traffic. One of the vaunted effects of this system is to increase the national industry. That is, to increase the labours of the poor and those luxuries of the rich which they supply, to make a manufacturer work 16 hours where he only worked 8, to turn children into lifeless and bloodless ma-

chines at an age when otherwise they would be at play
before the cottage doors of their parents, to augment indefinitely the proportion of those who enjoy the profit of
the labour of others as compared with those who exercise
this labour.

The consequences of this transaction have been the
establishment of a new aristocracy, which has its basis in
fraud as the old one has its basis in force. The hereditary
land-owners in England derived their title from royal
grants—they are fiefs bestowed by conquerors, or church-
lands, or they have been bought by bankers & merchants
from those persons. Now bankers & merchants are persons
whose . . . Since usage has consecrated the distinction
of the world aristocracy from its primitive meaning. . . .
Let me be assumed to employ the word aristocracy in that
ordinary sense which signifies that class of persons who
possess a right to the produce of the labour of others
without dedicating to the common service any labour in
return. This class of persons, whose existence is a prodigious anomaly in the social system, has ever constituted an
inseparable portion of it, and there has never been an
approach in practice towards any plan of political society
modelled on equal justice, at least in the complicated
mechanism of modern life. Mankind seem to acquiesce,
as in a necessary condition of the imbecility of their own
will and reason, in the existence of an aristocracy. With
reference to this imbecility, it has doubtless been the instrument of great social advantage, although that advantage would have been greater which might have been produced according to the forms of a just distribution of
the goods and evils of life. The object therefore of all
enlightened legislation and administration, is to enclose
within the narrowest practicable limits this order of drones.
The effect of the financial impostures of the modern rulers
of England has been to increase the numbers of the drones.
Instead of one aristocracy, the condition [to] which, in
the present state of human affairs, the friends of justice
and liberty are willing to subscribe as to an inevitable evil,
they have supplied us with two aristocracies. The one,
consisting [of] great land proprietors and merchants who
receive and interchange the produce of this country with
the produce of other countries; in this, because all other

great communities have as yet acquiesced in it, we acquiesce. Connected with the members of [it] is a certain generosity and refinement of manners and opinion which, although neither philosophy nor virtue, has been that acknowledged substitute for them, which at least is a religion which makes respected those venerable names. The other is an aristocracy of attornies and excisemen and directors and government pensioners, usurers, stock jobbers, country bankers, with their dependents and descendants. These are a set of pelting wretches in whose employment there is nothing to exercise, even to their distortion, the more majestic faculties of the soul. Though at the bottom it is all trick, there is something frank and magnificent in the chivalrous disdain of infamy connected with a gentleman. There is something to which—until you see through the base fals[e]hood upon which all inequality is founded—it is difficult for the imagination to refuse its respect, in the faithful and direct dealings of the substantial merchant. But in the habits and lives of this new aristocracy created out of an increase [in] the public calamities, and whose existence must be determined by their termination, there is nothing to qualify our disapprobation. They eat and drink and sleep, and in the intervals of those things performed with most ridiculous ceremony and accompaniments they cringe and lie. They poison the literature of the age in which they live by requiring either the antitype of their own mediocrity in books, or such stupid and distorted and inharmonious idealisms as alone have the power to stir their torpid imaginations. Their hopes and fears are of the narrowest description. Their domestic affections are feeble, and they have no others. They think of any commerce with their species but as a means, never as an end, and as a means to the basest forms of personal advantage.

If this aristocracy had arisen from a false and depreciated currency to the exclusion of the other, its existence would have been a moral calamity and disgrace, but it would not have constituted an oppression. But the hereditary aristocracy who held the political administration of affairs took the measures which created this other for purposes peculiarly its own. Those measures were so contrived as in no manner to diminish the wealth and power of the contrivers. The lord does not spare himself one luxury, but the peasant and artizan are assured of many needful things. To support the system of social order according to its supposed unavoidable constitution, those from whose labour all those external accommodations which distinguish a civilized being from a savage arise, worked, before the institution of this double aristocracy, eight hours. And of these only the healthy were compelled to labour, the efforts of the old, the sick, and the immature being dispensed with, and they maintained by the labour of the sane, for such is the plain English of the poor-rates. That labour procured a competent share of the decencies of life, and society seemed to extend the benefits of its institution even to its most unvalued instruments. Although deprived of those resources of sentiment and knowledge which might have been their lot could the wisdom of the institutions of social forms have established a system of strict justice, yet they earned by their labour a competency in those external materials of life which, and not the loss of moral and intellectual excellence, is supposed to be the legitimate object of the desires and murmurs of the poor. Since the institution of this double aristocracy, however, they have often worked not ten but twenty hours a day. Not that all the poor have rigidly worked twenty hours, but that the worth of the labour of twenty hours now, in food and clothing, is equivalent to the worth of ten hours then. And because twenty hours' labour cannot, from the nature of the human frame, be exacted from those who before performed ten, the aged and the sickly are compelled either to work or starve. Children who were exempted from labour are put in requisition, and the vigorous promise of the coming generation blighted by premature exertion. For fourteen hours' labour, which they do perform, they receive—no matter in what nominal amount—the price of seven. They eat less bread, wear worse clothes, are more ignorant, immoral, miserable, and desperate. This then is the condition of the lowest and the largest class, from whose labour the whole materials of life are wrought, of which the others are only the receivers or the consumers. They are more superstitious, for misery on earth begets a diseased expectation and panic-stricken faith in miseries beyond the grave. "God," they argue, "rules this world as well as that; and assuredly since his nature is immutable, and his powerful will unchangeable, he rules them by the same laws." The gleams of hope which speak of Paradise seem like the flames in Milton's hell only to make darkness visible, and all things take [their] colour from what surrounds them. They become revengeful . . .

But the condition of all classes of society, excepting those within the privileged pale, is singularly unprosperous, and even they experience the reaction of their own short-sighted tyranny in all those sufferings and deprivations which are not of a distinctly physical nature, in the loss of dignity, simplicity, and energy, and in the possession of all those qualities which distinguish a slave-driver from a proprietor. Right government being an institution for the purpose of securing such a moderate degree of happiness to men as has been experimentally practicable, the sure character of misgovernment is misery, and first discontent and, if that be despised, then insurrection, as the legitimate expression of that misery. The public ought to demand happiness; the labouring classes, when they cannot get food for their labour, are impelled to take it by force. Laws and assemblies and courts of justice and delegated powers placed in balance or in opposition are the means and the form, but public happiness is the substance and the end of political institution. Whenever this is attainted in a nation, not from external force, but from the internal arrangement and divisions of the common burthens of defence and maintenance, then there is oppression. And then arises an alternative between Reform, & the institution of a military Despotism, or a Revolution in which these two parties, one striving after ill-digested systems of democracy and the other clinging to the outworn abuses of power, leave the few who aspire to more than the former and who would overthrow the latter at whatever expense, to wait until that modified advantage which results from this conflict produces a small portion of that social improvement which, with the temperance and the toleration which both regard as a crime, might have resulted from the occasion which they let pass in a far more signal manner.

The propositions which are the consequences or the

corollaries, to which the preceding reasoning seems to have conducted us are:

—That the majority [of] the people of England are destitute and miserable, ill-clothed, ill-fed, ill-educated.

—That they know this, and that they are impatient to procure a reform of the cause of their abject and wretched state.

—That the cause of this peculiar misery is the unequal distribution which, under the form of the national debt, has been surreptitiously made of the products of their labour and the products of the labour of their ancestors; for all property is the produce of labour.

—That the cause of that cause is a defect in the government.

—That if they knew nothing of their condition, but believed that all they endured and all [they] were deprived of arose from the unavoidable condition of human life, this belief being an error, and [one] the endurance of [which] enforces an injustice, every enlightened and honourable person, whatever may be the imagined interest of his peculiar class, ought to excite them to the discovery of the true state of the case, and to the temperate but irresistible vindication of their rights.

It is better that they should be instructed in the whole truth, that they should see the clear grounds of their rights, the objects to which they ought to tend, and be impressed with the first persuasion, that patience and reason and endurance, and a calm yet invisible progress . . .

A Reform in England is most just and necessary. What ought to be that reform?

A writer of the present day (a priest of course, for his doctrines are those of a eunuch and of a tyrant) has stated that the evils of the poor arise from an excess of population,[24] and that after they have been stript naked by the

24 **A writer . . . population** Thomas Robert Malthus (1766–1834), British economist and author of the *Essay on the Principles of Population* (1798)

tax-gatherer and reduced to bread and tea and fourteen hours of hard labour by their masters, and after the frost has bitten their defenceless limbs, and the cramp has wrung like a disease within their bones, and hunger and the suppressed revenge of hunger has stamped the ferocity of want like the mark of Cain upon their countenance, that the last tie by which Nature holds them to benignant earth whose plenty is garnered up in the strongholds of their tyrants, is to be divided; that the single alleviation of their sufferings and their scorns, the one thing which made it impossible to degrade them below the beasts, which amid all their crimes and miseries yet separated a cynical and unmanly contamination, an anti-social cruelty, from all the soothing, elevating, and harmonious gentleness of the sexual intercourse and the humanizing charities of domestic life which are its appendages—that this is to be obliterated. They are required to abstain from marrying under penalty of starvation. And it is threatened to deprive them of that property which is as strictly their birthright as a gentleman's land is his birthright, without giving them any compensation but the insulting advice to conquer, with minds undisciplined in the habits of higher gratification, a propensity which persons of the most consummate wisdom have been unable to resist, and which it is difficult to admire a person for having resisted. The doctrine of this writer is that the principle of population, when under no dominion of moral restraint, [is] outstripping the sustenance produced by the labour of man, and that not in proportion to the number of inhabitants, but operating equally in a thinly peopled community as in one where the population is enormous, being not a prevention but a check.[25] So far a man might have been conducted by a train of reasoning which, though it may be shown to be defective, would argue in the reasoner no selfish and slavish feelings. But he has the hardened insolence to pro-

25 **after they have been . . . . check** this passage shows Shelley's antipathy to the theory of Malthus that goods increase in arithmetical progression, and population in geometrical progression; permanent removal of poverty, according to Malthus, is thus impossible, and the only alternative to overpopulation is an acceptance of war, poverty, and disease

pose as a remedy that the poor should be compelled (for what except compulsion is a threat of the confiscation of those funds which by the institutions of their country had been set apart for their sustenance in sickness or destitution?) to abstain from sexual intercourse, whilst the rich are to be permitted to add as many mouths to consume the products of the labour of the poor as they please. [The rights of all men are intrinsically and originally equal and they forgo the assertion of all of them only that they may the more securely enjoy a portion.] If any new disadvantages are found to attach to the condition of social existence, those disadvantages ought not to be borne exclusively by one class of men, nor especially by that class whose ignorance leads them to exaggerate the advantages of sensual enjoyment, whose callous habits render domestic endearments more important to dispose them to resist the suggestions to violence and cruelty by which their situation ever exposes them to be tempted, and all whose other enjoyments are limited and few, whilst their sufferings are various and many. In this sense I cannot imagine how the advocates of equality would so readily have conceded that the unlimited operation of the principle of population affects the truth of these theories. On the contrary, the more heavy and certain are the evils of life, the more injustice is there in casting the burden of them exclusively on one order in the community. They seem to have conceded it merely because their opponents have insolently assumed it. Surely it is enough that the rich should possess to the exclusion of the poor all other luxuries and comforts, and wisdom and refinement, the least envied but the most deserving of envy among all their privileges.

What is the Reform that we desire? Before we aspire after theoretical perfection in the amelioration of our political state, it is necessary that we possess those advantages which we have been cheated of and to which the experience of modern times has proved that nations even under the present [conditions] are susceptible. 1st. We would regain these. 2d. We would establish some form of government which might secure us against such a series of events as have conducted us to a persuasion that the forms according to which it is now administered are inadequate to that purpose.

We would abolish the national debt.

We would disband the standing army.

We would, with every possible regard to the existing interests of the holders, abolish sinecures.

We would, with every possible regard to the existing interests of the holders, abolish tithes, and make all religions, all forms of opinion respecting the origin and government of the Universe, equal in the eye of the law.

We would make justice cheap, certain, and speedy, and extend the institution of juries to every possible occasion of jurisprudence.

The national debt was chiefly contracted in two liberticide wars undertaken by the privileged classes of the country—the first for the ineffectual purpose of tyrannizing over one portion of their subjects, the second, in order to extinguish the resolute spirit of obtaining their rights in another. The labour which this money represents and that which is represented by the money wrung for purposes of the same detestable character out of the people since the commencement of the American war would, if properly employed, have covered our land with monuments of architecture exceeding the sumptuousness and the beauty of Egypt and Athens; it might have made every peasant's cottage, surrounded with its garden, a little paradise of comfort, with every convenience desirable in civilized life; neat tables and chairs, and good beds, and a nice collection of useful books; and our ships manned by sailors well-paid and well-clothed, might have kept watch round this glorious island against the less enlightened nations which assuredly would have envied, until they could have imitated, its prosperity. But the labour which is expressed by these sums has been diverted from these purposes of human happiness to the promotion of slavery, or the attempt at dominion, and a great portion of the sum in question is debt and must be paid. Is it to remain unpaid for ever, an eternal rent-charge upon the sacred soil from which the inhabitants of these islands draw their subsistence? This were to pronounce the perpetual institution of two orders of aristocracy, and men are in a temper to endure one with some reluctance. Is it to be paid now?

If so what are the funds, or when and how is it to be paid? The fact is that the national debt is a debt not contracted by the whole nation towards a portion of it, but a debt contracted by the whole mass of the privileged classes towards one particular portion of those classes. If the principal were paid, the whole property of those who possess property must be valued and the public creditor, whose property would have been included in this estimate, satisfied out of the proceeds. It has been said that all the land in the nation is mortgaged for the amount of the national debt. This is a partial statement. Not only all the land in the nation but all the property of whatever denomination, all the houses and the furniture and the goods and every article of merchandise, and the property which is represented by the very money lent by the fund-holder, who is bound to pay a certain portion as debtor whilst he is to receive another certain portion as creditor. The property of the rich is mortgaged; to use the language of the law, let the mortgagee foreclose.

If the principal of this debt were paid, after such reductions had been made so as to make an equal value, taking corn for the standard, be given as was received, it would be the rich who alone could, as justly they ought to, pay it. It would be a mere transfer among persons of property. Such a gentleman must lose a third of his estate, such a citizen a fourth of his money in the funds; the persons who borrowed would have paid and the juggling and complicated system of paper finance be suddenly at an end. As it is, the interest is chiefly paid by those who had no hand in the borrowing, and who are sufferers in other respects from the consequences of those transactions in which the money was spent.

The payment of the principal of what is called the national debt, which it is pretended is so difficult a problem, is only difficult to those who do not see who is the creditor, and who the debtor, and who the wretched sufferers from whom they both wring the taxes which under the form of interest is given by the [latter] and accepted by the [former]. It is from the labour of those who have no property that all the persons who possess property think to extort the perpetual interest of a debt, the whole of them to the part, which the [former] know they could not

persuade the [latter] to pay, but by conspiring with them
in an imposture which makes the third class pay what the
[second] neither received by their sanction nor spent for
their benefit, and what the [first] never lent to them. They
would both shift to the labour of the present and of all
succeeding generations the payment of the interest of their
own debt, from themselves and their posterity, because
the payment of the principal would be no more than a
compromise and transfer of property between each other,
by which the nation would be spared forty-four millions
a year, which now is paid to maintain in luxury and indolence the public debtors and to protect them from the
demand of their creditors upon them, who, being part of
the same body, and owing as debtors whilst they possess a
claim as creditors, agree to abstain from demanding the
principal which they must all unite to pay, for the sake of
receiving an enormous interest which is principally wrung
out of those who had no concern whatever in the transaction. One of the first acts of a reformed government would
undoubtedly be an effectual scheme for compelling these
to compromise their debt between themselves.

When I speak of persons of property I mean not every
man who possesses any right of property; I mean the rich.
Every man whose scope in society has a plebeian and intelligible utility, whose personal exertions are more valuable to him than his capital; every tradesman who is not
a monopolist, all surgeons and physicians and those me-
chanics and editors and literary men and artists, and farm-
ers, all those persons whose profits spring from honourably
and honestly exerting their own skill and wisdom or
strength in greater abundance than from the employment
of money to take advtanage of the necessity of the starvation of their fellow-citizens for their profit, are those who
pay, as well as those more obviously understood by the
labouring classes, the interest of the national debt. It is
the interest of all these persons as well as that of the
poor to insist upon the payment of the principal.

For this purpose the form ought to be as simple and
succinct as possible. The operations deciding who was to
pay, at what time, and how much, and to whom, are divested of financial chicanery, problems readily to be determined. The common tribunals may possess a legal

jurisdiction to award the proportion due upon the several claim of each.

There are two descriptions of property which, without entering into the subtleties of a more refined moral theory as applicable to the existing forms of society, are entitled to two very different measures of forbearance and regard. And this forbearance and regard have by political institutions usually been accorded in an inverse reason from what is just and natural. Labour, industry, economy, skill, genius, or any similar powers honourably and innocently exerted are the foundations of one description of property, and all true political institutions ought to defend every man in the exercise of his discretion with respect to property so acquired. Of this kind is the principal part of the property enjoyed by those who are but one degree removed from the class which subsists by daily labour. [Yet there are instances of persons in this class who have procured their property by fraudulent and violent means, as there are instances in the other of persons who have acquired their property by innocent or honourable exertion. All political science abounds with limitations and exceptions.] Property thus acquired men leave to their children. Absolute right becomes weakened by descent, first because it is only to avoid the greater evil of arbitrarily interfering with the discretion of any man in matters of property that the great evil of acknowledging any person to have an exclusive right to property who has not created it by his skill or labour is admitted, and secondly because the mode of its having been originally acquired is forgotten, and it is confounded with property acquired in a very different manner; and the principle upon which all property justly rests, after the great principle of the general advantage, becomes thus disregarded and misunderstood. Yet the privilege of disposing of property by will is one necessarily connected with the existing forms of domestic life and, exerted merely by those who have acquired property by industry or who have preserved it by economy, would never produce any great and invidious inequality of fortune. A thousand accidents would perpetually tend to level the accidental elevation, and the signs of property would perpetually recur to those whose deserving skill might attract or whose labour might create it.

But there is another species of property which has its foundation in usurpation, or imposture, or violence, without which, by the nature of things, immense possessions of gold or land could never have been accumulated. Of this nature is the principal part of the property enjoyed by the aristocracy and by the great fundholders, the great majority of whose ancestors never either deserved it by their skill and talents or acquired and created it by their personal labour. It could not be that they deserved it, for if the honourable exertion of the most glorious imperial faculties of our nature had been the criterion of the possession of property, the posterity of Shakespeare, of Milton, of Hampden, of Lor[d Bacon] would be the wealthiest proprietors in England. It could not be that they acquired it by legitimate industry, for—besides that the real mode of acquisition is matter of history—no honourable profession or honest trade, nor the hereditary exercise of it, ever in such numerous instances accumulated masses of property so vast as those enjoyed by the ruling orders in England. They were either grants from the feudal sovereigns whose right to what they granted was founded upon conquest or oppression, both a denial of all right; or they were the lands of the antient Catholic clergy which according to the most acknowledged principles of public justice reverted to the nation at their suppression; or they were the products of patents and monopolies, an exercise of sovereignty most [more?] pernicious that [than?] direct violence to the interests of a commercial nation; or in later times such property has been accumulated by dishonourable cunning and the taking advantage of a fictitious paper currency to obtain an unfair power over labour and the fruits of labour.

Property thus accumulated, being transmitted from father to son, acquires, as property of the more legitimate kind loses, force and sanction, but in a more limited manner. For not only on an examination and recurrence to first principles is it seen to have been founded on a violation of all that to which the latter owes its sacredness, but it is felt in its existence and perpetuation as a public burthen, and known as a rallying point to the ministers of tyranny, having the property of a snowball, gathering as it rolls, and rolling until it bursts. [It] is astonishing that

political theorists have not branded [it] as the most pernicious and odious. [Yet] there are three sets of people,
one who can place a thing to another in an intelligible
light, another who can understand it when so communicated, and a third who can neither discover or understand
it.

Labour and skill and the immediate wages of labour
and skill is a property of the most sacred and indisputable
right, and the foundation of all other property. And the
right of a man [to] property in the exertion of his own
bodily and mental faculties, or to the produce and free
reward from and for that exertion is the most [inalienable
of rights]. If however he takes by violence or appropri-
ates to himself through fraudulent cunning, or receives
from another property so acquired, his claim to that
property is of a far inferior force. We may acquiesce if
we evidently perceive an overbalance of public advantage
in submission under this claim; but if any public emergency should arise, at which it might be necessary as at
present by a tax on capital to satisfy the claims of a part
of the nation by a contribution from such national resources as may with the least injustice be appropriated to
that purpose, assuredly it would not be on labour and
skill, the foundation of all property, nor on the profits
and savings of labour and skill, which are property itself,
but on such possessions which can only be called property
in a modified sense, as have from their magnitude and their
nature an evident origin in violence or imposture.[26]

The national debt, as has been stated, is a debt contracted by the whole of a particular class in the nation
towards a portion of that class. It is sufficiently clear that
this debt was not contracted for the purpose of the public
advantage. Besides, there was no authority in the nation
competent to a measure of this nature. The usual vindication of national debts is that, [since] they are contracted
in an overwhelming measure for the purpose of defence
against a common danger, for the vindication of the rights
and liberties of posterity, it is just that posterity should

26 **Labour and skill . . . . imposture** agrees in general with
Adam Smith's view of labor as the sole basis for wealth; note also
the incisive analysis of the principle of taxation

bear the burthen of payment. This reasoning is most fallacious. The history of nations presents us with a succession of extraordinary emergencies, and thro their present imperfect organization their existence is perpetually threatened by new and unexpected combinations and developments of foreign or internal force. Imagine a situation of equal emergency to occur to England as that which the ruling party assume to have occurred as their excuse for burthening the nation with the perpetual payment of £45,000,000 annually. Suppose France, Russia, and America were to enter into a league against England, the first to revenge its injuries, the second to satisfy its ambition, the third to soothe its jealousy. Could the nation bear £90,000,000 of yearly interest? must there be twice as many luxurious and idle persons? must the labourer receive for twenty-eight hours' work what he now receives for fourteen, as he now receives for fourteen what he once received for seven? But this argument . . .

What is meant by a Reform of Parliament? If England were a Republic governed by one assembly; if there were no chamber of hereditary aristocracy which is at once an actual and a virtual representation of all who claim through rank or wealth superiority over their countrymen; if there were no king who is as the rallying point of those whose tendency is at once to [gather] and to confer that power which is consolidated at the expense of the nation, then . . .

The advocates of universal suffrage have reasoned correctly that no individual who is governed can be denied a direct share in the government of his country without supreme injustice. If we pursue the train of reasonings which have conducted to this conclusion, we discover that systems of social order still more incompatible than universal suffrage with any reasonable hope of instant accomplishment appear to be that which should result from a just combination of the elements of social life. I do not understand why those reasoners who propose at any price an immediate appeal to universal suffrage, because it is that which it is injustice to withhold, do not insist, on the same ground, on the immediate abolition, for instance, of monarchy and aristocracy, and the levelling of inordinate wealth, and an agrarian distribution, including the Parks and Chases of the rich, of the uncultivated districts of the country. No doubt the institution of universal suffrage would by necessary consequence *immediately* tend to the *temporary* abolition of these forms; because it is impossible that the people, having attained power, should fail to see what the demagogues now conceal from them, the legitimate consequence of the doctrines through which they had attained it. A Republic, however just in its principle and glorious in its object, would through violence and sudden change which must attend it, incur a great risk of being as rapid in its decline as in its growth. It is better that they should be instructed in the whole truth; that they should see the clear grounds of their rights, the objects to which they ought to tend; and be impressed with the just persuasion that patience and reason and endurance [are the means of] a calm yet irresistible progress. A civil war, which might be engendered by the passions attending on this mode of reform, would confirm in the mass of the nation those military habits which have been already introduced by our tyrants, and with which liberty is incompatible. From the moment that a man is a soldier, he becomes a slave. He is taught obedience; his will is no longer, which is the most sacred prerogative of man, guided by his own judgement. He is taught to despise human life and human suffering; this is the universal distinction of slaves. He is more degraded than a murderer; he is like the bloody knife which has stabbed and feels not: a murderer we may abhor and despise; a soldier is by profession beyond abhorrence and below contempt.

Chapter III

Probable Means

That Commons should reform itself, uninfluenced by any fear that the people would, on their refusal, assume to itself that office, seems a contradiction. What need of Reform if it expresses the will and watches over the interests of the public? And if, as is sufficiently evident, it despises that will and neglects that interest, what motives would incite it to institute a reform which the aspect of the times renders indeed sufficiently perilous, but without which there will speedily be no longer anything in England to distinguish it from the basest and most abject community of slaves that ever existed.

The great principle of Reform consists in every individual of mature age and perfect understanding giving his consent to the institution and the continued existence of the social system, which is instituted for his advantage and for the advantage of others in his situation. As in a great nation this is practically impossible, masses of individuals consent to qualify other individuals, whom they delegate to superintend their concerns. These delegates have constitutional authority to exercise the functions of sovereignty; they unite in the highest degree the legislative and executive functions. A government that is founded on any other basis is a government of fraud or force and ought on the first convenient occasion to be overthrown. The [?] broad principle of political reform is the natural equality of men, not with relation to their property but to their rights. That equality in possessions which Jesus Christ so passionately taught is a moral rather than a political truth and is such as social institutions cannot without mischief inflexibly secure. Morals and politics can only be considered as portions of the same science, with relation to a system of such absolute perfection as Christ and Plato and Rousseau and other reasoners have asserted, and as Godwin has, with irresistible eloquence, systematised and developed. Equality in possessions must be the last result of the utmost refinements of civilization; it is one of the conditions of that system of society towards which, with whatever hope of ultimate success, it is our duty to tend. We may and ought to advert to it as to the elementary principle, as to the goal, unattainable perhaps by us, but which, as it were, we revive in our posterity to pursue. We derive tranquillity and courage and grandeur of soul from contemplating an object which is, because we will it, and may be, because we hope and desire it, and must be if succeeding generations of the enlightened sincerely and earnestly seek it. We should with sincere and patient aspi[?ration] . . .

But our present business is with the difficult and unbending realities of actual life, and when we have drawn inspiration from the great object of our hopes, it becomes us with patience and resolution to apply ourselves to accommodating our theories to immediate practice.[27]

That Representative Assembly called the House of Commons ought questionless to be *immediately* nominated by the great mass of the people. The aristocracy and those who unite in their own persons the vast privileges conferred by the possession of inordinate wealth are sufficiently represented by the House of Peers and by the King. Those theorists who admire and would put into action the mechanism of what is called the British Constitution would acquiesce in this view of the question. For if the House of Peers be a permanent representation of the privileged classes, if the regal power be no more than another form, and a form still more jealously to be regarded, of the same representation, whilst the House of Commons be not chosen by the mass of the population, what becomes of that democratic element upon the presence of which it has been supposed that the waning superiority of England over the surrounding nations has depended?

Any sudden attempt at universal suffrage would produce an immature attempt at a Republic. It [is better] that [an] object so inexpressibly great and sacred should never have been attempted than that it should be attempted and fail. It is no prejudice to the ultimate establishment of the boldest political innovations that we temporize so as when they shall be accomplished they may be rendered permanent.

Considering the population of Great Britain and Ireland as twenty millions and the representative assembly as five hundred, each member ought to be the expression of the will of 40,000 persons; of these two-thirds would [consist of] women and children and persons under age; the actual number of voters therefore for each member would be 13,333. The whole extent of the empire might be divided into five hundred electoral departments or parishes, and

27 **But . . . practice** an important, representative example of Shelley's practicality, a quality too often overlooked by his critics

the inhabitants assemble on a certain day to exercise their rights of suffrage.

Mr. Bentham and other writers have urged the admission of females to the right of suffrage; this attempt seems somewhat immature.[28] Should my opinion be the result of despondency, the writer of these pages would be the last to withhold his vote from any system which might tend to an equal and full development of the capacities of all living beings.

The system of voting by ballot which some reasoners have recommended is attended with obvious inconveniences. [It withdraws the elector from the regard of his country and] his neighbors, and permits him to conceal the motives of his vote, which, if concealed, cannot but be dishonourable; when, if he had known that he had to render a public account of his conduct, he would have never permitted them to guide him.[29] There is in this system of voting by ballot and of electing a member of the *Representative Assembly* as a churchwarden is elected something too mechanical. The elector and the elected ought to meet one another face to face and interchange the meanings of actual presence and share some common impulses and, in a degree, understand each other. There ought to be the common sympathy of the excitements of a popular assembly among the electors themselves. The imagination would thus be strongly excited and a mass of generous and enlarged and popular sentiments be awakened, which would give the vitality of . . .

That republican boldness of censuring and judging one another, which has indeed [been] exerted in England under the title of "public opinion," though perverted from its true uses into an instrument of prejudice and calumny, would then be applied to its genuine purposes. Year by year the people would become more susceptible of assuming forms of government more simple and beneficial.

It is in this publicity of the exercise of sovereignty that the difference between the republics of Greece and the monarchies of Asia consisted. The actions of the times . . .

28 **immature** premature?   29 **The system . . . . guide him** an argument which, though logically valid, overlooks the protection afforded by the secret ballot against intimidation

If the existing government shall compel the Nation to take the task of reform into its own hands, one of the most obvious consequences of such a circumstance would be the abolition of monarchy and aristocracy. Why, it will then be argued, if the subsisting condition of social forms is to be thrown into confusion, should these things be endured? Then why do we now endure them? Is it because we think that an hereditary King is cheaper and wiser than an elected President, or a House of Lords and a Bench of Bishops are institutions modelled by the wisdom of the most refined and civilized periods, beyond which the wit of mortal man can furnish nothing more perfect? In case the subsisting Government should compel the people to revolt to establish a representative assembly in defiance of them, and to assume in that assembly an attitude of resistance and defence, this question would probably be answered in a very summary manner. No friend of mankind and of his country can desire that such a crisis should suddenly arrive; but still less, once having arrived, can he hesitate under what banner to array his person and his power. At the peace, the people would have been contented with strict economy and severe retrenchment and some direct and intelligible plan for producing that equilibrium between the capitalists and the landholders which is delusively styled the payment of the national debt; had this system been adopted, they probably would have refrained from exacting Parliamentary Reform, the only secure guarantee that it would have been pursued. Two years ago it might still have been possible to have commenced a system of gradual reform. The people were then insulted, tempted, and betrayed, and *the petitions of a million* of men rejected with disdain. Now they are more miserable, more hopeless, more impatient of their misery. Above all, they have become more universally aware of the true sources of their misery. It is possible that the period of conciliation is past and that, after having played with the confidence and cheated the expectations of the people, their passions will be too little under discipline to allow them to wait the slow, gradual, and certain operation of such a Reform as we can imagine the constituted authorities to concede.

Upon the issue of this question depends the species of

reform which a philosophical mind should regard with approbation. If Reform shall be begun by the existing government, let us be contented with a limited *beginning*, with any whatsoever opening; let the rotten boroughs be disfranchised and their rights transferred to the unrepresented cities and districts of the Nation; it is no matter how slow, gradual, and cautious be the change; we shall demand more and more with firmness and moderation, never anticipating but never deferring the moment of successful opposition, so that the people may become habituated [to] exercising the functions of sovereignty in proportion as they acquire the possession of it. If reform could begin from within the Houses of Parliament, as constituted at present, it appears to me that what is called moderate reform, that is a suffrage whose qualification should be the possession of a certain small property, and triennial parliaments, would be principles—a system in which for the sake of obtaining without bloodshed or confusion ulterior improvements of a more important character, all reformers ought to acquiesce. Not that such are first principles or that they would produce a system of perfect social institutions or one approaching to [such]. But nothing is more idle than to reject a limited benefit because we cannot without great sacrifices obtain an unlimited one. We might thus reject a Representative Republic, if it were obtainable, on the plea that the imagination of man can conceive of something more absolutely perfect. Towards whatsoever we regard as perfect, undoubtedly it is no less our duty than it is our nature to press forward; this is the generous enthusiasm which accomplishes not indeed the consummation after which it aspires, but one which approaches it in a degree far nearer than if the whole powers had not been developed by a delusion. It is in politics rather than in religion that faith is meritorious.

If the Houses of Parliament obstinately and perpetually refuse to concede any reform to the people, my vote is for universal suffrage and equal representation. My vote is— but, it is asked, how shall this be accomplished, in defiance of and in opposition to the constituted authorities of the Nation, they who possess whether with or without its consent the command of a standing army and of a legion of spies and police officers, and hold all the strings of that complicated mechanism with which the hopes and fears of men are moved like puppets? They would disperse any assembly really chosen by the people; they would shoot and hew down any multitude, without regard to sex or age, as the Jews did the Canaanites, which might be collected in its defence; they would calumniate, imprison, starve, ruin, and expatriate every person who wrote or acted, or thought, or might be suspected to think against them; misery and extermination would fill the country from one end to another. . . .

This question I would answer by another.

Will you endure to pay the half of your earnings to maintain in luxury and idleness the confederation of your tyrants as the reward of a successful conspiracy to defraud and oppress you? Will you make your tame cowardice and the branding record of it the everlasting inheritance of your posterity? Not only this; will you render by your torpid endurance this condition of things as permanent as the system of castes in India, by which the same horrible injustice is perpetrated under another form?

Assuredly no Englishmen by whom these propositions are understood will answer in the affirmative; and the opposite side of the alternative remains.

When the majority in any nation arrive at a conviction that it is their duty and their interest to divest the minority of a power employed to their disadvantage, and the minority are sufficiently mistaken as to believe that their superiority is tenable, a struggle must ensue.

If the majority are enlightened, united, impelled by a uniform enthusiasm, and animated by a distinct and powerful apprehension of their object—and full confidence in their undoubted power—the struggle is merely nominal. The minority perceive the approaches of the development of an irresistible force, by the influence of the public opinion of their weakness, on those political forms of which no government but an absolute despotism is devoid. They divest themselves of their usurped distinctions; the public tranquillity is not disturbed by the revolution.

But these conditions may only be imperfectly fulfilled by the state of a people grossly oppressed and impotent to cast off the load. Their enthusiasm may have been subdued by the killing weight of toil and suffering; they may be panic-stricken and disunited by their oppressors and the demagogues; the influence of fraud may have been sufficient to weaken the union of classes which compose them by suggesting jealousies; and the position of the conspirators, although it is to be forced by repeated assaults, may be tenable until the siege can be vigorously urged. The true patriot will endeavor to enlighten and to unite the nation and animate it with enthusiasm and confidence. For this purpose he will be indefatigable in promulgating political truth. He will endeavor to rally round one standard the divided friends of liberty and make them forget the subordinate objects with regard to which they differ by appealing to that respecting which they are all agreed. He will promote such open confederations among men of principle and spirit as may tend to make their intentions and their efforts converge to a common centre. He will discourage all secret associations, which have a tendency, by making national will develop itself in a partial and premature manner, to cause tumult and confusion. He will urge the necessity of exciting the people frequently to exercise their right of assembling, in such limited numbers as that all present may be actual parties to the proceedings of the day. Lastly, if circumstances had collected a more considerable number as at Manchester on the memorable 16th of August,[30] if the tyrants command their troops to fire upon them or cut them down unless they disperse, he will exhort them peaceably to risque the danger and to expect without resistance the onset of the cavalry and wait with folded arms the event of the fire of the artillery and receive with unshrinking bosoms the bayonets of the charging battalions. Men are every day persuaded to incur greater perils for a less manifest advantage. And this, not because active resistance is not justifiable when all other means shall have failed, but because in this instance temperance and courage would produce greater advantages than the most decisive victory. In the first place, the soldiers are men and Englishmen, and it is not to be believed that they would massacre an unresisting multitude of their countrymen

30 **at Manchester . . . August** reference to the massacre at Manchester (see Introduction, p. xvi)

drawn up in unarmed array before them and bearing in their looks the calm, deliberate resolution to perish rather than abandon the assertion of their rights. In the confusion of flight the ideas of the soldier become confused, and he massacres those who fly from him by the instinct of his trade. In the struggle of conflict and resistance he is irritated by a sense of his own danger, he is flattered by an apprehension of his magnanimity in incurring it, he considers the blood of his countrymen at once the price of his valour, the pledge of his security. He applauds himself by reflecting that these base and dishonourable motives will gain him credit among his comrades and his officers who are animated by the same as if they were something the same. But if he should observe neither resistance nor flight he would be reduced to impotence and indecision. Thus far, his ideas were governed by the same law as those of a dog who chases a flock of sheep to the corner of a field and keeps aloof when they make the firm parade of resistance. But the soldier is a man and an Englishman. This unexpected reception would probably throw him back upon a recollection of the true nature of the measures of which he was made the instrument, and the enemy might be converted into the ally.

The patriot will be foremost to publish the boldest truths in the most fearless manner, yet without the slightest tincture of personal malignity. He would encourage all others to the same efforts and assist them to the utmost of his power with the resources both of his intellect and fortune. He would call upon them to despise imprisonment and persecution and lose no opportunity of bringing public opinion and the power of the tyrants into circumstances of perpetual contest and opposition.

All might however be ineffectual to produce so uniform an impulse of the national will as to preclude a further struggle. The strongest argument, perhaps, for the necessity of Reform is the inoperative and unconscious abjectness to which the purposes of a considerable mass of the people are reduced. They neither know nor care. They are sinking into a resemblance with the Hindoos and the Chinese, who were once men as they are. Unless the cause which renders them passive subjects instead of active citizens be removed, they will sink with accelerated gradations into that barbaric and unnatural civilization which destroys all the differences among men. It is in vain to exhort us to wait until all men shall desire Freedom whose real interest will consist in its establishment. It is in vain to hope to enlighten them whilst their tyrants employ the utmost artifices of all their complicated engine to perpetuate the infection of every species of fanaticism and error from generation to generation. The advocates of Reform ought indeed to leave no effort unexerted, and they ought to be indefatigable in exciting all men to examine.

But if they wait until those neutral politicians, a class whose opinions represent the actions of this class, are persuaded that so soon [as] effectual reform is necessary, the occasion will have passed or will never arrive, and the people will have exhausted their strength in ineffectual expectation and will have sunk into incurable supineness. It was principally the [effect of] a similar quietism that the populous and extensive nations of Asia have fallen into their existing decrepitude; and that anarchy, insecurity, ignorance, and barbarism, the symptoms of the confirmed disease of monarchy, have reduced nations of the most delicate physical and intellectual organization and under the most fortunate climates of the globe to a blank in the history of man. The manufacturers[31] to a man are persuaded of the necessity of reform; An immense majority of the inhabitants of London. . . .

The reasoners who incline to the opinion that it is not sufficient that the innovators should produce a majority in the nation, but that we ought to expect such an unanimity as would preclude anything amounting to a serious dispute, are prompted to this view of the question by the dread of anarchy and massacre. Infinite and inestimable calamities belong to oppression, but the most fatal of them all is that mine of unexploded mischief which it has practiced beneath the foundations of society, and with which, "pernicious to one touch," it threatens to involve the ruin of the entire building together with its own. But delay merely renders these mischiefs more tremendous, not the less inevitable. For the utmost may now be the crisis of the

31 **manufacturers** factory laborers, or laboring class as a whole

social disease [which] is rendered thus periodical, chronic and incurable.

The savage brutality of the populance is proportioned to the arbitrary character of their government, and tumults and insurrections soon, as in Constantinople, become consistent with the permanence of the causing evil, of which they might have been the critical determination.

The public opinion in England ought first to [be] excited to action, and the durability of those forms within which the oppressors intrench themselves brought perpetually to the test of its operation. No law or institution can last if this opinion be distinctly pronounced against it. For this purpose government ought to be defied, in cases of questionable result, to prosecute for political libel. All questions relating to the jurisdiction of magistrates and courts of law respecting which any doubt could be raised ought to be agitated with indefatigable pertinacity. Some two or three of the popular leaders have shown the best spirit in this respect; they only want system and co-operation. The taxgatherer ought to be compelled in every practicable instance to distrain, whilst the right to impose taxes, as was the case in the beginning of the resistance to the tyranny of Charles the 1st is formally contested by an overwhelming multitude of defendants before the courts of common law. Confound the subtlety of lawyers with the subtlety of the law. All of the nation would thus be excited to develop itself and to declare whether it acquiesced in the existing forms of government. The manner in which all questions of this nature might be decided would develop the occasions, and afford a prognostic as to the success, of more decisive measures. Simultaneously with this active and vigilant system of opposition, means ought to be taken of solemnly conveying the sense of large bodies and various denominations of the people in a manner the most explicit to the existing depositaries of power. Petitions, couched in the actual language of the petitioners and emanating from distinct assemblies, ought to load the tables of the House of Commons. The poets, philosophers, and artists ought to remonstrate, and the memorials entitled their petitions might shew the diversit[y] [of] convictions they entertain of the inevitable connection between national prosperity and freedom, and the cultivation of the imagination and the cultivation of scientific truth, and the profound development of moral and metaphysical enquiry. Suppose these memorials to be severally written by Godwin, Hazlitt, Bentham, and Hunt; they would be worthy of the age and of the cause; these, radiant and irresistible like the meridian sun, would strike all but the eagles who dared to gaze upon its beams with blindness and confusion. These appeals of solemn and emphatic argument from those who have already a predestined existence among posterity would appal the enemies of mankind by their echoes from every corner of the world in which the majestic literature of England is cultivated; it would be like a voice from beyond the dead of those who will live in the memories of men, when they must be forgotten; it would be Eternity warning Time.

Let us hope that at this stage of the progress of Reform the oppressors would feel their impotence and reluctantly and imperfectly concede some limited portion of the rights of the people and disgorge some morsels of their undigested prey. In this case, the people ought to be exhorted by everything ultimately dear to them to pause until by the exercise of those rights which they have regained they become fitted to demand more. It is better that we gain what we demand by a process of negotiation which would occupy twenty years than that, by communicating a sudden shock to the interests of those who are the depositaries and dependents of power, we should incur the calamity which their revenge might inflict upon us by giving the signal of civil war. If, after all, they consider the chance of personal ruin and the infamy of figuring on the page of history as the promoters of civil war preferable to resigning any portion, how small soever, of their usurped authority, we are to recollect that we possess a right beyond remonstrance. It has been acknowledged by the most approved writers on the English constitution, which is in this instance merely [a] declaration of the superior decisions of eternal justice, that we possess a right of resistance. The claim of the [reigning] family is founded upon a memorable exertion of this solemnly recorded right.

The last resort of resistance is undoubtedly insurrection. The right of insurrection is derived from the employment of armed force to counteract the will of the nation. Let the government disband the standing army, and the purpose of resistance would be sufficiently fulfilled by the incessant agitation of the points of dispute before the courts of common law and by an unwarlike display of the irresistible number and union of the people.

Before we enter into a consideration of the measures which might terminate in civil war, let us for a moment consider the nature and the consequences of war. This is the alternative which the unprincipled cunning of the tyrants has presented to us, from which we must not sh[rink]. There is secret sympathy between Destruction and Power, between Monarchy and War; and the long experience of the history of all recorded time teaches us with what success they have played into each other's hands. War is a kind of superstition; the pageantry of arms and badges corrupts the imagination of men. How far more appropriate would be the symbols of an inconsolable grief —muffled drums, and melancholy music, and arms reversed, and the livery of sorrow rather than of blood. When men mourn at funerals, for what do they mourn in comparison with the calamities which they hasten with all circumstance of festivity to suffer and to inflict! Visit in imagination the scene of a field of battle or a city taken by assault; collect into one group the groans and the distortions of the innumerable dying, the inconsolable grief and horror of their surviving friends, the hellish exultation, and unnatural drunkenness of destruction of the conquerors, the burning of the harvests and the obliteration of the traces of cultivation. To this, in civil war, is to be added the sudden disruption of the bonds of social life, and "father against son."

If there had never been war, there could never have been tyranny in the world; tyrants take advantage of the mechanical organization of armies to establish and defend their encroachments. It is thus that the mighty advantages of the French Revolution have been almost compensated by a succession of tyrants (for demagogues, oligarchies, usurpers and legitimate kings are merely varieties of the same class) from Robespierre to Louis 18. War, waged from whatever motive, extinguishes the sentiment of reason and justice in the mind. The motive is forgotten or only adverted to in a mechanical and habitual manner. A sentiment of confidence in brute force and in a contempt of death and danger is considered as the highest virtue, when in truth, and however indispensable, they are merely the means and the instruments, highly capable of being perverted to destroy the cause they were assumed to promote. It is a foppery the most intolerable to an amiable and philosophical mind. It is like what some reasoners have observed of religious faith; no false and indirect motive to action can subsist in the mind without weakening the effect of those which are genuine and true. The person who thinks it virtuous to believe will think a less degree of virtue attaches to good actions than if he had considered it as indifferent. The person who has been accustomed to subdue men by force will be less inclined to the trouble of convincing or persuading them.

These brief considerations suffice to show that the true friend of mankind and of his country would hesitate before he recommended measures which tend to bring down so heavy a calamity as war.

I imagine however that before the English Nation shall arrive at that point of moral and political degradation now occupied by the Chinese, it will be necessary to appeal to an exertion of physical strength. If the madness of parties admits no other mode of determining the question at issue, . . .

When the people shall have obtained, by whatever means, the victory over their oppressors, and when persons appointed by them shall have taken their seats in the Representative Assembly of the nation and assumed the control of public affairs according to constitutional rules, there will remain the great task of accommodating all that can be preserved of antient forms with the improvements of the knowledge of a more enlightened age in legislation, jurisprudence, government, and religious and academical institution. The settlement of the national debt is on the principles before elucidated merely circumstance of form and, however necessary and important, is an affair of mere arithmetical proportions readily determined; nor can I see how those who, being deprived of their unjust advantages, will probably inwardly murmur, can oppose one word of open expostulation to a measure of such inescapable justice.

There is one thing which certain vulgar agitators endeavour to flatter the most uneducated part of the people by assiduously proposing, which they ought not to do nor to require; and that is Retribution. Men having been injured desire to injure in return. This is falsely called an universal law of human nature; it is a law from which many are exempt, and all in proportion to their virtue and cultivation. The savage is more revengeful than the civilized man, the ignorant and uneducated than the person of a refined and cultivated intellect; the generous and . . .

Fragments on Reform

That our country is on the point of submitting to some momentous change in its internal government is a fact which few who observe and compare the [?] of human society will dispute. The distribution of wealth, no less than the spirit by which it is upheld and that by which it is assailed, render[s] the event inevitable. Call it reform or revolution, as you will; a change must take place; one of the consequences of which will be the wresting of political power from those who are at present the depositories of it. A strong sentiment [prevails] in the nation at large that they have been guilty of enormous malversations of their trust. It is a commonplace of political reformers to say that it is the measures, not the men, they abhor; and it is a general practice, so soon as the party shall have gained the victory, to inflict the severest punishments upon their predecessors and to pursue measures not less selfish and pernicious than those a protest against which was the ladder that conducted them to power. The people sympathise with the passions of their liberators without reflecting that these in turn may become their tyrants, and without perceiving that the same motives and excitements to act or to feel can never, except by a perverse imitation, belong to both.

The hopes of the world were bound up in the claims which the people of England made to be delivered from the oppression under which they groaned, and to abolish the symbols of those impostures which surrounded their tyrants with sanctity. The claim on the part of the people was that the institutions of government should be provided for, at certain limited periods, by the people themselves; those for whose benefit alone it was declared or declaimed that any of the regulations of social life ought to be permitted to subsist. The voice of public opinion had by no means decided as to the precise form of the political institutions which should supersede that already existing; but a general persuasion prevailed that the multitude was deluded and oppressed by its rulers; thousands of miserable men and women and children wandered through the streets famished, naked, and homeless; the cottages and farm houses became tenanted whilst [new] . . .

A System of
Government by Juries

A FRAGMENT

Government, as it now subsists, is perhaps an engine at once the most expensive and inartificial that could have been devised as a remedy for the imperfections of society. Immense masses of the product of labour are committed to the discretion of certain individuals for the purpose of executing its intentions or interpreting its meaning. These have not been consumed but wasted in the principal part of the past history of political society.

Government may be distributed into two parts: First —the fundamental—that is, the permanent forms, which regulate the deliberation or the action of the whole; from which it results that a state is democratical, or aristocratical, or despotic, or a combination of all these principles.

And Secondly—the necessary or accidental—that is, those that determine, *not* the forms according to which the deliberation or the action of the mass of the community is to be regulated but the opinions or moral principles which are to govern the particular instances of such action or deliberation. These may be called, with little violence to the popular acceptation of those terms, Constitution, and Law—understanding by the former the collection of those written institutions or traditions which determine the individuals who are to exercise in a nation the discretionary right of peace and war, of death or imprisonment, fines and penalties, and the imposition and collection of taxes and their application thus vested in a king, or an hereditary senate, or in a representative assembly, or in a

combination of all; and by the latter, the mode of determining those opinions according to which the constituted
authorities are to decide on any action; for law is either a
collection of opinions expressed by individuals without
constitutional authority, or the decision of a constitutional
body of men, the opinion of some or all of whom it expresses—and no more.

To the former, or constitutional topics, this treatise has
no direct reference. Law may be considered simply an
opinion regulating political power. It may be divided into
two parts: General Law, or that which relates to the external and integral concerns of a nation and decides on
the competency of a particular person or collection of persons to discretion in matters of war and peace, the assembling of the representative body, the time, place, manner, form, of holding judicial courts, and other concerns
enumerated before and in reference to which this community is considered as a whole; and Particular Law, or that
which decides upon contested claims of property, which
punishes or restrains violence and fraud, which enforces
compacts and preserves to every man that degree of liberty
and security the enjoyment of which is judged not to be
inconsistent with the liberty and security of another.

To the former, or what is here called general law, this
treatise has no direct reference. How far law in its general
form or constitution, as it at present exists in the greater
part of the nations of Europe, may be affected by inferences
from the ensuing reasonings it is foreign to the present
purpose to inquire—let us confine our attention to particular law, or law strictly so termed.

The only defensible intention of law, like that of every
other human institution, is very simple and clear—the good
of the whole. If law is found to accomplish this object very
imperfectly, that imperfection makes no part of the design
with which men submit to its institution. Any reasonings
which tend to throw light on a subject hitherto so dark
and intricate cannot fail, if distinctly stated, to impress
mankind very deeply, because it is a question in which the
life and property and liberty and reputation of every man
are vitally involved.

For the sake of intelligible method, let us assume the
ordinary distinctions of law, those of civil and criminal

law and of the objects of it, private and public wrongs. The author of these pages ought not to suppress his conviction that the principles on which punishment is usually inflicted are essentially erroneous; and that, in general, ten times more is apportioned to the victims of law than is demanded by the welfare of society under the shape of reformation or example. He believes that, although universally disowned, the execrable passion of vengeance, exasperated by fear, exists as a chief source among the secret causes of this exercise of criminal justice. He believes also that in questions of property there is a vague but most effective favouritism in courts of law and among lawyers, against the poor to the advantage of the rich—against the tenant in favour of the landlord—against the creditor in favour of the debtor; thus enforcing and illustrating that celebrated maxim, against which moral science is a perpetual effort: *To whom much is given, of him shall much be required; and to whom men have committed much, of him they will ask the more*.

But the present purpose is not the exposure of such mistakes as actually exist in public opinion but an attempt to give to public opinion its legitimate dominion, and an uniform and unimpeded influence to each particular case which is its object.

When law is once understood to be no more than the recorded opinion of men, no more than the apprehensions of individuals on the reasoning of a particular case, we may expect that the sanguinary or stupid mistakes which disgrace the civil and criminal jurisprudence of civilized nations will speedily disappear. How long, under its present sanctions, do not the most exploded violations of humanity maintain their ground in courts of law after public opinion has branded them with reprobation; sometimes even until, by constantly maintaining their post under the shelter of venerable names, they out-weary the very scorn and abhorrence of mankind or subsist unrepealed and silent until some check in the progress of human improvement awakens them, and that public opinion from which they should have received their reversal is infected by their influence. Public opinion would never long stagnate in error were it not fenced about and frozen over by forms and superstitions. If men were accustomed to reason, and to hear the

arguments of others upon each particular case that concerned the life, or liberty, or property, or reputation of their
peers, those mistakes, which at present render these possessions so insecure to all but those who enjoy enormous
wealth, never could subsist. If the administration of law
ceased to appeal from the common sense or the enlightened minds of twelve contemporary *good and true
men* who should be the peers of the accused or, in cases of
property, of the claimant, to the obscure records of dark
and barbarous epochs or the precedents of what venal and
enslaved judges might have decreed to please their tyrants,
or the opinion of any man or set of men who lived when
bigotry was virtue and passive obedience that discretion
which is the better part of valour, all those mistakes now
fastened in the public opinion would be brought at each
new case to the. . . .

A Defense of Poetry

PART I

According to one mode of regarding those two classes of mental action which are called reason and imagination, the former may be considered as mind contemplating the relations borne by one thought to another, however produced, and the latter as mind acting upon those thoughts so as to colour them with its own light, and composing from them, as from elements, other thoughts, each containing within itself the principle of its own integrity. The one is the τὸ ποιειν, or the principle of synthesis, and has for its objects those forms which are common to universal nature and existence itself; the other is the τὸ λογιζειν, or principle of analysis, and its action regards the relations of things, simply as relations—considering thoughts not in their integral unity but as the algebraical representations which conduct to certain general results. Reason is the enumeration of quantities already known; imagination is the perception of the value of those quantities, both separately and as a whole. Reason respects the differences and imagination the similitudes of things. Reason is to imagination as the instrument to the agent, as the body to the spirit, as the shadow to the substance.

Poetry in a general sense may be defined to be "the expression of the imagination," and poetry is connate with the origin of man. Man is an instrument over which a series of external and internal impressions are driven, like the alternations of an everchanging wind over an Æolian lyre,[1] which move it by their motion to ever-changing melody. But there is a principle within the human being, and perhaps within all sentient beings, which acts other-

1 **Æolian lyre** named after Æolus, god of the winds; romantic concept of an instrument whose music is produced by the passage of the wind over its strings

wise than in the lyre and produces not melody alone, but harmony, by an internal adjustment of the sounds or motions thus excited to the impressions which excite them. It is as if the lyre could accommodate its chords to the motions of that which strikes them, in a determined proportion of sound, even as the musician can accommodate his voice to the sound of the lyre. A child at play by itself will express its delight by its voice and motions; and every inflexion of tone and every gesture will bear exact relation to a corresponding antitype in the pleasurable impressions which awakened it; it will be the reflected image of that impression; and as the lyre trembles and sounds after the wind has died away, so the child seeks, by prolonging in its voice and motions the duration of the effect, to prolong also a consciousness of the cause. In relation to the objects which delight a child, these expressions are what poetry is to higher objects. The savage (for the savage is to ages what the child is to years) expresses the emotions produced in him by surrounding objects in a similar manner; and language and gesture, together with plastic or pictorial imitation, become the image of the combined effect of those objects and of his apprehension of them. Man in society, with all his passions and his pleasures, next becomes the object of the passions and pleasures of man; an additional class of emotions produces an augmented treasure of expressions; and language, gesture, and the imitative arts become at once the representation and the medium, the pencil and the picture, the chisel and the statue, the chord and the harmony. The social sympathies, or those laws from which, as from its elements, society results, begin to develop themselves from the moment that two human beings coexist; the future is contained within the present as the plant within the seed; and equality, diversity, unity, contrast, mutual dependence become the principles alone capable of affording the motives according to which the will of a social being is determined to action, inasmuch as he is social, and constitute pleasure in sensation, virtue in sentiment, beauty in art, truth in reasoning, and love in the intercourse of kind. Hence men, even in the infancy of society, observe a certain order in their words and actions, distinct from that of the objects and the impressions represented by them, all expression being subject to the laws of that from which it proceeds. But let us dismiss those more general considerations, which might involve an inquiry into the principles of society itself, and restrict our view to the manner in which the imagination is expressed upon its forms.

In the youth of the world, men dance and sing and imitate natural objects, observing in these actions as in all others a certain rhythm or order. And although all men observe a similar, they observe not the same order in the motions of the dance, in the melody of the song, in the combinations of language, in the series of their imitations of natural objects. For there is a certain order or rhythm belonging to each of these classes of mimetic representation, from which the hearer and the spectator receive an intenser and purer pleasure than from any other; the sense of an approximation to this order has been called taste by modern writers. Every man, in the infancy of art, observes an order which approximates more or less closely to that from which this highest delight results; but the diversity is not sufficiently marked as that its gradations should be sensible, except in those instances where the predominance of this faculty of approximation to the beautiful (for so we may be permitted to name the relation between this highest pleasure and its cause) is very great. Those in whom it exists in excess are poets in the most universal sense of the word, and the pleasure resulting from the manner in which they express the influence of society or nature upon their own minds communicates itself to others and gathers a sort of reduplication from that community. Their language is vitally metaphorical; that is, it marks the before unapprehended relations of things and perpetuates their apprehension until the words which represent them become, through time, signs for portions or classes of thoughts instead of pictures of integral thoughts; and then if no new poets should arise to create afresh the associations which have been thus disorganised, language will be dead to all the nobler purposes of human intercourse. These similitudes or relations are finely said by Lord Bacon to be "the same footsteps of nature impressed upon the various subjects of the world" [2]—and he con-

2 *De Augment. Scient.*, cap. 1, lib. iii. [Shelley's note]

siders the faculty which perceives them as the storehouse of axioms common to all knowledge. In the infancy of society every author is necessarily a poet, because language itself is poetry; and to be a poet is to apprehend the true and the beautiful, in a word, the good which exists in the relation subsisting, first between existence and perception, and secondly between perception and expression. Every original language near to its source is in itself the chaos of a cyclic poem; the copiousness of lexicography and the distinctions of grammar are the works of a later age and are merely the catalogue and the form of the creations of poetry.

But poets, or those who imagine and express this indestructible order, are not only the authors of language and of music, of the dance and architecture, and statuary, and painting; they are the institutors of laws, and the founders of civil society, and the inventors of the arts of life, and the teachers, who draw into a certain propinquity with the beautiful and the true that partial apprehension of the agencies of the invisible world which is called religion. Hence all original religions are allegorical, or susceptible of allegory, and, like Janus,[3] have a double face of false and true. Poets, according to the circumstances of the age and nation in which they appeared, were called, in the earlier epochs of the world, legislators or prophets; a poet essentially comprises and unites both these characters. For he not only beholds intensely the present as it is and discovers those laws according to which present things ought to be ordered, but he beholds the future in the present, and his thoughts are the germs of the flower and the fruit of latest time. Not that I assert poets to be prophets in the gross sense of the word, or that they can foretell the form as surely as they foreknow the spirit of events; such is the pretence of superstition, which would make poetry an attribute of prophecy rather than prophecy an attribute of poetry. A poet participates in the eternal, the infinite, and the one; as far as relates to his conceptions, time and place and number are not. The grammatical forms which express the moods of time, and the

3 ancient Roman deity of gates and doors, and of beginnings, represented as having two faces

difference of persons, and the distinction of place are convertible with respect to the highest poetry without injuring it as poetry; and the choruses of Æschylus, and the book of Job, and Dante's Paradise, would afford, more than any other writings, examples of this fact if the limits of this essay did not forbid citation. The creations of sculpture, painting, and music are illustrations still more decisive.

Language, colour, form, and religious and civil habits of action are all the instruments and materials of poetry; they may be called poetry by that figure of speech which considers the effect as a synonym of the cause. But poetry in a more restricted sense expresses those arrangements of language, and especially metrical language, which are created by that imperial faculty whose throne is curtained within the invisible nature of man. And this springs from the nature itself of language, which is a more direct representation of the actions and passions of our internal being, and is susceptible of more various and delicate combinations than colour, form, or motion, and is more plastic and obedient to the control of that faculty of which it is the creation. For language is arbitrarily produced by the imagination, and has relation to thoughts alone; but all other materials, instruments, and conditions of art have relations among each other which limit and interpose between conception and expression. The former is as a mirror which reflects, the latter as a cloud which enfeebles, the light of which both are mediums of communication. Hence the fame of sculptors, painters, and musicians, although the intrinsic powers of the great masters of these arts may yield in no degree to that of those who have employed language as the hieroglyphic of their thoughts, has never equalled that of poets in the restricted sense of the term; as two performers of equal skill will produce unequal effects from a guitar and a harp. The fame of legislators and founders of religions, so long as their institutions last, alone seems to exceed that of poets in the restricted sense; but it can scarcely be a question whether, if we deduct the celebrity which their flattery of the gross opinions of the vulgar usually conciliates, together with that which belonged to them in their higher character of poets, any excess will remain.

We have thus circumscribed the meaning of the word

Poetry within the limits of that art which is the most familiar and the most perfect expression of the faculty itself. It is necessary, however, to make the circle still narrower, and to determine the distinction between measured and unmeasured language, for the popular division into prose and verse is inadmissible in accurate philosophy.

Sounds as well as thoughts have relation both between each other and towards that which they represent, and a perception of the order of those relations has always been found connected with a perception of the order of those relations of thoughts. Hence the language of poets has ever affected a certain uniform and harmonious recurrence of sound, without which it were not poetry and which is scarcely less indispensable to the communication of its action than the words themselves, without reference to that peculiar order. Hence the vanity of translation; it were as wise to cast a violet into a crucible that you might discover the formal principle of its colour and odour as seek to transfuse from one language into another the creations of a poet. The plant must spring again from its seed, or it will bear no flower—and this is the burthen of the curse of Babel.[4]

An observation of the regular mode of the recurrence of this harmony in the language of poetical minds, together with its relation to music, produced metre, or a certain system of traditional forms of harmony of language. Yet it is by no means essential that a poet should accommodate his language to this traditional form, so that the harmony, which is its spirit, be observed. The practice is indeed convenient and popular and to be preferred, especially in such composition as includes much form and action; but every great poet must inevitably innovate upon the example of his predecessors in the exact structure of his peculiar versification. The distinction between poets and prose writers is a vulgar error. The distinction between philosophers and poets has been anticipated. Plato was essentially a poet—the truth and splendour of his imagery, and the melody of his language, is the most intense that it is possible to conceive. He rejected the measure of the epic, dramatic, and lyrical forms because he sought to

4 **curse of Babel** the confusion of languages (Gen. 11:9)

kindle a harmony in thoughts divested of shape and action, and he forbore to invent any regular plan of rhythm which should include, under determinate forms, the varied pauses of his style. Cicero sought to imitate the cadence of his periods, but with little success. Lord Bacon was a poet.[5] His language has a sweet and majestic rhythm which satisfies the sense no less than the almost superhuman wisdom of his philosophy satisfies the intellect; it is a strain which distends and then bursts the circumference of the hearer's mind and pours itself forth together with it into the universal element with which it has perpetual sympathy. All the authors of revolutions in opinion are not only necessarily poets as they are inventors, nor even as their words unveil the permanent analogy of things by images which participate in the life of truth, but as their periods are harmonious and rhythmical and contain in themselves the elements of verse, being the echo of the eternal music. Nor are those supreme poets who have employed traditional forms of rhythm on account of the form and action of their subjects less capable of perceiving and teaching the truth of things than those who have omitted that form. Shakspeare, Dante, and Milton (to confine ourselves to modern writers) are philosophers of the very loftiest power.

A poem is the image of life expressed in its eternal truth. There is this difference between a story and a poem, that a story is a catalogue of detached facts which have no other bond of connexion than time, place, circumstance, cause, and effect; the other is the creation of actions according to the unchangeable forms of human nature, as existing in the mind of the creator, which is itself the image of all other minds. The one is partial, and applies only to a definite period of time and a certain combination of events which can never again recur; the other is universal and contains within itself the germ of a relation to whatever motives or actions have place in the possible varieties of human nature. Time, which destroys the beauty and the use of the story of particular facts stript of the poetry which should invest them, augments that of

5 See the *Filum Labyrinthi* and the *Essay on Death* particularly. [Shelley's note]

Poetry and forever develops new and wonderful applications of the eternal truth which it contains. Hence epitomes have been called the moths of just history; they eat out the poetry of it. The story of particular facts is as a mirror which obscures and distorts that which should be beautiful; Poetry is a mirror which makes beautiful that which is distorted.

The parts of a composition may be poetical without the composition as a whole being a poem. A single sentence may be considered as a whole, though it be found in a series of unassimilated portions; a single word even may be a spark of inextinguishable thought. And thus all the great historians, Herodotus, Plutarch, Livy, were poets; and although the plan of these writers, especially that of Livy, restrained them from developing this faculty in its highest degree, they make copious and ample amends for their subjection by filling all the interstices of their subjects with living images.

Having determined what is poetry, and who are poets, let us proceed to estimate its effects upon society.

Poetry is ever accompanied with pleasure: all spirits on which it falls open themselves to receive the wisdom which is mingled with its delight. In the infancy of the world, neither poets themselves nor their auditors are fully aware of the excellence of poetry: for it acts in a divine and unapprehended manner, beyond and above consciousness; and it is reserved for future generations to contemplate and measure the mighty cause and effect in all the strength and splendour of their union. Even in modern times, no living poet ever arrived at the fulness of his fame; the jury which sits in judgment upon a poet, belonging as he does to all time, must be composed of his peers; it must be impanneled by Time from the selectest of the wise of many generations. A Poet is a nightingale who sits in darkness and sings to cheer its own solitude with sweet sounds; his auditors are as men entranced by the melody of an unseen musician, who feel that they are moved and softened, yet know not whence or why. The poems of Homer and his contemporaries were the delight of infant Greece; they were the elements of that social system which is the column upon which all succeeding civilization has reposed. Homer embodied the ideal perfection of his age in human character; or can we doubt that those who read his verses were awakened to an ambition of becoming like to Achilles, Hector, and Ulysses; the truth and beauty of friendship, patriotism, and persevering devotion to an object were unveiled to the depths in these immortal creations; the sentiments of the auditors must have been refined and enlarged by a sympathy with such great and lovely impersonations, until from admiring they imitated, and from imitation they identified themselves with the objects of their admiration. Nor let it be objected that these characters are remote from moral perfection and that they can by no means be considered as edifying patterns for general imitation. Every epoch, under names more or less specious, has deified its peculiar errors; Revenge is the naked Idol of the worship of a semi-barbarous age; and Self-deceit is the veiled Image of unknown evil, before which luxury and satiety lie prostrate. But a poet considers the vices of his contemporaries as the temporary dress in which his creations must be arrayed, and which cover without concealing the eternal proportions of their beauty. An epic or dramatic personage is understood to wear them around his soul as he may the antient armour or the modern uniform around his body—whilst it is easy to conceive a dress more graceful than either. The beauty of the internal nature cannot be so far concealed by its accidental vesture but that the spirit of its form shall communicate itself to the very disguise and indicate the shape it hides from the manner in which it is worn. A majestic form and graceful motions will express themselves through the most barbarous and tasteless costume. Few poets of the highest class have chosen to exhibit the beauty of their conceptions in its naked truth and splendour; and it is doubtful whether the alloy of costume, habit, &c., be not necessary to temper this planetary music for mortal ears.

The whole objection, however, of the immorality of poetry rests upon a misconception of the manner in which poetry acts to produce the moral improvement of man.[6]

6 **The whole . . . man** a repetition of Shelley's frequent declaration of poetry's function of elevating by creating sympathy and moral courage, here made in response to Plato's criticism of poets and specifically to Peacock's ambiguous attack on poetry

Ethical science arranges the elements which poetry has created and propounds schemes and proposes examples of civil and domestic life; nor is it for want of admirable doctrines that men hate, and despise, and censure, and deceive, and subjugate one another. But Poetry acts in another and diviner manner. It awakens and enlarges the mind itself by rendering it the receptacle of a thousand unapprehended combinations of thought. Poetry lifts the veil from the hidden beauty of the world and makes familiar objects be as if they were not familiar; it reproduces all that it represents, and the impersonations clothed in its Elysian[7] light stand thenceforward, in the minds of those who have once contemplated them, as memorials of that gentle and exalted content which extends itself over all thoughts and actions with which it coexists. The great secret of morals is love, or a going out of our own nature, and an identification of ourselves with the beautiful which exists in thought, action, or person not our own. A man, to be greatly good, must imagine intensely and comprehensively; he must put himself in the place of another and of many others; the pains and pleasures of his species must become his own. The great instrument of moral good is the imagination; and poetry administers to the effect by acting upon the cause. Poetry enlarges the circumference of the imagination by replenishing it with thoughts of ever new delight, which have the power of attracting and assimilating to their own nature all other thoughts, and which form new intervals and interstices whose void forever craves fresh food. Poetry strengthens that faculty which is the organ of the moral nature of man, in the same manner as exercise strengthens a limb. A Poet therefore would do ill to embody his own conceptions of right and wrong, which are usually those of his place and time, in his poetical creations, which participate in neither. By this assumption of the inferior office of interpreting the effect, in which perhaps after all he might acquit himself but imperfectly, he would resign the glory in a participation in the cause. There was little danger that Homer, or any of the eternal Poets, should have so far misunderstood them-

7 **Elysian** pertaining to Elysium, in Greek mythology, the blissful abode of the good after death

selves as to have abdicated this throne of their widest dominion. Those in whom the poetical faculty, though great, is less intense, as Euripides, Lucan, Tasso, Spenser, have frequently affected a moral aim, and the effect of their poetry is diminished in exact proportion to the degree in which they compel us to advert to this purpose.

Homer and the cyclic poets were followed at a certain interval by the dramatic and lyrical Poets of Athens, who flourished contemporaneously with all that is most perfect in the kindred expressions of the poetical faculty: architecture, painting, music, the dance, sculpture, philosophy, and we may add, the forms of civil life. For although the scheme of Athenian society was deformed by many imperfections which the poetry existing in Chivalry and Christianity have erased from the habits and institutions of modern Europe, yet never at any other period has so much energy, beauty, and virtue been developed; never was blind strength and stubborn form so disciplined and rendered subject to the will of man, or that will less repugnant to the dictates of the beautiful and the true, as during the century which preceded the death of Socrates. Of no other epoch in the history of our species have we records and fragments stamped so visibly with the image of the divinity in man. But it is Poetry alone, in form, in action, or in language, which has rendered this epoch memorable above all others, and the storehouse of examples to everlasting time. For written poetry existed at that epoch simultaneously with the other arts, and it is an idle enquiry to demand which gave and which received the light which all, as from a common focus, have scattered over the darkest periods of succeeding age. We know no more of cause and effect than a constant conjunction of events; Poetry is ever found to coexist with whatever other arts contribute to the happiness and perfection of man. I appeal to what has already been established to distinguish between the cause and the effect.

It was at the period here adverted to that the Drama had its birth; and however a succeeding writer may have equalled or surpassed those few great specimens of the Athenian drama which have been preserved to us, it is indisputable that the art itself never was understood or practised according to the true philosophy of it, as at

Athens. For the Athenians employed language, action, music, painting, the dance, and religious institutions to produce a common effect in the representation of the loftiest idealisms of passion and of power; each division in the art was made perfect in its kind by artists of the most consummate skill and was disciplined into a beautiful proportion and unity one towards another. On the modern stage a few only of the elements capable of expressing the image of the poet's conception are employed at once. We have tragedy without music and dancing, and music and dancing without the high impersonations of which they are the fit accompaniment, and both without religion and solemnity; religious institution has indeed been usually banished from the stage. Our system of divesting the actor's face of a mask, on which the many expressions appropriated to his dramatic character might be moulded into one permanent and unchanging expression, is favourable only to a partial and inharmonious effect; it is fit for nothing but a monologue, where all the attention may be directed to some great master of ideal mimicry. The modern practice of blending comedy with tragedy, though liable to great abuse in point of practice, is undoubtedly an extension of the dramatic circle; but the comedy should be as in King Lear, universal, ideal, and sublime. It is perhaps the intervention of this principle which determines the balance in favour of King Lear against the Œdipus Tyrannus or the Agamemnon, or if you will, the trilogies with which they are connected; unless the intense power of the choral poetry, especially that of the latter, should be considered as restoring the equilibrium. King Lear, if it can sustain this comparison, may be judged to be the most perfect specimen of the dramatic art existing in the world, in spite of the narrow conditions to which the poet was subjected by the ignorance of the philosophy of the drama which has prevailed in modern Europe. Calderon, in his religious Autos, has attempted to fulfil some of the high conditions of dramatic representation neglected by Shakspeare, such as the establishing a relation between the drama and religion and the accommodating them to music and dancing, but he omits the observation of conditions still more important, and more is lost than gained by a substitution of the rigidly-defined and ever-repeated idealisms of a distorted superstition for the living impersonations of the truth of human passion.

But we disgress. The Author of the Four Ages of Poetry has prudently omitted to dispute on the effect of the Drama upon life and manners. For if I know the Knight by the device of his shield, I have only to inscribe Philoctetes or Agamemnon or Othello[8] upon mine to put to flight the giant sophisms which have enchanted him, as the mirror of intolerable light though on the arm of one of the weakest of the Paladines[9] could blind and scatter whole armies of necromancers and pagans. The connexion of scenic exhibitions with the improvement or corruption of the manners of men has been universally recognised; in other words, the presence or absence of poetry in its most perfect and universal form has been found to be connected with good and evil in conduct and habit. The corruption which has been imputed to the drama as an effect begins when the poetry employed in its constitution ends, I appeal to the history of manners whether the gradations of the growth of the one and the decline of the other have not corresponded with an exactness equal to any other example of moral cause and effect.

The drama at Athens, or wheresoever else it may have approached to its perfection, coexisted with the moral and intellectual greatness of the age. The tragedies of the Athenian poets are as mirrors in which the spectator beholds himself under a thin disguise of circumstance, stript of all but that ideal perfection and energy which every one feels to be the internal type of all that he loves, admires, and would become. The imagination is enlarged by a sympathy with pains and passions so mighty that they distend in their conception the capacity of that by which they are conceived; the good affections are strengthened by pity, indignation, terror, and sorrow; and an exalted calm is prolonged from the satiety of this high exercise of them into the tumult of familiar life; even crime is disarmed of half its horror and all its contagion by being represented as the fatal consequence of the unfathomable agencies of nature: Error is thus divested of its wilfulness;

8 heroes of drama   9 champions or legendary heroes, especially those in the Charlemagne romances

men can no longer cherish it as the creation of their choice.
In a drama of the highest order there is little food for
censure or hatred; it teaches rather self-knowledge and
self-respect. Neither the eye nor the mind can see itself
unless reflected upon that which it resembles. The drama,
so long as it continues to express poetry, is as a prismatic
and many-sided mirror which collects the brightest rays
of human nature and divides and reproduces them from
the simplicity of these elementary forms, and touches
them with majesty and beauty, and multiplies all that it
reflects, and endows it with the power of propagating its
like wherever it may fall.

But in periods of the decay social life, the drama
sympathises with that decay. Tragedy becomes a cold
imitation of the form of the great masterpieces of antiquity,
divested of all harmonious accompaniment of the kindred
arts, and often the very form misunderstood, or a weak
attempt to teach certain doctrines which the writer considers as moral truths and which are usually no more than
specious flatteries of some gross vice or weakness with
which the author, in common with his auditors, are infected. Hence what has been called the classical and
domestic drama. Addison's "Cato" [10] is a specimen of the
one; and would it were not superfluous to cite examples
of the other! To such purposes poetry cannot be made
subservient. Poetry is a sword of lightning, ever unsheathed,
which consumes the scabbard that would contain it. And
thus we observe that all dramatic writings of this nature
are unimaginative in a singular degree; they affect sentiment and passion, which, divested of imagination, are
other names for caprice and appetite. The period in our
own history of the grossest degradation of the drama is
the reign of Charles II, when all forms in which poetry
had been accustomed to be expressed became hymns to
the triumph of kingly power over liberty and virtue.
Milton stood alone illuminating an age unworthy of him.
At such periods the calculating principle pervades all the
forms of dramatic exhibition, and poetry ceases to be ex-

10 **Addison's "Cato"** a tragedy by Joseph Addison (produced in
1713) dealing with the last days of Marcus Porcius Cato, the
Roman republican

pressed upon them. Comedy loses its ideal universality; wit succeeds to humour; we laugh from self-complacency and triumph, instead of pleasure; malignity, sarcasm, and contempt succeed to sympathetic merriment; we hardly laugh, but we smile. Obscenity, which is ever blasphemy against the divine beauty in life, becomes, from the very veil which it assumes, more active if less disgusting; it is a monster for which the corruption of society forever brings forth new food, which it devours in secret.

The drama being that form under which a greater number of modes of expression of poetry are susceptible of modes of being combined than any other, the connexion of poetry and social good is more observable in the drama than in whatever other form. And it is indisputable that the highest perfection of human society has ever corresponded with the highest dramatic excellence, and that the corruption or the extinction of the drama in a nation where it has once flourished is a mark of a corruption of manners and an extinction of the energies which sustain the soul of social life. But, as Machiavelli[11] says of political institutions, that life may be preserved and renewed if men should arise capable of bringing back the drama to its principles. And this is true with respect to poetry in its most extended sense; all language, institution, and form require not only to be produced but to be sustained; the office and character of a poet participates in the divine nature as regards providence no less than as regards creation.

Civil war, the spoils of Asia, and the fatal predominance first of the Macedonian and then of the Roman arms were so many symbols of the extinction or suspension of the creative faculty in Greece. The bucolic writers,[12] who found patronage under the lettered tyrants of Sicily and Egypt, were the latest representatives of its most glorious reign. Their poetry is intensely melodious; like the odour of the tuberose, it overcomes and sickens the spirit with excess of sweetness; whilst the poetry of the preceding age was as a meadow-gale of June which mingles the fragrance of all the flowers of the field and adds a quickening and

11 author of *The Prince* (1513), a treatise on statecraft   12 the Greek elegiac, or pastoral poets: Theocritus, Bion, and Moschus

harmonising spirit of its own which endows the sense with a power of sustaining its extreme delight. The bucolic and erotic delicacy in written poetry is correlative with that softness in statuary, music, and the kindred arts, and even in manners and institutions, which distinguished the epoch to which we now refer. Nor is it the poetical faculty itself, or any misapplication of it, to which this want of harmony is to be imputed. An equal sensibility to the influence of the senses and the affections is to be found in the writings of Homer and Sophocles; the former, especially, has clothed sensual and pathetic images with irresistible attractions. Their superiority over these succeeding writers consists in the presence of those thoughts which belong to the inner faculties of our nature, not in the absence of those which are connected with the external: their incomparable perfection consists in an harmony of the union of all. It is not what the erotic writers have, but what they have not, in which their imperfection consists. It is not inasmuch as they were Poets, but inasmuch as they were not Poets, that they can be considered with any plausibility as connected with the corruption of their age. Had that corruption availed so as to extinguish in them the sensibility to pleasure, passion, and natural scenery, which is imputed to them as an imperfection, the last triumph of evil would have been achieved. For the end of social corruption is to destroy all sensibility to pleasure, and therefore it is corruption. It begins at the imagination and the intellect as at the core and distributes itself thence as a paralysing venom through the affections into the very appetites, till all become a torpid mass in which sense hardly survives. At the approach of such a period, Poetry ever addresses itself to those faculties which are the last to be destroyed, and its voice is heard, like the footsteps of Astræa,[13] departing from the world. Poetry ever communicates all the pleasure which men are capable of receiving; it is ever still the light of life; the source of whatever of beautiful or generous or true can have place in an evil time. It will readily be confessed that those among the luxurious citizens of Syracuse and Alexandria who were delighted with the poems of

13 **Greek** goddess of Justice

Theocritus were less cold, cruel, and sensual than the remnant of their tribe. But corruption must have utterly destroyed the fabric of human society before poetry can ever cease. The sacred links of that chain have never been entirely disjoined, which descending through the minds of many men is attached to those great minds, whence as from a magnet the invisible effluence is sent forth, which at once connects, animates, and sustains the life of all. It is the faculty which contains within itself the seeds at once of its own and of social renovation. And let us not circumscribe the effects of the bucolic and erotic poetry within the limits of the sensibility of those to whom it was addressed. They may have perceived the beauty of those immortal compositions simply as fragments and isolated portions; those who are more finely organised or born in a happier age may recognise them as episodes to that great poem which all poets, like the co-operating thoughts of one great mind, have built up since the beginning of the world.

The same revolutions within a narrower sphere had place in antient Rome, but the actions and forms of its social life never seem to have been perfectly saturated with the poetical element. The Romans appear to have considered the Greeks as the selectest treasuries of the selectest forms of manners and of nature and to have abstained from creating in measured language, sculpture, music, or architecture, anything which might bear a particular relation to their own condition whilst it might bear a general one to the universal constitution of the world. But we judge from partial evidence, and we judge perhaps partially. Ennius, Varro, Pacuvius, and Accius, all great poets, have been lost. Lucretius is in the highest, and Virgil in a very high sense, a creator. The chosen delicacy of the expressions of the latter are as a mist of light which conceal from us the intense and exceeding truth of his conceptions of nature. Livy is instinct with poetry. Yet Horace, Catullus, Ovid, and generally the other great writers of the Virgilian age, saw man and nature in the mirror of Greece. The institutions also and the religion of Rome were less poetical than those of Greece, as the shadow is less vivid than the substance. Hence poetry in Rome seemed to follow rather than accompany the perfection of political and domestic society. The true poetry of Rome lived in its institutions; for whatever of beautiful, true, and majestic they contained could have sprung only from the faculty which creates the order in which they consist. The life of Camillus, the death of Regulus; the expectation of the Senators, in their godlike state, of the victorious Gauls; the refusal of the Republic to make peace with Hannibal after the battle of Cannæ were not the consequences of a refined calculation of the probable personal advantage to result from such a rhythm and order in the shews of life to those who were at once the poets and the actors of these immortal dramas. The imagination, beholding the beauty of this order, created it out of itself according to its own idea; the consequence was empire, and the reward ever-living fame. These things are not the less poetry, *quia carent vate sacro*.[14] They are the episodes of that cyclic poem written by Time upon the memories of men. The Past like an inspired rhapsodist fills the theatre of everlasting generations with their harmony.

At length the antient system of religion and manners had fulfilled the circle of its revolution. And the world would have fallen into utter anarchy and darkness but that there were found poets among the authors of the Christian and Chivalric systems of manners and religion who created forms of opinion and action never before conceived, which, copied into the imaginations of men, became as generals to the bewildered armies of their thoughts. It is foreign to the present purpose to touch upon the evil produced by these systems, except that we protest on the ground of the principles already established that no portion of it can be imputed to the poetry they contain.

It is probable that the astonishing poetry of Moses, Job, David, Solomon, and Isaiah had produced a great effect upon the mind of Jesus and his disciples. The scattered fragments preserved to us by the biographers of this extraordinary person are all instinct with the most vivid poetry. But his doctrines seem to have been quickly distorted. At a certain period after the prevalence of doctrines founded upon those promulgated by him, the three forms into which Plato had distributed the faculties of

14 "they lack a sacred poet" (from Horace's *Ode IV*)

mind [15] underwent a sort of apotheosis and became the object of the worship of Europe. Here it is to be confessed that "Light seems to thicken," and

> The crow makes wing to the rooky wood,
> Good things of day begin to droop and drowse,
> And night's black agents to their preys do rouse.[16]

But mark how beautiful an order has sprung from the dust and blood of this fierce chaos! how the World, as from a resurrection, balancing itself on the golden wings of knowledge and of hope, has reassumed its yet unwearied flight into the Heaven of time. Listen to the music, unheard by outward ears, which is as a ceaseless and invisible wind nourishing its everlasting course with strength and swiftness.

The poetry in the doctrines of Jesus Christ and the mythology and institutions of the Celtic conquerors of the Roman empire outlived the darkness and the convulsions connected with their growth and victory and blended themselves into a new fabric of manners and opinion. It is an error to impute the ignorance of the dark ages to the Christian doctrines or the predominance of the Celtic nations.[17] Whatever of evil their agencies may have contained sprang from the extinction of the poetical principle, connected with the progress of despotism and superstition. Men, from causes too intricate to be here discussed, had become insensible and selfish; their own will had become feeble, and yet they were its slaves and thence the slaves of the will of others; lust, fear, avarice, cruelty, and fraud characterised a race amongst whom no one was to be found capable of *creating* in form, language, or institution. The moral anomalies of such a state of society are not justly to be charged upon any class of events immediately connected with them, and those events are most entitled to our approbation which could dissolve it most expedi-

15 **the three forms . . . mind** reference to Plato's *Timaeus*
16 **The crow . . . rouse** inaccurate quotation of *Macbeth*, III, 2, 50–53   17 **It is an error . . . nations** Shelley's declaration against Gibbon's contention in *The Decline and Fall of the Roman Empire*, ch. XV

to the worship of which Chivalry was the law and poets the prophets.

The poetry of Dante may be considered as the bridge thrown over the stream of time, which unites the modern and antient World. The distorted notions of invisible things which Dante and his rival Milton have idealised are merely the mask and the mantle in which these great poets walk through eternity enveloped and disguised. It is a difficult question to determine how far they were conscious of the distinction which must have subsisted in their minds between their own creeds and that of the people. Dante at least appears to wish to mark the full extent of it by placing Riphæus, whom Virgil calls *justissimus unus*, in Paradise, and observing a most heretical caprice in his distribution of rewards and punishments. And Milton's poem contains within itself a philosophical refutation of that system[19] of which, by a strange and natural antithesis, it has been a chief popular support. Nothing can exceed the energy and magnificence of the character of Satan as expressed in "Paradise Lost." It is a mistake to suppose that he could ever have been intended for the popular personification of evil. Implacable hate, patient cunning, and a sleepless refinement of device to inflict the extremest anguish on an enemy, these things are evil; and, although venial in a slave, are not to be forgiven in a tyrant—although redeemed by much that ennobles his defeat in one subdued, are marked by all that dishonours his conquest in the victor. Milton's Devil as a moral being is as far superior to his God as One who perseveres in some purpose which he has conceived to be excellent in spite of adversity and torture, is to One who in the cold security of undoubted triumph inflicts the most horrible revenge upon his enemy, not from any mistaken notion of inducing him to repent of a perseverance in enmity but with the alleged design of exasperating him to deserve new torments. Milton has so far violated the popular creed (if this shall be judged to be a violation) as to have alleged no superiority of moral virtue to his God over his Devil. And this bold neglect of a direct moral purpose is the most decisive proof of the supremacy of Milton's

19 **that system** Christianity

genius. He mingled as it were the elements of human nature as colours upon a single pallet and arranged them in the composition of his great picture according to the laws of epic truth; that is, according to the laws of that principle by which a series of actions of the external universe and of intelligent and ethical beings is calculated to excite the sympathy of succeeding generations of mankind. The Divina Commedia and Paradise Lost have conferred upon modern mythology a systematic form; and when change and time shall have added one more superstition to the mass of those which have arisen and decayed upon the earth, commentators will be learnedly employed in elucidating the religion of ancestral Europe, only not utterly forgotten because it will have been stamped with the eternity of genius.

Homer was the first and Dante the second epic poet: that is, the second poet, the series of whose creations bore a defined and intelligible relation to the knowledge and sentiment and religion and political conditions of the age in which he lived and of the ages which followed it— developing itself in correspondence with their development. For Lucretius had limed the wings of his swift spirit in the dregs of the sensible world;[20] and Virgil, with a modesty which ill became his genius, had affected the fame of an imitator even whilst he created anew all that he copied; and none among the flock of Mock-birds, though their notes were sweet, Apollonius Rhodius, Quintus Calaber Smyrnetheus, Nonnus, Lucan, Statius, or Claudian, have sought even to fulfil a single condition of epic truth. Milton was the third epic poet. For if the title of epic in its highest sense be refused to the Æneid, still less can it be conceded to the Orlando Furioso, the Gerusalemme Liberata, the Lusiad, or the Fairy Queen.[21]

Dante and Milton were both deeply penetrated with the antient religion of the civilized world, and its spirit exists in their poetry probably in the same proportion as

20 **For Lucretius . . . world** not a condemnation of Lucretius (who was always admired by Shelley), but a statement explaining why he is not ranked second among epic poets   21 **Æneid . . . Fairy Queen** five poems by Virgil, Ariosto, Tasso, Camoëns, and Spenser, respectively

its forms survived in the unreformed worship of modern Europe. The one preceded and the other followed the Reformation at almost equal intervals. Dante was the first religious reformer, and Luther surpassed him rather in the rudeness and acrimony than in the boldness of his censures of papal usurpation. Dante was the first awakener of entranced Europe; he created a language, in itself music and persuasion, out of a chaos of inharmonious barbarisms. He was the congregator of those great spirits who presided over the resurrection of learning, the Lucifer of that starry flock which in the thirteenth century shone forth from republican Italy as from a heaven into the darkness of the benighted world. His very words are instinct with spirit; each is as a spark, a burning atom of inextinguishable thought; and many yet lie covered in the ashes of their birth and pregnant with a lightning which has yet found no conductor. All high poetry is infinite; it is as the first acorn, which contained all oaks potentially. Veil after veil may be undrawn and the inmost naked beauty of the meaning never exposed. A great poem is a fountain forever overflowing with the waters of wisdom and delight; and after one person and one age has exhausted all its divine effluence which their peculiar relations enable them to share, another and yet another succeeds, and new relations are ever developed, the source of an unforeseen and an unconceived delight.

The age immediately succeeding to that of Dante, Petrarch, and Boccaccio was characterized by a revival of painting, sculpture, music, and architecture. Chaucer caught the sacred inspiration, and the superstructure of English literature is based upon the materials of Italian invention.

But let us not be betrayed from a defence into a critical history of Poetry and its influence on Society. Be it enough to have pointed out the effects of poets, in the large and true sense of the word, upon their own and all succeeding times and to revert to the partial instances cited as illustrations of an opinion the reverse of that attempted to be established by the Author of the Four Ages of Poetry.

But poets have been challenged to resign the civic crown to reasoners and mechanists on another plea. It is admitted that the exercise of the imagination is most delightful, but it is alleged that that of reason is more useful. Let us examine as the grounds of this distinction what is here meant by utility. Pleasure or good, in a general sense, is that which the consciousness of a sensitive and intelligent being seeks and in which, when found, it acquiesces. There are two modes or degrees of pleasure, one durable, universal, and permanent; the other transitory and particular. Utility may either express the means of producing the former or the latter. In the former sense, whatever strengthens and purifies the affections, enlarges the imagination, and adds spirit to sense is useful. But the meaning in which the Author of the Four Ages of Poetry seems to have employed the word utility is the narrower one of banishing the importunity of the wants of our animal nature, the surrounding men with security of life, the dispersing the grosser delusions of superstition, and the conciliating such a degree of mutual forbearance among men as may consist with the motives of personal advantage.

Undoubtedly the promoters of utility, in this limited sense, have their appointed office in society. They follow the footsteps of poets and copy the sketches of their creations into the book of common life. They make space and give time. Their exertions are of the highest value so long as they confine their administration of the concerns of the inferior powers of our nature within the limits due to the superior ones. But whilst the sceptic destroys gross superstitions, let him spare to deface, as some of the French writers have defaced, the eternal truths charactered upon the imaginations of men. Whilst the mechanist abridges and the political economist combines labour, let them beware that their speculations, for want of correspondence with those first principles which belong to the imagination, do not tend, as they have in modern England, to exasperate at once the extremes of luxury and want. They have exemplified the saying, "To him that hath, more shall be given; and from him that hath not, the little that he hath shall be taken away." [22] The rich have become richer, and the poor have become poorer; and the vessel of the state is driven between the Scylla and Charybdis of anarchy and despotism. Such are the effects

22 adaptation of Matt. 25:29

which must ever flow from an unmitigated exercise of the calculating faculty.

It is difficult to define pleasure in its highest sense, the definition involving a number of apparent paradoxes. For, from an inexplicable defect of harmony in the constitution of human nature, the pain of the inferior is frequently connected with the pleasures of the superior portions of our being. Sorrow, terror, anguish, despair itself, are often the chosen expressions of an approximation to the highest good. Our sympathy in tragic fiction depends on this principle; tragedy delights by affording a shadow of the pleasure which exists in pain. This is the source also of the melancholy which is inseparable from the sweetest melody. The pleasure that is in sorrow is sweeter than the pleasure of pleasure itself. And hence the saying, "It is better to go to the house of mourning, than to the house of mirth." [23] Not that this highest species of pleasure is necessarily linked with pain. The delight of love and friendship, the ecstasy of the admiration of nature, the joy of the perception and still more of the creation of poetry is often wholly unalloyed.

The production and assurance of pleasure in this highest sense is true utility. Those who produce and preserve this pleasure are Poets or poetical philosophers.

The exertions of Locke, Hume, Gibbon, Voltaire, Rousseau,[24] and their disciples, in favour of oppressed and deluded humanity are entitled to the gratitude of mankind. Yet it is easy to calculate the degree of moral and intellectual improvement which the world would have exhibited had they never lived. A little more nonsense would have been talked for a century or two and perhaps a few more men, women, and children, burnt as heretics. We might not at this moment have been congratulating each other on the abolition of the Inquisition in Spain.[25] But it exceeds all imagination to conceive what would have been the moral condition of the world if neither Dante, Petrarch,

23 Eccles. 7:2 (misquoted)   24 I follow the classification adopted by the Author of the Four Ages of Poetry; but he was essentially a Poet. The others, even Voltaire, were mere reasoners. [Shelley's note]   25 **We might . . . Spain** finally achieved in 1820

Boccaccio, Chaucer, Shakspeare, Calderon, Lord Bacon, nor Milton, had ever existed; if Raphael and Michael Angelo had never been born; if the Hebrew poetry had never been translated; if a revival of the study of Greek literature had never taken place; if no monuments of antient sculpture had been handed down to us; and if the poetry of the religion of the antient world had been extinguished together with its belief. The human mind could never, except by the intervention of these excitements, have been awakened to the invention of the grosser sciences and that application of analytical reasoning to the aberrations of society which it is now attempted to exalt over the direct expression of the inventive and creative faculty itself.

We have more moral, political, and historical wisdom than we know how to reduce into practice; we have more scientific and economical knowledge than can be accommodated to the just distribution of the produce which it multiplies. The poetry in these systems of thought is concealed by the accumulation of facts and calculating processes. There is no want of knowledge respecting what is wisest and best in morals, government, and political economy, or at least what is wiser and better than what men now practise and endure. But we let "*I dare not* wait upon *I would*, like the poor cat i' the adage." We want the creative faculty to imagine that which we know; we want the generous impulse to act that which we imagine; we want the poetry of life; our calculations have outrun conception; we have eaten more than we can digest. The cultivation of those sciences which have enlarged the limits of the empire of man over the external world has, for want of the poetical faculty, proportionally circumscribed those of the internal world; and man, having enslaved the elements, remains himself a slave. To what but a cultivation of the mechanical arts in a degree disproportioned to the presence of the creative faculty, which is the basis of all knowledge, is to be attributed the abuse of all invention for abridging and combining labour to the exasperation of the inequality of mankind? From what other cause has it arisen that these inventions which should have lightened have added a weight to the curse imposed on Adam? Thus Poetry and the principle of Self, of which

Money is the visible incarnation, are the God and Mammon of the world.

The functions of the poetical faculty are twofold; by one it creates new materials for knowledge and power and pleasure; by the other it engenders in the mind a desire to reproduce and arrange them according to a certain rhythm and order which may be called the beautiful and the good. The cultivation of poetry is never more to be desired than at periods when, from an excess of the selfish and calculating principle, the accumulation of the materials of external life exceed the quantity of the power of assimilating them to the internal laws of human nature. The body has then become too unwieldy for that which animates it.

Poetry is indeed something divine. It is at once the centre and circumference of knowledge; it is that which comprehends all science and that to which all science must be referred. It is at the same time the root and blossom of all other systems of thought; it is that from which all spring and that which adorns all, and that which, if blighted, denies the fruit and the seed and withholds from the barren world the nourishment and the succession of the scions of the tree of life. It is the perfect and consummate surface and bloom of things; it is as the odour and the colour of the rose to the texture of the elements which compose it, as the form and the splendour of unfaded beauty to the secrets of anatomy and corruption. What were Virtue, Love, Patriotism, Friendship—what were the scenery of this beautiful Universe which we inhabit; what were our consolations on this side of the grave, and what were our aspirations beyond it, if Poetry did not ascend to bring light and fire from those eternal regions where the owl-winged faculty of calculation dare not ever soar? Poetry is not, like reasoning, a power to be exerted according to the determination of the will. A man cannot say, "I will compose poetry." The greatest poet even cannot say it, for the mind in creation is as a fading coal, which some invisible influence, like an inconstant wind, awakens to transitory brightness; this power arises from within like the colour of a flower which fades and changes as it is developed, and the conscious portions of our natures are unprophetic either of its approach or its departure. Could this influence be durable in its original purity and force, it is impossible to predict the greatness of the results; but when composition begins, inspiration is already on the decline, and the most glorious poetry that has ever been communicated to the world is probably a feeble shadow of the original conception of the Poet. I appeal to the great poets of the present day, whether it be not an error to assert that the finest passages of poetry are produced by labour and study. The toil and the delay recommended by critics can be justly interpreted to mean no more than a careful observation of the inspired moments and an artificial connexion of the spaces between their suggestions by the intertexture of conventional expressions, a necessity only imposed by the limitedness of the poetical faculty itself. For Milton conceived the Paradise Lost as a whole before he executed it in portions. We have his own authority also for the Muse having "dictated" to him the "unpremeditated song," and let this be an answer to those who would allege the fifty-six various readings of the first line of the Orlando Furioso. Compositions so produced are to poetry what mosaic is to painting. This instinct and intuition of the poetical faculty is still more observable in the plastic and pictorial arts; a great statue or picture grows under the power of the artist as a child in the mother's womb; and the very mind which directs the hands in formation is incapable of accounting to itself for the origin, the gradations, or the media of the process.

Poetry is the record of the best and happiest moments of the happiest and best minds. We are aware of evanescent visitations of thought and feeling sometimes associated with place or person, sometimes regarding our own mind alone, and always arising unforeseen and departing unbidden, but elevating and delightful beyond all expression; so that even in the desire and the regret they leave, there cannot but be pleasure, participating as it does in the nature of its object. It is as it were the interpenetration of a diviner nature through our own; but its footsteps are like those of a wind over a sea, which the coming calm erases and whose traces remain only as on the wrinkled sand which paves it. These and corresponding conditions of being are experienced principally by those of the most delicate sensibility and the most enlarged imagination, and the state of mind produced by them is at war with every base desire. The enthusiasm of virtue, love, patriotism, and friendship is essentially linked with these emotions; and whilst they last, self appears as what it is, an atom to a Universe.[26] Poets are not only subject to these experiences as spirits of the most refined organisation, but they can colour all that they combine with the evanescent hues of this ethereal world; a word or a trait in the representation of a scene or a passion will touch the enchanted chord and reanimate, in those who have ever experienced these emotions, the sleeping, the cold, the buried image of the past. Poetry thus makes immortal all that is best and most beautiful in the world; it arrests the vanishing apparitions which haunt the interlunations of life and, veiling them or in language or in form sends them forth among mankind, bearing sweet news of kindred joy to those with whom their sisters abide—abide, because there is no portal of expression from the caverns of the spirit which they inhabit into the universe of things. Poetry redeems from decay the visitations of the divinity in Man.

Poetry turns all things to loveliness; it exalts the beauty of that which is most beautiful, and it adds beauty to that which is most deformed; it marries exultation and horror, grief and pleasure, eternity and change; it subdues to union under its light yoke all irreconcilable things. It transmutes all that it touches, and every form moving within the radiance of its presence is changed by wondrous sympathy to an incarnation of the spirit which it breathes; its secret alchemy turns to potable gold the poisonous waters which flow from death through life; it strips the veil of familiarity from the world and lays bare the naked and sleeping beauty which is the spirit of its forms.

All things exist as they are perceived; at least in relation to the percipient. "The mind is its own place, and of itself can make a Heaven of Hell, a Hell of Heaven." [27] But poetry defeats the curse which binds us to be subjected to the accident of surrounding impressions. And whether it spreads its own figured curtain or withdraws life's dark veil from before the scene of things, it equally creates for us a being within our being. It makes us the inhabitants

26 **We are . . . . Universe** a prose version of Shelley's "Hymn to Intellectual Beauty" 27 *Paradise Lost*, 1. 254–255

of a world to which the familiar world is a chaos. It reproduces the common Universe of which we are portions and
percipients and it purges from our inward sight the film
of familiarity which obscures from us the wonder of our
being. It compels us to feel that which we perceive and to
imagine that which we know. It creates anew the universe
after it has been annihilated in our minds by the recurrence of impressions blunted by reiteration. It justifies that
bold and true word of Tasso: *Non merita nome di creatore,
se non Iddio ed il Poeta.*[28]

A poet, as he is the author to others of the highest
wisdom, pleasure, virtue, and glory, so he ought personally
to be the happiest, the best, the wisest, and the most illustrious of men. As to his glory, let Time be challenged to
declare whether the fame of any other institutor of human life be comparable to that of a poet. That he is the
wisest, the happiest, and the best, inasmuch as he is a
poet, is equally incontrovertible: the greatest Poets have
been men of the most spotless virtue, of the most consummate prudence, and, if we could look into the interior of
their lives, the most fortunate of men; and the exceptions,
as they regard those who possessed the imaginative faculty
in a high yet inferior degree, will be found on consideration
to confirm rather than destroy the rule. Let us for a moment stoop to the arbitration of popular breath, and usurp-
ing and uniting in our own persons the incompatible
characters of accuser, witness, judge, and executioner, let
us without trial, testimony, or form determine that certain
motives of those who are "there sitting where we dare not
soar" [29] are reprehensible. Let us assume that Homer was
a drunkard, that Virgil was a flatterer, that Horace was a
coward, that Tasso was a madman, that Lord Bacon was
a peculator, that Raphael was a libertine, that Spenser was
a poet laureate. It is inconsistent with this division of our
subject to cite living poets, but Posterity has done ample
justice to the great names now referred to. Their errors

28 "No one merits the name of Creator but God and the poet"
(in substance, though not verbatim, in Tasso's *Discorsi del
Poema Eroico*)—used by Shelley also in his letters and in the
Essay on Life 29 **"there . . . soar"** approximation to Shelley's
Adonais, l. 337; see also *Paradise Lost*, l. 828–829)

have been weighed and found to have been dust in the balance; if their sins were as scarlet, they are now white as snow; they have been washed in the blood of the mediator and the redeemer, Time. Observe in what a ludicrous chaos the imputations of real or fictitious crime have been confused in the contemporary calumnies against poetry and poets; consider how little is as it appears—or appears as it is; look to your own motives, and judge not, lest ye be judged.

Poetry, as has been said, in this respect differs from logic, that it is not subject to the controul of the active powers of the mind and that its birth and recurrence has no necessary connexion with consciousness or will. It is presumptuous to determine that these are the necessary conditions of all mental causation, when mental effects are experienced insusceptible of being referred to them. The frequent recurrence of the poetical power, it is obvious to suppose, may produce in the mind an habit of order and harmony correlative with its own nature and with its effects upon other minds. But in the intervals of inspiration, and they may be frequent without being durable, a Poet becomes a man, and is abandoned to the sudden reflux of the influences under which others habitually live. But as he is more delicately organized than other men and sensible to pain and pleasure, both his own and that of others, in a degree unknown to them, he will avoid the one and pursue the other with an ardour proportioned to this difference. And he renders himself obnoxious to calumny when he neglects to observe the circumstances under which these objects of universal pursuit and flight have disguised themselves in one another's garments.

But there is nothing necessarily evil in this error, and thus cruelty, envy, revenge, avarice, and the passions purely evil have never formed any portion of the popular imputations on the lives of poets.

I have thought it most favourable to the cause of truth to set down these remarks according to the order in which they were suggested to my mind by a consideration of the subject itself, instead of following that of the treatise that excited me to make them public. Thus although devoid of the formality of a polemical reply, if the view they contain be just, they will be found to involve a refutation of the doctrines of the Four Ages of Poetry so far at least as regards the first division of the subject. I can readily conjecture what should have moved the gall of the learned and intelligent author of that paper; I confess myself, like him, unwilling to be stunned by the Theseids[30] of the hoarse Codri[31] of the day. Bavius and Mævius[32] undoubtedly are, as they ever were, insufferable persons. But it belongs to a philosophical critic to distinguish rather than confound.

The first part of these remarks has related to Poetry in its elements and principles; and it has been shewn, as well as the narrow limits assigned them would permit, that what is called poetry in a restricted sense has a common source with all other forms of order and of beauty according to which the materials of human life are susceptible of being arranged and which is Poetry in an universal sense.

The second part[33] will have for its object an application of these principles to the present state of the cultivation of Poetry, and a defence of the attempt to idealize the modern forms of manners and opinions, and compel them into a subordination to the imaginative and creative faculty. For the literature of England, an energetic development of which has ever preceded or accompanied a great and free development of the national will, has arisen as it were from a new birth. In spite of the low-thoughted envy which would undervalue contemporary merit, our own will be a memorable age in intellectual achievements, and we live among such philosophers and poets as surpass beyond comparison any who have appeared since the last national struggle for civil and religious liberty. The most unfailing herald, companion, and follower of the awakening of a great people to work a beneficial change in opinion or institution is Poetry. At such periods there is an accumulation of the power of communicating and receiving intense and impassioned conceptions respecting man and nature. The persons in whom this power resides may

30 poems in honor of the god Theseus   31 an unimaginative writer satirized in Juvenal's *First Satire*   32 two versifiers ridiculed in Virgil's *Third Eclogue*   33 **The second part** of A *Defence of Poetry*—never written

often, as far as regards many portions of their nature, have little apparent correspondence with that spirit of good of which they are the ministers. But even whilst they deny and abjure, they are yet compelled to serve the Power which is seated upon the throne of their own soul. It is impossible to read the compositions of the most celebrated writers of the present day without being startled with the electric life which burns within their words. They measure the circumference and sound the depths of human nature with a comprehensive and all-penetrating spirit, and they are themselves perhaps the most sincerely astonished at its manifestations; for it is less their spirit than the spirit of the age. Poets are the hierophants of an unapprehended inspiration; the mirrors of the gigantic shadows which futurity casts upon the present; the words which express what they understand not; the trumpets which sing to battle and feel not what they inspire; the influence which is moved not, but moves. Poets are the unacknowledged legislators of the world.

Fragments

In one mode of considering these two classes of action of the human mind which are called reason and imagination, the former may be considered as mind employed upon the relations borne by one thought to another, however produced, and imagination as mind combining the elements of thought itself. It has been termed the power of association; and on an accurate anatomy of the functions of the mind, it would be difficult to assign any other origin to the mass of what we perceive and know than this power. Association is, however, rather a law according to which this power is exerted than the power itself, in the same manner as gravitation is a passive expression of the reciprocal tendency of heavy bodies towards their respective centres. Were these bodies conscious of such a tendency, the name which they would assign to that consciousness would express the cause of gravitation; and it were a vain inquiry as to what might be the cause of that cause. Association bears the same relation to imagination as a mode to a source of action; when we look upon shapes in the fire or the clouds and imagine to ourselves the resemblance of familiar objects, we do no more than seize the relation of certain points of visible objects, and fill up, blend together . . .

The imagination is a faculty not less imperial and essential to the happiness and dignity of the human being, than the reason.

It is by no means indisputable that what is true, or rather that which the disciples of a certain mechanical and superficial philosophy call true, is more excellent than the beautiful.

These fragments are probably connected with A *Defence of Poetry*, and a part of the original exordium

appendix a

selected prefaces to poems

Laon and Cythna;

OR, THE REVOLUTION OF THE GOLDEN CITY,
A VISION OF THE NINETEENTH CENTURY

(1817)

PREFACE (in part)

The Poem which I now present to the world [1] is an
attempt from which I scarcely dare to expect success, and
in which a writer of established fame might fail without
disgrace. It is an experiment on the temper of the public
mind, as to how far a thirst for a happier condition of
moral and political society survives, among the enlightened and refined, the tempests which have shaken the
age in which we live. I have sought to enlist the harmony
of metrical language, the etherial combinations of the
fancy, the rapid and subtle transitions of human passion,
all those elements which essentially compose a Poem, in
the cause of a liberal and comprehensive morality: and in
the view of kindling within the bosoms of my readers a
virtuous enthusiasm for those doctrines of liberty and

These selections from Shelley's prefaces and letters have been
chosen because of their relevance to and reenforcement of the
political concepts expressed in the essays 1 reissued, after slight
revision, as *The Revolt of Islam*

199

justice, that faith and hope in something good, which neither violence, nor misrepresentation, nor prejudice, can ever totally extinguish among mankind.

For this purpose I have chosen a story of human passion in its most universal character, diversified with moving and romantic adventures, and appealing, in contempt of all artificial opinions or institutions, to the common sympathies of every human breast. I have made no attempt to recommend the motives which I would substitute for those at present governing mankind by methodical and systematic argument. I would only awaken the feelings, so that the reader should see the beauty of true virtue and be incited to those inquiries which have led to my moral and political creed, and that of some of the sublimest intellects in the world. The Poem, therefore (with the exception of the first Canto, which is purely introductory), is narrative, not didactic. It is a succession of pictures illustrating the growth and progress of individual mind aspiring after excellence, and devoted to the love of mankind; its influence in refining and making pure the most daring and uncommon impulses of the imagination, the understanding, and the senses; its impatience at "all the oppressions which are done under the sun"; its tendency to awaken public hope and to enlighten and improve mankind; the rapid effects of the application of that tendency; the awakening of an immense nation from their slavery and degradation to a true sense of moral dignity and freedom; the bloodless dethronement of their oppressors, and the unveiling of the religious frauds by which they had been deluded into submission; the tranquillity of successful patriotism, and the universal toleration and benevolence of true philanthropy; the treachery and barbarity of hired soldiers; vice not the object of punishment and hatred, but kindness and pity; the faithlessness of tyrants; the confederacy of the Rulers of the World, and the restoration of the expelled Dynasty by foreign arms; the massacre and extermination of the Patriots, and the victory of established power; the consequences of legitimate despotism, civil war, famine, plague, superstition, and an utter extinction of the domestic affections; the judicial murder of the advocates of Liberty; the temporary triumph of oppression, that secure earnest of its final and inevitable fall; the transient nature of ignorance and error, and the eternity of genius and virtue. Such is the series of delineations of which the Poem consists. And if the lofty passions with which it has been my scope to distinguish this story shall not excite in the reader a generous impulse, an ardent thirst for excellence, an interest profound and strong, such as belongs to no meaner desires—let not the failure be imputed to a natural unfitness for human sympathy in these sublime and animating themes. It is the business of the Poet to communicate to others the pleasure and the enthusiasm arising out of those images and feelings, in the vivid presence of which within his own mind, consists at once his inspiration and his reward.

The panic which, like an epidemic transport, seized upon all classes of men during the excesses consequent upon the French Revolution, is gradually giving place to sanity. It has ceased to be believed that whole generations of mankind ought to consign themselves to a hopeless inheritance of ignorance and misery because a nation of men who had been dupes and slaves for centuries were incapable of conducting themselves with the wisdom and tranquillity of freemen so soon as some of their fetters were partially loosened. That their conduct could not have been marked by any other characters than ferocity and thoughtlessness is the historical fact from which liberty derives all its recommendations, and falsehood the worst features of its deformity. There is a reflux in the tide of human things which bears the shipwrecked hopes of men into a secure haven, after the storms are past. Methinks, those who now live have survived an age of despair.

The French Revolution may be considered as one of those manifestations of a general state of feeling among civilized mankind, produced by a defect of correspondence between the knowledge existing in society and the improvement or gradual abolition of political institutions. The year 1788 may be assumed as the epoch of one of the most important crises produced by this feeling. The sympathies connected with that event extended to every bosom. The most generous and amiable natures were those which participated the most extensively in these sympathies. But such a degree of unmingled good was expected as it was impossible to realize. If the Revolution had been in every respect prosperous, then misrule and superstition would lose half their claims to our abhorrence, as fetters which the captive can unlock with the slightest motion of his fingers, and which do not eat with poisonous rust into the soul. The revulsion occasioned by the atrocities of the demagogues and the re-establishment of successive tyrannies in France was terrible, and felt in the remotest corner of the civilized world. Could they listen to the plea of reason who had groaned under the calamities of a social state, according to the provisions of which one man riots in luxury whilst another famishes for want of bread? Can he who the day before was a trampled slave suddenly become liberal-minded, forbearing, and independent? This is the consequence of the habits of a state of society to be produced by resolute perseverance and indefatigable hope, and long-suffering and long believing courage, and the systematic efforts of generations of men of intellect and virtue. Such is the lesson which experience teaches now. But on the first reverses of hope in the progress of French liberty, the sanguine eagerness for good overleapt the solution of these questions and for a time extinguished itself in the unexpectedness of their result. Thus many of the most ardent and tender-hearted of the worshippers of public good have been morally ruined by what a partial glimpse of the events they deplored, appeared to shew as the melancholy desolation of all their cherished hopes. Hence gloom and misanthropy have become the characteristics of the age in which we live, the solace of a disappointment that unconsciously finds relief only in the wilful exaggeration of its own despair. This influence has tainted the literature of the age with the hopelessness of the minds from which it flows. Metaphysics[2] and enquiries into moral and political science have become little else than vain attempts to revive exploded superstitions, or sophisms like those[3] of Mr. Malthus, cal-

2 I ought to except Sir W. Drummond's "Academical Questions"; a volume of very acute and powerful metaphysical criticism. [Shelley's note]   3 It is remarkable, as a symptom of the revival of public hope, that Mr. Malthus has assigned, in the later editions of his work, an indefinite dominion to moral restraint over the principle of population. This concession answers all the inferences from his doctrine unfavourable to human improvement

culated to lull the oppressors of mankind into a security of everlasting triumph. Our works of fiction and poetry have been overshadowed by the same infectious gloom. But mankind appear to me to be emerging from their trance. I am aware, methinks, of a slow, gradual, silent change. In that belief I have composed the following Poem. . . .

I trust that the reader will carefully distinguish between those opinions which have a dramatic propriety in reference to the characters which they are designed to elucidate and such as are properly my own. The erroneous and degrading idea which men have conceived of a Supreme Being, for instance, is spoken against, but not the Supreme Being itself. The belief which some superstitious persons whom I have brought upon the stage entertain of the Deity, as injurious to the character of his benevolence, is widely different from my own. In recommending also a great and important change in the spirit which animates the social institutions of mankind, I have avoided all flattery to those violent and malignant passions of our nature which are ever on the watch to mingle with and to alloy the most beneficial innovations. There is no quarter given to Revenge, or Envy, or Prejudice. Love is celebrated everywhere as the sole law which should govern the moral world.

In the personal conduct of my Hero and Heroine there is one circumstance which was intended to startle the reader from the trance of ordinary life. It was my object to break through the crust of those outworn opinions on which established institutions depend. I have appealed therefore to the most universal of all feelings, and have endeavoured to strengthen the moral sense by forbidding it to waste its energies in seeking to avoid actions which are only crimes of convention. It is because there is so great a multitude of artificial vices that there are so few real virtues. Those feelings alone which are benevolent or malevolent are essentially good or bad. The circumstance of which I speak was introduced, however, merely to accustom men to that charity and toleration which the ex-

---

and reduces the *Essay on Population* to a commentary illustrative of the unanswerableness of *Political Justice*. [Shelley's note]

hibition of a practice widely differing from their own has a tendency to promote.[4] Nothing indeed can be more mischievous than many actions, innocent in themselves, which might bring down upon individuals the bigoted contempt and rage of the multitude.

Prometheus Unbound

A LYRICAL DRAMA IN FOUR ACTS

(1818–1819)

PREFACE

The Greek tragic writers, in selecting as their subject any portion of their national history or mythology, employed in their treatment of it a certain arbitrary discretion. They by no means conceived themselves bound to adhere to the common interpretation or to imitate in story as in title their rivals and predecessors. Such a system would have amounted to a resignation of those claims to preference over their competitors which incited the composition. The Agamemnonian story was exhibited on the Athenian theatre with as many variations as dramas.

I have presumed to employ a similar license. The "Prometheus Unbound" of Æschylus supposed the reconciliation of Jupiter with his victim as the price of the disclosure of the danger threatened to his empire by the consummation of his marriage with Thetis. Thetis, according to this view of the subject, was given in marriage to Peleus, and Prometheus, by the permission of Jupiter, delivered from his captivity by Hercules. Had I framed my story on this model, I should have done no more than have attempted to restore the lost drama of Æschylus—an ambition, which, if my preference to this mode of treating the

4 The sentiments connected with and characteristic of this circumstance have no personal reference to the writer. [Shelley's note]

subject had incited me to cherish, the recollection of the
high comparison such an attempt would challenge might
well abate. But, in truth, I was averse from a catastrophe
so feeble as that of reconciling the Champion with the
Oppressor of mankind. The moral interest of the fable,
which is so powerfully sustained by the sufferings and
endurance of Prometheus, would be annihilated if we
could conceive of him as unsaying his high language and
quailing before his successful and perfidious adversary.
The only imaginary being resembling in any degree
Prometheus is Satan; and Prometheus is, in my judgment,
a more poetical character than Satan because, in addition
to courage, and majesty, and firm and patient opposition
to omnipotent force, he is susceptible of being described
as exempt from the taints of ambition, envy, revenge, and
a desire for personal aggrandisement, which, in the Hero
of Paradise Lost, interfere with the interest. The character
of Satan engenders in the mind a pernicious casuistry
which leads us to weigh his faults with his wrongs and to
excuse the former because the latter exceed all measure.
In the minds of those who consider that magnificent fiction
with a religious feeling it engenders something worse. But
Prometheus is, as it were, the type of the highest perfection
of moral and intellectual nature, impelled by the purest
and the truest motives to the best and noblest ends.

This Poem was chiefly written upon the mountainous
ruins of the Baths of Caracalla, among the flowery glades
and thickets of odoriferous blossoming trees which are
extended in ever winding labyrinths upon its immense
platforms and dizzy arches suspended in the air. The
bright blue sky of Rome and the effect of the vigorous
awakening spring in that divinest climate, and the new
life with which it drenches the spirits even to intoxication,
were the inspiration of this drama.

The imagery which I have employed will be found, in
many instances, to have been drawn from the operations
of the human mind or from those external actions by
which they are expressed. This is unusual in modern
poetry, although Dante and Shakspeare are full of instances
of the same kind; Dante indeed more than any other poet,
and with greater success. But the Greek poets, as writers
to whom no resource of awakening the sympathy of their

contemporaries was unknown, were in the habitual use of this power; and it is the study of their works (since a higher merit would probably be denied me) to which I am willing that my readers should impute this singularity.

One word is due in candour to the degree in which the study of contemporary writings may have tinged my composition, for such has been a topic of censure with regard to poems far more popular, and indeed more deservedly popular, than mine. It is impossible that any one who inhabits the same age with such writers as those who stand in the foremost ranks of our own can conscientiously assure himself that his language and tone of thought may not have been modified by the study of the productions of those extraordinary intellects. It is true that not the spirit of their genius, but the forms in which it has manifested itself, are due less to the peculiarities of their own minds than to the peculiarity of the moral and intellectual condition of the minds among which they have been produced. Thus a number of writers possess the form whilst they want the spirit of those whom, it is alleged, they imitate; because the former is the endowment of the age in which they live, and the latter must be the uncommunicated lightning of their own mind.

The peculiar style of intense and comprehensive imagery which distinguishes the modern literature of England has not been, as a general power, the product of the imitation of any particular writer. The mass of capabilities remains at every period materially the same; the circumstances which awaken it to action perpetually change. If England were divided into forty republics, each equal in population and extent to Athens, there is no reason to suppose but that, under institutions not more perfect than those of Athens, each would produce philosophers and poets equal to those who (if we except Shakspeare) have never been surpassed. We owe the great writers of the golden age of our literature to that fervid awakening of the public mind which shook to dust the oldest and most oppressive form of the Christian religion. We owe Milton to the progress and development of the same spirit; the sacred Milton was, let it ever be remembered, a republican and a bold inquirer into morals and religion. The great writers of our own age are, we have reason to suppose, the companions and forerunners of some unimagined change in our social condition, or the opinions which cement it. The cloud of mind is discharging its collected lightning, and the equilibrium between institutions and opinions is now restoring, or is about to be restored.

As to imitation, poetry is a mimetic art. It creates, but it creates by combination and representation. Poetical abstractions are beautiful and new, not because the portions of which they are composed had no previous existence in the mind of man or in nature, but because the whole produced by their combination has some intelligible and beautiful analogy with those sources of emotion and thought, and with the contemporary condition of them; one great poet is a masterpiece of nature which another not only ought to study but must study. He might as wisely and as easily determine that his mind should no longer be the mirror of all that is lovely in the visible universe as exclude from his contemplation the beautiful which exists in the writings of a great contemporary. The pretence of doing it would be a presumption in any but the greatest; the effect, even in him, would be strained, unnatural, and ineffectual. A poet is the combined product of such internal powers as modify the nature of others; and of such external influences as excite and sustain these powers; he is not one, but both. Every man's mind is, in this respect, modified by all the objects of nature and art; by every word and every suggestion which he ever admitted to act upon his consciousness; it is the mirror upon which all forms are reflected and in which they compose one form. Poets, not otherwise than philosophers, painters, sculptors, and musicians, are in one sense the creators and in another the creations of their age. From this subjection the loftiest do not escape. There is a similarity between Homer and Hesiod, between Æschylus and Euripides, between Virgil and Horace, between Dante and Petrarch, between Shakspeare and Fletcher, between Dryden and Pope; each has a generic resemblance under which their specific distinctions are arranged. If this similarity be the result of imitation, I am willing to confess that I have imitated.

Let this opportunity be conceded to me of acknowledging that I have what a Scotch philosopher characteristically terms "a passion for reforming the world"; what passion incited him to write and publish his book, he omits to explain. For my part, I had rather be damned with Plato and Lord Bacon than go to Heaven with Paley and Malthus. But it is a mistake to suppose that I dedicate my poetical compositions solely to the direct enforcement of reform, or that I consider them in any degree as containing a reasoned system on the theory of human life. Didactic poetry is my abhorrence; nothing can be equally well expressed in prose that is not tedious and supererogatory in verse. My purpose has hitherto been simply to familiarize the highly refined imagination of the more select classes of poetical readers with beautiful idealisms of moral excellence; aware that until the mind can love, and admire, and trust, and hope, and endure, reasoned principles of moral conduct are seeds cast upon the highway of life which the unconscious passenger tramples into dust, although they would bear the harvest of his happiness. Should I live to accomplish what I purpose, that is, produce a systematical history of what appear to me to be the genuine elements of human society, let not the advocates of injustice and superstition flatter themselves that I should take Æschylus rather than Plato as my model.

The having spoken of myself with unaffected freedom will need little apology with the candid; and let the uncandid consider that they injure me less than their own hearts and minds by misrepresentation. Whatever talents a person may possess to amuse and instruct others, be they ever so inconsiderable, he is yet bound to exert them; if his attempt be ineffectual, let the punishment of an unaccomplished purpose have been sufficient; let none trouble themselves to heap the dust of oblivion upon his efforts; the pile they raise will betray his grave which might otherwise have been unknown.

Hellas

A LYRICAL DRAMA

(1821)

PREFACE

The poem of Hellas, written at the suggestion of the events of the moment, is a mere improvise, and derives its interest (should it be found to possess any) solely from the intense sympathy which the Author feels with the cause he would celebrate.

The subject, in its present state, is insusceptible of being treated otherwise than lyrically, and if I have called this poem a drama, from the circumstance of its being composed in dialogue, the licence is not greater than that which has been assumed by other poets who have called their productions epics only because they have been divided into twelve or twenty-four books.

The Persæ of Æschylus afforded me the first model of my conception, although the decision of the glorious contest now waging in Greece being yet suspended forbids a catastrophe parallel to the return of Xerxes and the desolation of the Persians. I have, therefore, contented myself with exhibiting a series of lyric pictures, and with having wrought upon the curtain of futurity, which falls upon the unfinished scene, such figures of indistinct and visionary delineation as suggest the final triumph of the Greek cause as a portion of the cause of civilisation and social improvement.

The drama (if drama it must be called) is, however, so inartificial that I doubt whether, if recited on the Thespian waggon to an Athenian village at the Dionysiaca, it would have obtained the prize of the goat. I shall bear with equanimity any punishment greater than the loss of such a reward which the Aristarchi of the hour may think fit to inflict.

The only *goat-song* which I have yet attempted has, I confess, in spite of the unfavourable nature of the subject,[1] received a greater and a more valuable portion of applause than I expected or than it deserved.

Common fame is the only authority which I can allege for the details which form the basis of the poem, and I must trespass upon the forgiveness of my readers for the display of newspaper erudition to which I have been reduced. Undoubtedly, until the conclusion of the war,[2] it will be impossible to obtain an account of it sufficiently authentic for historical materials; but poets have their privilege, and it is unquestionable that actions of the most exalted courage have been performed by the Greeks—that they have gained more than one naval victory, and that their defeat in Wallachia was signalised by circumstances of heroism more glorious even than victory.

The apathy of the rulers of the civilised world, to the astonishing circumstance of the descendants of that nation to which they owe their civilisation—rising as it were from the ashes of their ruin, is something perfectly inexplicable to a mere spectator of the shows of this mortal scene. We are all Greeks. Our laws, our literature, our religion, our arts, have their root in Greece. But for Greece —Rome the instructor, the conqueror, or the metropolis of our ancestors, would have spread no illumination with her arms, and we might still have been savages and idolaters; or, what is worse, might have arrived at such a stagnant and miserable state of social institutions as China and Japan possess.

The human form and the human mind attained to a perfection in Greece, which has impressed its image on those faultless productions whose very fragments are the despair of modern art and has propagated impulses which cannot cease, through a thousand channels of manifest or imperceptible operation, to ennoble and delight mankind until the extinction of the race.

The modern Greek is the descendant of those glorious beings whom the imagination almost refuses to figure to

1 **The only . . . subject** reference to Shelley's drama *The Cenci*, which deals with the subject of incest   2 **the war** for independence then being waged by Greece against the Turks

itself as belonging to our kind, and he inherits much of their sensibility, their rapidity of conception, their enthusiasm, and their courage. If in many instances he is degraded by moral and political slavery to the practice of the basest vices it engenders, and that below the level of ordinary degradation, let us reflect that the corruption of the best produces the worst, and that habits which subsist only in relation to a peculiar state of social institution may be expected to cease as soon as that relation is dissolved. In fact, the Greeks, since the admirable novel of "Anastatius" could have been a faithful picture of their manners, have undergone most important changes; the flower of their youth returning to their country from the universities of Italy, Germany, and France, have communicated to their fellow-citizens the latest results of that social perfection of which their ancestors were the original source. The university of Chios contained before the breaking out of the revolution eight hundred students, and among them several Germans and Americans. The munificence and energy of many of the Greek princes and merchants, directed to the renovation of their country with a spirit and a wisdom which has few examples, is above all praise.

The English permit their own oppressors to act according to their natural sympathy with the Turkish tyrant and to brand upon their name the indelible blot of an alliance with the enemies of domestic happiness, of Christianity and civilisation.

Russia desires to possess, not to liberate Greece; and is contented to see the Turks, its natural enemies, and the Greeks, its intended slaves, enfeeble each other until one or both fall into its net. The wise and generous policy of England would have consisted in establishing the independence of Greece, and in maintaining it both against Russia and the Turk; but when was the oppressor generous or just?

Should the English people ever become free, they will reflect upon the part which those who presume to represent their will have played in the great drama of the revival of liberty, with feelings which it would become them to anticipate. This is the age of the war of the oppressed against the oppressors, and everyone of those ringleaders of the privileged gangs of murderers and swindlers, called

Sovereigns, look to each other for aid against the common enemy and suspend their mutual jealousies in the presence of a mightier fear. Of this holy alliance all the despots of the earth are virtually members. But a new race has arisen throughout Europe, nursed with abhorrence of the opinions which are its chains, and she will continue to produce fresh generations to accomplish that destiny which tyrants foresee and dread.

The Spanish Peninsula is already free. France is tranquil in the enjoyment of a partial exemption from the abuses which its unnatural and feeble government are vainly attempting to revive. The seed of blood and misery has been sown in Italy, and a more vigorous race is arising to go forth to the harvest. The world waits only the news of a revolution of Germany, to see the tyrants who have pinnacled themselves on its supineness precipitated into the ruin from which they shall never arise. Well do these destroyers of mankind know their enemy when they impute the insurrection in Greece to the same spirit before which they tremble throughout the rest of Europe, and that enemy well knows the power and cunning of its opponents and watches the moment of their approaching weakness and inevitable division to wrest the bloody sceptres from their grasp.

appendix b

selections from Shelley's letters

To Leigh Hunt

(As Editor of *The Examiner*)

University College, Oxford,
March 2, 1811.

SIR,

Permit me, although a stranger, to offer my sincerest congratulations on the occasion of that triumph[1] so highly to be prized by men of liberality; permit me also to submit to your consideration, as to one of the most fearless enlighteners of the public mind at the present time, a scheme of mutual safety and mutual indemnification for men of public spirit and principle, which if carried into effect would evidently be productive of incalculable advantages; of the scheme the enclosed is an address to the public, the proposal for a meeting, and shall be modified according to your judgment, if you will do me the honour to consider the point.

The ultimate intention of my aim is to induce a *meeting* of such enlightened unprejudiced members of the community, whose independent principles expose them to evils which might thus become alleviated, and to form a

1 **that triumph** Hunt's acquittal (with his brother John) on a charge of seditious libel for publishing in the *Examiner* for February 24, 1811, an article on the savagery of military floggings

methodical society which should be organized so as to resist the coalition of the enemies of liberty which at present renders any expression of opinion on matters of policy dangerous to individuals. It has been for want of societies of this nature that corruption has attained the height at which we now behold it, nor can any of us bear in mind the very great influence which some years since was gained by *Illuminism*, without considering that a society of equal extent might establish *rational liberty* on as firm a basis as that which would have supported the visionary schemes of a completely equalized community.

Although perfectly unacquainted privately with you, I address you as a common friend of *Liberty*, thinking that in cases of this urgency and importance, that etiquette ought not to stand in the way of usefulness.

My father is in parliament, and on attaining 21 I shall, in all probability, fill his vacant seat. On account of the responsibility to which my residence at this University subjects me, I of course dare not publicly to avow all that I think, but the time will come when I hope that my every endeavour, insufficient as this may be, will be directed to the advancement of liberty.

To William Godwin

London

Keswick, Cumberland,
January 3, 1812.

You will be surprised at hearing from a stranger. No introduction has, nor in all probability ever will authorize that which common thinkers would call a liberty; it is, however, a liberty which, although not sanctioned by custom, is so far from being reprobated by reason that the dearest interests of mankind imperiously demand that a certain etiquette of fashion should no longer keep "man at a distance from man" or impose its flimsy fancies between the free communication of intellect.

The name of Godwin has been used to excite in me feelings of reverence and admiration. I have been accustomed to consider him a luminary too dazzling for the darkness which surrounds him. From the earliest period of my knowledge of his principles, I have ardently desired to share, on the footing of intimacy, that intellect which I have delighted to contemplate in its emanations.

Considering, then, these feelings, you will not be surprised at the inconceivable emotions with which I learned your existence and your dwelling. I had enrolled your name in the list of the honourable dead. I had felt regret that the glory of your being had passed from this earth of ours. It is not so; you still live and, I firmly believe, are still planning the welfare of human kind.

I have but just entered on the scene of human operations; yet my feelings and my reasonings correspond with what yours were. My course has been short, but eventful. I have seen much of human prejudice, suffered much from human persecution, yet I see no reason hence inferable which should alter my wishes for their renovation. The ill-treatment I have met with has more than ever impressed the truth of my principles on my judgment. I am young, I am ardent in the cause of philanthropy and truth; do not suppose that this is vanity; I am not conscious that it influences this portraiture. I imagine myself dispassionately describing the state of my mind. I am young; you have gone before me, I doubt not are a veteran to me in the years of persecution. Is it strange that, defying prejudice as I have done, I should outstep the limits of custom's prescription and endeavour to make my desire useful by a friendship with William Godwin?

I pray you to answer this letter. Imperfect as may be my capacity, my desire is ardent and unintermitted. Half an hour would be at least humanely employed in the experiment. I may mistake your residence; certain feelings of which I may be an inadequate arbiter may induce you to desire concealment; I may not, in fine, have an answer to this letter. If I do not, when I come to London, I shall seek for you. I am convinced I could represent myself to you in such terms as not to be thought wholly unworthy of your friendship; at least, if desire for universal happiness has any claim upon your preference, that desire I can exhibit. Adieu! I shall earnestly await your answer.

To Thomas Love Peacock

[Naples,
January 24, 1819.]

My Dear Peacock,
Your two letters arrived within a few days of each other, one being directed to Naples, and the other to Livorno. They are more welcome visitors to me than mine can be to you. I writing as from sepulchres, you from the habitations of men yet unburied; tho the Sexton, Castlereagh, after having dug their grave, stands with his spade in his hand, evidently doubting whether he will not be forced to occupy it himself. . . .

. . . O, if I had health, and strength, and equal spirits, what boundless intellectual improvement might I not gather in this wonderful country! At present I write little else but poetry, and little of that. My 1st act of Prometheus is complete, and I think you would like it. I consider Poetry very subordinate to moral and political science, and if I were well, certainly I should aspire to the latter; for I can conceive a great work, embodying the discoveries of all ages, and harmonising the contending creeds by which mankind have been ruled. Far from me is such an attempt, and I shall be content, by exercising my fancy, to amuse myself, and perhaps some others, and cast what weight I can into the right scale of that balance, which the Giant of Arthegall holds[1]. . . .

1 Explaining this passage, Peacock adds the following note: "The allusion is to the *Fairy Queen*, Book V, canto 3. The Giant has

To Leigh Hunt

Florence,
November 3, 1819.

MY DEAR FRIEND,

The event of Carlisle's trial [1] has filled me with an indignation that will not and ought not to be suppressed.

In the name of all we hope for in human nature what are the people of England about? Or rather how long will they, and those whose hereditary duty it is to lead them, endure the enormous outrages of which they are one day made the victim and the next the instrument? Post succeeds post, and fresh horrors are ever detailed. First we hear that a troop of the enraged master-manufacturers are let loose with sharpened swords upon a multitude of their starving dependents and in spite of the remonstrances of the regular troops that they ride over them and massacre without distinction of sex or age, and cut off women's breasts and dash the heads of infants against the stones. Then comes information that a man has been found guilty of some inexplicable crime, which his prosecutors call blasphemy; one of the features of which, they inform us,

---

scales, in which he professes to weigh right and wrong, and rectify the physical and moral evils which result from inequality of condition. Shelley once pointed out this passage to me, observing, 'Artegall argues with the Giant; the Giant has the best of the argument; Artegall's iron man knocks him over into the sea and drowns him. This is the usual way in which power deals with opinion.' I said, 'That was not the lesson Spenser intended to convey.' 'Perhaps not,' he said; 'it is the lesson which he conveys to me. I am of the Giant's faction.' In the same feeling with respect to Thomson's *Castle of Indolence*, he held that the Enchanter in the first canto was a true philanthropist, and the Knight of Arts and Industry in the second an oligarchical imposter overthrowing truth by power." *Fraser's Magazine*, March 1860, p. 319. 1 **Carlisle's trial** correct spelling: Carlile; see p. xii, Introduction, for mention of trial

is the denying that the massacring of children and the ravishing of women was done by the immediate command of the author and preserver of all things. And thus at the same time we see on one hand men professing to act by the public authority who put in practise the trampling down and murdering an unarmed multitude without distinction of sex or age, and on the other a tribunal which punishes men for asserting that deeds of the same character, transacted in a distant age and country, were not done by the command of God. If not for this, for what was Mr. Carlisle prosecuted? For impugning the Divinity of Jesus Christ? I impugn it. For denying that the whole mass of antient Hebrew literature is of divine authority? I deny it. I hope this is no blasphemy and that I am not to be dragged home by the enmity of our political adversaries to be made a sacrifice to the superstitious fury of the ruling sect. But I am prepared both to do my duty and abide by whatever consequences may be attached to its fulfilment.

It is said that Mr. Carlisle has been found guilty by a jury. Juries are frequently in cases of libel illegally and partially constituted, and whenever this can be proved the party accused has a title to a new trial. A view of the question, so simple that it is in danger of being overlooked from its very obviousness, has presented itself to me, by which I think it will clearly appear that this illegal and partial character belonged to the jury which pronounced a verdict of guilty against Mr. Carlisle, and that he is entitled to a new trial.

It is the privilege of an Englishman to be tried not only by a jury, but by a jury of his peers. Who are the *peers* of any man and what is the legal import of this word? Let us illustrate the letter by the spirit of the law. A nobleman has a right to be tried by his peers, a gentleman, a tradesman, a farmer—the like; the peers of a man are men of the same station, class denomination with himself. The reason on which this provision is founded is that the persons called upon to determine the guilt or innocence of the accused might be so alive to a tender sympathy towards him, through common interests, habits, and opinions, as to render it impossible, either that thro[ugh] neglect or aversion they would commit injustice towards him, or that they might be incapable of knowing and weighing the merits of the case. Butchers and surgeons are excluded on this ground from juries, it being supposed by the law that they are engaged in occupations foreign to that delicate sensibility respecting human life and suffering exacted in those selected as arbiters for inflicting it. From the dictation of this spirit, in all cases where foreigners are criminally accused, the jury impanelled are half Englishmen and half foreigners. And the reason why they are not all foreigners is manifest; not that it is theoretically just that any men not strictly his peers should determine between the accused and the country, but because the practical disadvantage arising from the inexperience of foreigners in this admirable form peculiar to English law would overbalance the advantage of adhering to the shadow, by letting the substance of justice escape. This therefore is the law, and the spirit of the law, of juries; and thus plainly and clearly it is illustrated by the antient and perpetual practice of the English courts of Justice.

Who were Mr. Carlisle's peers? Mr. Carlisle was a Deist accused of blaspheming the religion of men professing themselves Christians. Who were his peers? Christians? Surely not. Such a proposition is refuted by the very terms of which it is composed. It were to constitute a jury out of the men who are parties to the prosecution; it were to make those who are offended judges of the cause of him by whom they profess themselves to have been offended; it were less absurd to impannell the nearest relations of a murdered man to try the guilt or innocence of a person on whom circumstances attach a strong suspicion of the deed. No honest Christian would sit on such a jury except he felt himself thoroughly imbued with the universal toleration preached by the alledged founder of his religion—a state of feeling which we are not warranted by experience to presume to belong except to extraordinary men. He must know he could not be impartial. He sees before him the enemy of his God, one already predestined to the tortures of Hell and who by the most specious arguments is seducing every one around him into the same peril. He probably feels that his own faith is tottering whilst he listens to the prisoner's defense, and this naturally redoubles his indignation. How is such a person to be considered as the *peer* of

the other, if by peer be meant one who from common
habits and interests would be likely to weigh the merits of
the cause dispassionately? He is a person of the same sect
with him who framed the indictment in which the culprit
is accused as a malicious blasphemer. He is evidently less
his *peer* with reference to the circumstances of the case
than a ploughman would be the peer of a nobleman, and
it is less probable that the one would give an unconscien-
tious verdict from envy towards rank, that the other from
abhorrence from the speculative opinions of the prisoner.
The Christian may be the peer of the Deist with reference
to any matter not involving a question of his guilt in expressing contumelious sentiments concerning the Christian's own belief (for this if anything is meant by
blasphemy) because he may have those common interests
and feelings which make one man alive to render justice
to another; but with regard to the matter in question he
cannot be his peer, because he is one of the persons whom
he is charged as having injured, because what he boasts to
consider as his most important interests compel him to
judge harshly of the accused, and to impersonate the
character of the injured party, the accuser and the judge,
[rather] than the impartial juryman.

Neither therefore the practice of law, nor the reason of
law on which lawyers profess to ground that practice, nor
the universal reason of all men which is the foundation not
only of law but of all human society, admit that a professed
Christian should be the peer of a Deist in a case where
the uttering contumelious expressions against the opinions
of the Christian is the crime of which the Deist is accused. Suppose a Deist brought an action against a Christian for reviling *his* opinions; how would an English court
of justice endure to be told that the jury must not be
Christians but Deists, and what weight would they give
to the prosecutor's objections to such and such a juryman
because he suspected that he believed the Bible to be of
divine authority? And yet Christianity, or that system
which is founded on the maxim of "Do unto others as
thou wouldst they should do unto thee," has been declared
to be part of the law of the land.

Who then are the peers of the Deist? We must admit I
fear the existence of a law against *blasphemy*. Let us hope

that some legislative enactment will speedily be passed to erase this scandal from our age. Meanwhile there is a law that men should be censured for what is called blasphemy. But who are to be the judges of blasphemy? Not the blasphemer; still less the blasphemed, or the persons who are injured and provoked by the blasphemy? The peers of the accused. Who are the peers of the Deist? Deists, to be sure. "No," objects the Christian, "they will assuredly acquit him." But the Christian would condemn him right or wrong. Well, let there be that same compromise between the theoretical justice and the practical convenience of the case as already obtains in the instance of foreigners. Let them be half Deists and half Christians. As in the case of foreigners accused of crimes of universally acknowledged enormity let there be impannelled a jury one moiety consisting of such as have interests and feelings common with his own and the other of such as are uninfluenced by those interests. Anything short of this is an open mockery, an unfeeling denial of justice. "But," says the Christian, "You would not insist on impannelling murderers to try a murderer on the pretence that they are alone his peers, because they alone have the same interests and feelings. Why impannell Deists to try a Deist?" My reply to the insolent bigot is simple. Deism is no crime by the law of England any more than Sandimonianism or Unitarianism is a crime. The indictment does not accuse him of Deism but of blasphemy. He is accused of speaking injuriously of a certain religious persuasion and not of avowing his disbelief in that persuasion. Mere disbelief is perfectly legal. And it is so legal that if a man be asked in public "Do you believe the Bible to be of divine authority?" and he should deliberately answer, "I am from my soul convinced that it is not" no legal punishment could be inflicted on him for that avowal. . . .

bibliography

editions

Brett-Smith, H. F. B., ed. *Peacock's Four Ages of Poetry, Shelley's Defence of Poetry, and Browning's Essay on Shelley*. London, 1929.

Cameron, K. N., ed. *The Carl H. Pforzheimer Library: Shelley and His Circle, 1773–1822*, vols. I & II. Cambridge, Massachusetts, 1961. [Correspondence and writings up to 1811.]

Clark, David L., ed. *Shelley's Prose; or, The Trumpet of a Prophecy*, Corrected edition. Albuquerque, 1966.

Forman, H. Buxton, ed. *The Complete Works of Percy Bysshe Shelley*, 8 vols. London, 1876–1880. [Prose works re-issued, with added memoir, in five volumes in 1892.]

Ingpen, Roger, and Peck, W. E., eds. *The Complete Works of Percy Bysshe Shelley*, 10 vols. New York, 1926–1930.

Jones, Frederick L., ed. *The Letters of Percy Bysshe Shelley*, 2 vols. Oxford, 1964.

McElderry, Bruce R., Jr., ed. *Shelley's Critical Prose*. Lincoln, Nebraska, 1967.

Rolleston, T. W., ed. *A Philosophical View of Reform*. London, 1920. [The first edition.]

Shawcross, John, ed. *Shelley's Literary and Philosophical Criticism*. London, 1909.

Shelley, Mary W., ed. *Essays, Letters from Abroad, Translations, and Fragments*. London, 1840. [With Mary Shelley's introduction and notes.]

White, R. J., ed. *Political Tracts of Wordsworth, Coleridge, and Shelley*. Cambridge, England, 1953.

Entries in this bibliography have been chosen with Shelley's political thought as the specific point of focus.

biographies

Blunden, Edmund. *Shelley: A Life Story*. London, 1946.
Dowden, Edward. *The Life of P. B. Shelley*. 2 vols. London, 1886; abridged one volume edition, 1896.
White, Newman Ivey. *Shelley*. 2 vols. New York, 1940.
———. *Portrait of Shelley*. New York, 1945.

criticism

Baker, Carlos. *Shelley's Major Poetry*. Princeton, 1948.
Baker, Joseph Ellis. *Shelley's Platonic Answer to a Platonic Attack on Poetry*. Iowa City, 1965.
Barnard, Ellsworth. *Shelley's Religion*. Minneapolis, 1936.
Barrell, Joseph. *Shelley and the Thought of His Time: A Study in the History of Ideas*. New Haven, 1947; London, 1948.
Brailsford, Henry N. *Shelley, Godwin, and Their Circle*. New York, 1913.
Brinton, Clarence Crane. *The Political Ideas of English Romanticism*. London, 1926.
Cameron, Kenneth N. "Shelley and the Reformers." *Journal of English Literary History*, XII (1945), 62–86.
———. "The Social Philosophy of Shelley," *Sewanee Review*, L (1942), 457–466.
———. *The Young Shelley*. New York, 1950.
Duerksen, Roland A. "Shelley's 'Defence' and Whitman's 1855 'Preface': A Comparison." *Walt Whitman Review*, X (1964), 51–60.
———. *Shelleyan Ideas in Victorian Literature*. The Hague, 1966.
Grabo, Carl. *The Magic Plant: The Growth of Shelley's Thought*. Chapel Hill, North Carolina, 1936.
Guinn, John Pollard. *Shelley's Political Thought*. The Hague, 1969.
Ingpen, Roger. *Shelley in England*. Boston and New York, 1917.
King-Hele, Desmond. *Shelley: His Thought and Work*. London, 1960.

Lea, F. A. *Shelley and the Romantic Revolution*. London, 1945; Folcroft, Pennsylvania, 1969.

McNiece, Gerald. *Shelley and the Revolutionary Idea*. Cambridge, Massachusetts, 1969.

Norman, Sylva. *Flight of the Skylark: The Development of Shelley's Reputation*. Norman, Oklahoma, 1954.

Notopoulos, James A. "The Dating of Shelley's Prose," *PMLA*, LVIII (June, 1943), 477–498.

Salt, Henry S. *Percy Bysshe Shelley: Poet and Pioneer*. London, 1896.

Walker, Stanley A. "Peterloo, Shelley and Reform," *PMLA*, XL (March, 1925), 128–164.

Weaver, Bennett. "Pre-Promethean Thought in the Prose of Shelley," *Philosophical Quarterly*, XXVII (July, 1948), 193–208.

———. *Toward the Understanding of Shelley*. Ann Arbor, 1932.

White, Newman Ivey. *The Unextinguished Hearth*. Durham, North Carolina, 1938.

Wilson, Milton. *Shelley's Later Poetry: A Study of His Prophetic Imagination*. New York, 1959.

Wylie, Laura Johnson. "Shelley's Democracy," *Social Studies in English Literature*. Boston, 1916.